PLANNING POLITICS IN TORONTO

The Ontario Municipal Board and Urban Development

The Ontario Municipal Board is an independent provincial planning appeals body that has wielded major influence on Toronto's urban development. In this book, Aaron A. Moore examines the effect that the OMB has had on the behaviour and relationships of Toronto's main political actors, including city planners, developers, neighbourhood associations, and local politicians.

Moore's findings draw on a quantitative analysis of all OMB decisions and settlements from 2000 through 2006, as well as eight in-depth case studies. The cases, which examine a variety of development proposals that resulted in OMB appeals, compare the decisions of Toronto's political actors to those typified in American local political economy analyses.

A much-needed contribution to the literature on the politics of urban development in Toronto since the 1970s, *Planning Politics in Toronto* challenges popular preconceptions of the OMB's role in Toronto's patterns of growth and change.

AARON A. MOORE is a fellow of the Institute on Municipal Finance and Governance at the Munk School of Global Affairs and a research affiliate at the Cities Centre at the University of Toronto.

Planning Politics in Toronto

The Ontario Municipal Board and Urban Development

AARON A. MOORE

UNIVERSITY OF TORONTO PRESS
Toronto Buffalo London

ISBN 978-1-4426-4423-6 (cloth)
ISBN 978-1-4426-1259-4 (paper)

Printed on acid-free, 100% post-consumer recycled paper with vegetable-based inks.

Library and Archives Canada Cataloguing in Publication

Moore, Aaron A., 1979–
Planning politics in Toronto : the Ontario Municipal Board and urban development / Aaron A. Moore.

Includes bibliographical references and index.
ISBN 978-1-4426-4423-6 (bound). – ISBN 978-1-4426-1259-4 (pbk.)

1. City planning – Political aspects – Ontario – Toronto – History. 2. Ontario Municipal Board. I. Title.

HT169.C32T67 2013   307.1'21609713541   C2012-908100-0

This book has been published with the help of a grant from the Canadian Federation for the Humanities and Social Sciences, through the Awards to Scholarly Publications Program, using funds provided by the Social Sciences and Humanities Research Council of Canada.

University of Toronto Press acknowledges the financial assistance to its publishing program of the Canada Council for the Arts and the Ontario Arts Council.

 Canada Council   Conseil des Arts
for the Arts   du Canada

University of Toronto Press acknowledges the financial support of the Government of Canada through the Canada Book Fund for its publishing activities.

For Bridget Melissa Whipple

Contents

Illustrations

Tables

Acknowledgments

The process of preparing this book for publication, while easier because of Andrew Sancton's guidance, involved feedback and insight from a number of individuals. Andrew Sancton was and continues to be a great mentor and guide, and I could not have achieved what I did without his support. Laura Stephenson and Martin Horak provided important counterpoints to Andy, and I think my final work was much stronger from having to balance very different perspectives. Bridget Whipple, who now knows far more about the OMB and Toronto than a woman from a small town in Quebec could ever want to know, provided useful feedback throughout, and I regret not using her editing skills more often. I would also like to thank Richard Stren, Michael Buzzelli, and Cameron Anderson, and the two anonymous reviewers who read the first draft of my manuscript (you know who you are). Their feedback and suggestions made my work that much stronger. I was not able to address all their suggestions when producing this book, but will move forward in future research with them in mind. Richard Stren, in particular, has also become something of a champion of my work outside of Western, and I greatly appreciate the exposure he has given me. Speaking of Western, I benefited greatly from my time at the University of Western Ontario, and the funding the school provided. I would also like to thank the whole of the Department of Political Science for their help. I evolved from a bright student to a veritable academic during my time there. I am also indebted to all of my interviewees for their insight into the politics and machinations of urban development in Toronto. I am also indebted to Matthew Brian at the OMB and Rita Marrazzo at the City of Toronto for their aid in my research. I have become particularly indebted to Daniel Quinlan from the University of Toronto Press, who has made the process of publishing this work far too easy on me. I am lucky he saw something in my work early on, so I was able to avoid the process of creating a manuscript without a guide or a sense of direction. Lastly, I would like to thank my parents Geoff Moore and Pego McKenzie for all of their years of support.

Abbreviations

ABC	ABC Residents' Association
ACII	Alderwood Community Involvement Inc.
APAB	Assessment and Planning Appeal Board
ARA	Annex Residents' Association
BVA	Bayview Village Association
CMQ	Commission Municipale Québec
CORRA	Confederation of Residents' and Ratepayers' Associations
CP	Comprehensive Plan
CPA	Comprehensive Plan Amendment
DAB	Development Appeals Board
DLCD	Department of Land Conservation and Development
DOAH	Division of Administrative Hearings
EYCA	Edithvale-Yonge Community Association
EYCC	Etobicoke York Community Council
FoNTRA	Federation of North Toronto Residents Associations
GTA	Greater Toronto Area
GYRA	Greater Yorkville Residents Association
ICBL	Interim Control By-law
LCDC	Land Conservation and Development Commission
LPE	Local Political Economy
LUBA	Land Use Board of Appeal
MCC	Midtown Community Council
MHA	Markland Homes Association
MMB	Manitoba Municipal Board
MPS	Municipal Planning Strategies
MSSB	Metropolitan Separate School Board
NSURB	Nova Scotia Utility and Review Board

NYCC	North York Community Council
PAC	Planning Appeals Commission
OMB	Ontario Municipal Board
OP	Official Plan
OPA	Official Plan Amendment
ORMB	Ontario Railway and Municipal Board
SGDC	Sherway Gate Development Corporation
SMB	Saskatchewan Municipal Board
SSSOCCC	Stop Spadina, Save Our City Co-ordinating Committee
SYHA	Save Yorkville Heritage Association
SYN	Save Yorkville Now
TEYCC	Toronto East York Community Council
TPA	Toronto Parking Authority
ZBL	Zoning By-law
ZBLA	Zoning By-law Amendment

PLANNING POLITICS IN TORONTO

The Ontario Municipal Board and Urban Development

1 Introduction

In a scathing editorial entitled "the curse of the OMB," the *Globe and Mail* recounted the tale of the Ontario Municipal Board's "most recent affront to democracy," a decision to allow a new visitor centre in one of Toronto's largest cemeteries despite the City's refusal of the proposal and opposition from residents (Globe and Mail 2007, A22). The article proceeded to recount other instances where the OMB overturned Toronto City Council's land-use planning decisions. In its conclusion, the newspaper quoted a former premier of British Columbia, who characterized the OMB as "a medieval abomination" (ibid.). The Ontario Municipal Board looms large in Toronto urban development. The city is Canada's largest, and the fifth largest municipality in North America. However, as with all municipalities in Ontario, Toronto City Council's planning decisions are subject to appeal to the Ontario Municipal Board, which functions as a powerful quasi-judicial appeal body for land-use planning. Despite the board's obvious importance to planning and development in Ontario, and the animosity it generates, few authors have rigorously examined the role it plays in urban planning in the province. More important, those few have stopped short of analysing the OMB's broader influence over the politics of urban development. This book, in part, is my attempt to address this lack of research.

My larger purpose, however, extends beyond the City of Toronto and the Province of Ontario. I consider how the existence of a distinct institution for planning distorts the way we conceive of political behaviour at the local level in political science and related fields. Since the emergence of the "community power" debate in the 1950s and 1960s, local government scholars have devoted significant time to analysing the behaviour of, and interaction among, actors involved in the politics of urban development in North American cities. This literature has since evolved to incorporate the role of the economy and basic institutions that shape and direct actors' behaviour. This local political economy (LPE) approach has come to dominate the discourse on the politics of urban development in North America. However, the prevailing assumptions in LPE theories regarding the distribution of resources among political actors severely constrain their explanatory power. Despite such limitations, I believe the broader local political economy framework is capable of accounting for such variations, so long as one accounts for the institutional and structural differences that affect resource distribution.

Robert Dahl introduced the notion of unequal resource distribution when articulating his pluralist theory, a precursor to the LPE approach. According to Dahl, the distribution of resources among different actors in local politics drives the pluralist system of politics in the United States. Dahl's list of resources includes wealth, legality, popularity, and control over sources of information (Dahl 1961). Though many scholars later criticized Dahl's pluralist theory, variations on his theme of political resources remain a pivotal element of LPE theories, and are a defining element of the LPE approach to studying urban politics. In the majority of such theories, business and developers' control of wealth offer them means to win the support of local politicians; neighbourhood associations and other citizen-led groups use their ability to mobilize the electorate to influence local politicians; and local politicians control policy decision making, offering legitimacy and legality to policies benefiting different groups in the politics of urban development.

Various LPE theories allow for the waxing and waning of developers' and citizen groups' influence over local politicians, but the latter's role as final decision-maker over land use remains integral to most of these theories. However, not all municipalities and local politicians in North America enjoy the same authority over planning and development. For instance, in the case of Boston, the State of Massachusetts invests the power to adopt and amend the City's zoning codes and map in the Zoning Commission, and has left appeals and variances to the Zoning Board of Appeal, both of which are unelected bodies (Frug and Barron 2008). As in Ontario and Toronto, institutional differences may distort the regular pattern of political behaviour LPE theories depict, because these institutional variations change the distribution of resources and subsequently the political game.

The Province of Ontario technically invests planning authority in local politicians (municipal councils). At the same time, however, it allows any actors upset with the decision of a municipal council to appeal the council's decision to the Ontario Municipal Board. The OMB is the most powerful board of its kind in North America. The board's role as an appeal body in planning disputes – its ability to overturn or alter the decisions of democratically elected councils – is a cause for consternation among many Ontario communities, including its capital, Toronto. The board's existence undoubtedly alters the role of local politicians and the behaviour of other actors in the politics of urban development such that urban development politics in Canada's largest city may differ significantly from that which LPE literature portrays.

The OMB in North America

In 1906 the Province of Ontario created the Ontario Railway and Municipal Board (ORMB). The ORMB's main purpose was to regulate municipal street railways in the province's rapidly growing cities. By the early 1930s, the purpose and name of the board (now the Ontario Municipal Board) had changed. The OMB acquired considerable powers over municipalities (Chipman 2002). Today, the OMB spends the bulk of its time adjudicating disputes over development and planning. While other jurisdictions in Canada and the United States have such quasi-judicial boards in place for resolving disputes, none has the same scope of power as the OMB.

Given the primacy of property and development issues in North American municipal politics (see Lorimer 1970; Sancton 1983; Logan and Molotch 1987; Swanstrom 1988), the OMB's ability to undermine and overturn the will of municipal politicians suggests that the board may play an important role in shaping the politics of Ontario's municipalities. The City of Toronto is Canada's most populous municipality, larger than a majority of the country's provinces; yet, the OMB can overturn Toronto City Council's decisions regarding development just as it can the decisions of the province's smallest municipalities. Both the OMB's position as the final decision-maker on development and planning issues and the procedural requirements of appealing to the board may substantially shape and direct the politics of urban development in the City of Toronto. While the board likely influences the politics of urban development in other Ontario cities, this book focuses on Toronto because of its size, its significant urban development in recent years, and its prominence in local government literature in Canada. In addition, it seeks to rectify the failure of past works to account for the influence of the OMB on the politics of urban development in the city.

Land-use planning is one of the fundamental responsibilities of most municipal governments in both the United States and Canada. In most jurisdictions in both countries, municipal governments have the power to determine and direct the development of their built environment and planning law and policy. Accordingly, in Philadelphia, the city council chose to support a proposal for an office and hotel development that would soar over 1500 feet high, 500 feet higher than the city's largest existing building and over ten times greater than the existing height limit for the site (125 feet). The developer and city councillors championed the development as capable of transforming the city into a new hub for the American financial industry (Shields 2008a). The city council, and the councillor in whose ward the site is located, supported the development despite almost immediate opposition from an area neighbourhood association, and even opposition from the district's state senator (Shields 2008).

In Seattle, processes exist to encourage and incorporate neighbourhood concerns into planning, and neighbourhood associations traditionally have significant influence on local politicians' decision making. However, city council ignored significant opposition from local neighbourhood associations and supported a number of changes to the city's zoning to encourage development. Newspaper accounts of development politics in 2003–4 suggest a shift in the city's politics from an orientation towards community groups and neighbourhood associations to a focus on generating new jobs in the city and development (Young 2003a, 2003b; Sommerfeld 2003). The shift, notably, was one led by city politicians, a necessity for any changes in the direction of growth and development due to council's authority to allow, refuse, and control development in the city.

Although LPE theories traditionally depict local politicians as important allies for developers, councils just as often use their authority to combat development. For instance, in 2004, Vancouver City Council utilized its authority over planning to scuttle Home Depot's plans to build a new store in one of the city's neighbourhoods. The company spent $22 million for the site of a former IGA supermarket. Local residents opposed the development for fear that it would damage the character of the existing community (Greenwood 2004). The hardware retailer proposed to replace the existing 28,000 square foot supermarket with a 72,000 square foot store (Vancouver Sun 2004). Initially, City staff proposed a limit of 40,000 square feet for any new development in the area. Over 5000 neighbourhood residents signed a petition in opposition to the development. Many residents in turn demanded a limit of 10,000 square feet, a third the size of the former IGA (Chu 2004). City council decided against the development. In addition, council imposed the 10,000 square foot limit residents demanded, though exempting grocery stores, which could be as large as 30,000 square feet (ibid.).

Similarly, in Chicago, a city comparable in size to Toronto, where authority over planning clearly rests with the city's local politicians, the city council has repeatedly frustrated some of its local developers. Many of Chicago's development projects are equal to or greater in size and scope than Toronto's. In the late 1970s, 1350 Lakeshore Development Associates applied for and received a zoning amendment allowing the company to construct a building upwards of forty storeys high along the city's Gold Coast. The developer chose to wait for two decades before actually developing the land, however. In late 1997, the developer submitted plans to the city for a new high-rise condominium for the site. Local residents opposed the development. The following year, Chicago City Council passed an ordinance that reduced the allowable height for development to eight storeys (Quine 2004). The developer took the City to court, arguing that it stood to lose almost $10 million from the zoning change, which it believed was unjust (Rooney 2004). For almost a decade, the developer has fought the City, with little success (Sachdev 2006).

These cases demonstrate the more controversial and heavy-handed uses of municipal power over land use and development. However, they are indicative of the important role municipal governments and local politicians have as the final decision-makers on development and land-use planning (excluding the role of courts, which assess the legality of municipalities' decisions). The municipal governments in each example wield authority to decide the fate of development projects within their borders. Local politicians in these cities enjoy the powers assumed in the LPE literature. They are the final decision-makers on issues of planning, and, as such, have significant influence over the development of their cities, and the politics of urban development. Given the presence of the OMB, had developers introduced any of these development proposals in Ontario, or had citizens opposed any such developments, the outcome of any of these cases could have differed significantly. Both developer and citizen could appeal the decision to the Ontario Municipal Board. Even in instances where municipalities have yet to render a decision, the board has the final say on planning and development in Ontario's municipalities. Had either of the first two examples, where local politicians in Philadelphia and Seattle ignored significant resident opposition to development, occurred in Ontario, local residents and neighbourhood associations could have appealed the council's decision. An OMB hearing would judge the planning merits of the proposal, not the legal grounds for a council's decision. In the Vancouver case, Home Depot would likely have successfully appealed council's decision, given that the existing zoning and planning experts supported a larger proposal than city council was willing to allow. Lastly, even if the City of Chicago had never approved a forty-storey building for the Gold Coast in the first place and had maintained an eight-storey limit since the late seventies, a tribunal with the OMB's powers could have overturned the council's decision with impunity. The idea that such an institution could overturn the decisions of democratically elected officials in cities the size of Chicago and Philadelphia may seem absurd to some, but this is precisely the power the OMB wields over the fifth most populous municipality in North America, Toronto.[1]

Existing Literature on the OMB

A number of academics, especially those interested in land use planning regulation, have written extensively on the OMB. Most of the books and articles written in this vein are either normative or prescriptive in nature. For instance, Adler (1971) attempts to discern what factors influence the OMB's decisions, notably, whether political factors have influence. He also examines the OMB's influence on municipalities' built environment, and suggests a number of ways to reform the board's methods of operation and decision making. Chipman (2002) argues vehemently for the dismemberment of the board, as he documents the board's self-devised criteria for decision making. Neither of these authors addresses the board's potential influence on local politics, though Adler (1971) makes note of such a possibility. Only Cullingworth (1987), in his survey of urban and regional planning practices across Canada, addresses the OMB's potential to influence political behaviour. He notes, in passing, that "the OMB nicely allows politicians to abrogate the responsibilities which properly fall on them" (440).

Given that these authors are interested primarily in the administration and effects of land-use planning, not the politics of development, the fact that they do not address whether the OMB influences local politics is not surprising. However, literature devoted to the politics of Toronto usually makes the same omission. Ample writing devoted to local politics in the City of Toronto and the former Metro Toronto exists.[2] Broader surveys of the history of Toronto and Metro politics all include mention of the OMB, particularly in conjunction with its role in the creation of Metropolitan Toronto (see Kaplan 1965, 1967; Rose 1972; Magnusson 1983; Frisken 2001). However, only Rose touches on the broader implications of the OMB's existence, suggesting that the board, at least for a time, had become an alternative tool of citizen activism, as local politicians seemed enthralled by developers. However, he does not elaborate on this point.

Important changes to the political environment of the city that took place in the late 1960s and early 1970s spawned a number of books and articles focused more specifically on the politics of urban development in the city (Lorimer 1970; Sewell 1972; Caulfield 1974; Goldrick 1982). More recently, particularly since the amalgamation of Metropolitan Toronto in 1998, a number of academics have returned to the issues of development policy making (Frisken 1988), and the political relations between city council and development interests (Keil 1998; Filion 1999; Kipfer and Keil 2002). Few of these authors omit the OMB from their discussion, or fail to discuss the board's extraordinary powers. Kipfer and Keil (2002) make note of developers' ability to by-pass city council and City Planning by appealing to the OMB. However, none of these authors directly addresses the actual role or influence the OMB has on the politics of urban development in the city. Such literature recognizes the board's direct influence on development in the city, given its significant powers to shape planning. However, it does not address how, well before an appeal, the very existence of the board may alter the behaviour and strategies of actors involved in the politics of urban development. In other jurisdictions in the United States and Canada, developers' and neighbourhood associations' main strategies focus on influencing local politicians, as few other avenues exist for achieving their interests. In Ontario and Toronto, both actors have the additional option of appealing to the OMB. In fact, given the likelihood of an appeal in Toronto, both actors could be more interested in securing planning expertise for a board hearing than in swaying local politicians.

Local Political Economy Literature

Land-use planning is of special importance to municipal government in North America as a means to direct development patterns, influence the local economy, and raise revenue. This corresponds to the importance of development politics at the local level in both the United States and Canada. The role that local politicians play in shaping planning policy is an important factor when analysing the politics of urban development in North American cities. Land-use planning helps shape the politics of urban development while the politics of urban development shapes land-use planning. Understanding the possible influence of a quasi-judicial body that removes final decision-making power on development proposals from local politicians is, thus, of importance to the study of any municipalities that fall within the jurisdiction of such a board. To understand properly the politics of urban development in Toronto, one must address whether and how the OMB influences its politics. Furthermore, the existence of such a powerful decision-making and quasi-judicial body warrants attention in itself as a means to gain a broader understanding of local political behaviour and processes of decision making.

A necessary corollary of such an analysis is a general understanding of how the politics of urban development unfolds in similar cities where councils have the final say on land use and planning. For instance, what motivates and drives the actors involved in development politics in Chicago? What incentives or disincentives do various interests have in working with or against one another in Los Angeles? Without a benchmark for comparison, establishing how and to what degree the OMB shapes and influences Toronto's developmental politics would be a frustrating task. Moreover, examining Toronto in complete isolation would also limit the development of broader insights from the analysis, especially as many other jurisdictions have similar if less powerful bodies that can also affect the politics of urban development.

Although this book questions whether current local political economy theories or analyses account for the role of quasi-judicial institutions on the politics of urban development, it also aims to extend the existing LPE approach to urban politics to account for such institutional variation. As a result, I draw on the basic elements and assumptions of LPE literature, which offers compelling accounts of the basic motivations of political actors in the politics of urban development. Although the institutional context of local development politics in Toronto differs from most accounts in the LPE literature, the basic interests of actors in Toronto are similar. The LPE approach focuses on the self-interest of political actors, the resources that they command, and the incentive structures that develop from the confluence of their self-interest, resources, and broader structures and institutions that direct or limit local politics, such as the free market and the relationship between municipal government and higher levels of government.

Numerous authors in the United States and Canada utilize the local political economy approach in various guises such that it has become one of the most influential approaches for studying urban and local politics in North America.[3] Whether deriving from a structuralist approach (Logan and Molotch 1987; Keil 1998; Harvey 1989) or building upon traditional behaviouralist literature (Stone 1989; Kantor with David 1988), local political economy theories focus on the interests of particular political actors, and the institutional and socio-economic constraints that shape their behaviour.

Accordingly, the LPE approach portrays the development industry's main goal as developing property for profit. To this end, developers will seek out the best means for realizing this goal. In North America, working with or co-opting local politicians (the terms used to describe such relationships often reflect the author's attitude towards the industry) is, according to most local political economy literature, the main method of choice for developers given local politicians' decision-making power. Regardless of their motivations, developers form relationships with local politicians, using their wealth to do so, because the latter make the final decision on whether development projects will or will not proceed. Citizens whose interests may be jeopardized by development tend to become the most vocal opponents of developers. They will organize, often in the form of a neighbourhood association, and seek to mobilize the electorate for or against local politicians in a bid to influence the latter's decision making. Academics are often at odds over what constitutes neighbourhood associations' interests. Some authors portray citizen or neighbourhood activists as progressive groups, while others are more critical of their role.[4] Regardless, citizen groups, for much the same reason as developers, prefer to target local politicians in order to prevent development.

Politicians, therefore, have a choice between working with developers or working with citizens. Many academics, regardless of their ideological disposition, suggest that local politicians in North America will choose the former. However, academics disagree as to what drives politicians to make this choice. While some suggest that the arrangement derives from local government's need of business and developers' resources to govern effectively, others argue that contributions to political campaigns and other more selfish reasons predominate.[5] As for citizen groups, a growing body of literature suggests that politicians will choose to work with them instead of business.[6] The clash between these groups (developers and neighbourhood associations) has come to dominate the politics of urban development in many North American cities, as local politicians lose their leverage over the former, while local government becomes increasingly open to the input and influence of the latter.[7]

Local Political Economy in Toronto

The resources each group has to offer to one another provide the incentive for cooperation or collaboration. The main resources politicians control are legitimacy and authority. According to most LPE specialists, local politicians have the final decision-making authority regarding development. In Ontario, the OMB effectively removes this authority from municipal government and local politicians. Although municipalities render decisions on development proposals, given that almost anyone can appeal the decision to the OMB, the board is, in effect, the final decision maker, especially as it can force municipalities to implement its decisions in place of their own. Precisely because of the powerful role of the OMB, the politics of urban development in Toronto likely unfold in a different manner than in most other North American cities. Furthermore, the OMB's process of appeals and decision making adds another dimension that may affect the politics of urban development in Toronto. The procedures of the appeals process place significant importance on expert testimony (Chipman 2002; Krushelnicki 2007), possibly increasing the importance of planning experts, particularly city planners, and limiting the influence of parties with little expertise.

If appeals to the board were not a regular occurrence, then the board's influence on development politics might be in question. However, an additional element of land-use planning in Ontario ensures a bevy of appeals to the OMB, especially from Toronto. Municipalities in Ontario can amend the policies and laws that govern development within their jurisdiction on a whim, and provincial legislation even offers them incentives to do so. Section 37 of the Ontario Planning Act, 1990 allows municipalities to require additional services and facilities from

developers for permission to build developments exceeding municipalities' height and density limits. Breaking one's own laws and policies can be very lucrative for a municipality (Barber 2008). The lucrative
nature of this power makes it appealing to local politicians and its existence could affect their decision making. However, constantly amending or changing the policies and laws that govern development in a
municipality erodes the legitimacy of these policies, in turn, providing
far greater scope for appeals, and for OMB decisions, than would otherwise be available if such policies and laws were more sacrosanct.

Given the important differences between the system of decision making on development issues in Toronto and Ontario and the system depicted in the LPE literature, the incentive structure and behaviour of
local political actors in Toronto should differ from that portrayed in
local political economy theories. However, the basic elements inherent
in the LPE approach to studying urban politics (actors' interests, the
focus on resource distribution, and the effect of constraints on actors'
behaviour) provide a strong framework for analysis. Consequently, this
book adopts this approach, comparing the expected behaviour of actors
in local political economy theories with the behaviour of political actors
in Toronto. I premise the following four questions on such a comparison with LPE theories:

Question 1: Does the existence of the OMB affect the role Toronto's
   planning community plays in the politics of urban development?
Question 2: Does the existence of the OMB affect the behaviour of developers in Toronto?
Question 3: Does the existence of the OMB affect the behaviour of
   neighbourhood associations in Toronto?
Question 4: Does the existence of the OMB affect local politicians' decision making and behaviour towards other actors?

The final three questions derive from the local political economy approach. The first deviates somewhat by adding a fourth actor for analysis. That city planners are important to city planning is nothing new.
However, most local political economy literature tends to ignore their
political significance. Perhaps their absence from the literature arises
from a sense among scholars that planners are subject to the whims of
politicians and their allies. Alternatively, just as the LPE literature does
not address local planning institutions, so too may scholars have omitted an important actor in the planning process. Even had the influence

of planners proved minimal in this analysis, omitting them would have been an error given their potential for influence under the OMB. In fact, this research indicates that land-use planners do play an important role in the politics of urban development in Toronto, suggesting that the issue of planners' omission from local political economy literature is an important one.

The politics of urban planning in Toronto are complex. More complex than either the LPE models or my own expectations suggest. The importance of planning experts, in particular the land-use planners employed by the City, to the politics of urban development in Toronto is a key finding of this research. Given the existing literature and conventional wisdom regarding the OMB process, that planning experts are pivotal for victory at the OMB is probably unsurprising to those familiar with the board and its practices. However, the significant role the city planners play throughout the planning process and their influence on political and policy outcomes suggests that either Toronto substantially differs from the cities portrayed in the local political economy literature, or the literature is missing a key actor when addressing urban politics. I suspect the reality is somewhere in between; however, the absence of any cases for comparison on this point makes any decisive conclusion difficult.

The Ontario Municipal Board does not completely alter the landscape of urban development politics in Toronto. Rather, the board alters the resources available to the actors involved in the politics of urban development, creating a moderate shift in influence away from local politicians and towards the City's land-use planners. The OMB, in rendering its decision, focuses heavily on expert testimony. Its reliance on the technical jargon of the land-use planning profession increases the overall importance of the planning profession, while limiting the influence of other actors on its decisions, whether local politicians, developers, or residents. City planners enjoy relatively greater autonomy in comparison to their private-sector counterparts, as their professional opinion is not as constrained by their employers' demands. This autonomy can result in an advantage for city planners when going before the board.

Contrary to expectations, developers in Toronto do not simply bypass local politicians in favour of the OMB. Rather, developers will shift some of their attention away from winning the support of local politicians towards gaining the approval of the City's planners. The support of City planners is an important safety net for developers in Toronto.

With City planners' support, developers have significantly greater success at the OMB, should the city council decide against them, and more often than not, council will support the recommendations of City Planning. Local politicians in Toronto do not necessarily object to this subtle shift in influence, as the spectre of the OMB allows them far greater flexibility when navigating the dangerous waters of urban development politics.

This book will not be the last word on the politics of urban development. I hope, however, that it helps broaden the descriptive power of the local political economy framework by demonstrating the importance of institutional variation in shaping urban politics, and by introducing (or perhaps re-introducing) a key actor to the study of the politics of urban development.

2 Local Political Economy Theory and Toronto

Local Political Economy can denote a wide variety of theories of local politics. The uniting element of the LPE approach to studying local politics is an understanding of the important role economic structure plays in shaping political behaviour at the local level and in distributing resources among political actors. Increasingly, such literature also focuses on the importance of institutional constraints on actors' behaviour.[1] Diverse theories, such as governance theory (see Peter 2001; Stoker 1998) and regulation theory (see Painter 1995, Harvey 1989), all fall within the auspices of the LPE approach. I focus mostly, however, on the two most prominent LPE theories in the United States, urban regime theory (Elkin 1987; Stone 1989) and growth machine theory (see Molotch 1976; and Logan and Molotch 1987). Although a number of scholars have questioned the applicability of these two theories to a Canadian setting, the politics of urban development unfolds in a very similar fashion in both countries. While neither theory may be directly applicable to Toronto, their shared understanding of the role of the economy, institutions, and actors' behaviour in the United States apply north of the border.

The scope of urban regime theory is greater than the focus of my own research, the politics of urban development, but it, along with growth machine theory, provides the most developed account of the politics of urban development in American cities. The significant literature drawing on both theories provide ample evidence of actors' interests and behaviour in American cities. This book synthesizes these accounts of political behaviour into a benchmark I can compare and contrast to the politics of urban development in the City of Toronto. I hope to use such comparisons to offer insights into the OMB's influence on the politics of urban development in Toronto.

As Elizabeth Strom (1996) suggests, even if these theories are not entirely applicable to situations outside of the United States, they can still be useful tools for analysing and understanding political behaviour. One of the three main issues I seek to address is whether the LPE approach to studying urban politics, which informs all LPE theories, can accommodate divergent planning institutions that shape and direct planning policy and decision making. Rather than testing the direct applicability of either urban regime or growth machine theory to the City of Toronto, I adopt certain basic assumptions contained in both theories regarding actors' interests. I use these assumptions to generate questions concerning the behaviour of actors in Toronto in light of the existence of the OMB. While the explanatory power of individual theories in a Canadian context may be limited, the approach to studying urban politics these theories adopt (the LPE approach) is applicable to the City of Toronto, as are many of the assumptions these theories make regarding the behaviour of political actors and the institutions and structures that shape their behaviour.

Both growth machine and urban regime theories emerged, in part, as a response to traditional behaviouralist analysis (see Hunter 1953 and Dahl 1961) and economic determinist theory (especially Peterson 1981) of urban politics. According to local political economy literature, the former ignored the limiting effect of economic structure on political behaviour, while the latter overemphasized such constraints, allowing for little flexibility in the decision making of local politicians. Harvey Molotch (1976) first advanced his growth machine theory in the mid-seventies, and developed it further with John Logan a decade later (Logan and Molotch 1987). Urban regime theory appeared in a number of sources, including Fainstein and Fainstein (1983) and Stephen Elkin (1985, 1987) in the early eighties. However, Clarence Stone's (1989) *Regime Politics* emerged as the most influential interpretation of the theory.

The following draws heavily on a number of authors with a variety of perspectives on both urban regimes and growth machines. However, Molotch (1976) and Logan and Molotch's (1987) initial portrayal of the growth machine and Stone's (1989) version of urban regime theory form the core of my conception of each theory. The two theories are distinct, though some authors suggest the growth machine is a subset or type of urban regime (Logan, Whaley, Crowder 1997). Stone's urban regime focuses on the relationship between local politicians and local businesses (not exclusively developers), and how it can permeate

diverse policy areas of local government. In contrast, Logan and Molotch's (1987) growth machine focuses exclusively on the issue of urban
(and suburban) development. Developers (or place entrepreneurs) are
the central protagonists of their theory.

Despite the broader focus of urban regime theory, Stone's (1989) depiction of Atlanta's governing regime suggests a close proximation
between it and Logan and Molotch's growth machine model. This proximation is important because, while the authors come to very similar
findings, they nevertheless come from disparate backgrounds. Logan
and Molotch adopt a structuralist approach that borrows from Marxist
literature.[2] In contrast, Stone's work develops and expands upon the
behaviouralist theories of authors like Dahl and Hunter.[3] That authors
with divergent starting points and different theoretical perspectives
come to depict the behaviour and interest of actors in the same manner
offers stronger evidence of the validity of their findings than a single
theoretical perspective would.

Machines and Regimes

Both growth machine and urban regime theory share a political economic focus that suggests the importance of external economic and institutional factors as well as the importance of political behaviour in
shaping local government policy. They also reject the notion that the
economy so constrains local government that government lacks real
policy-making power. For instance, Molotch (1976) argues that a shared
desire for growth provides the impetus necessary to unite a city's local
elite. This provides for a far more active relationship between local politicians and a city's business sector than economic determinist·theories
allow. In addition, as Stone (1989) suggests, the combination of local
government and businesses' resources allows for far more flexibility in
policy making. At the same time, all three authors, Logan, Molotch, and
Stone, argue that economic and institutional pressures (particularly the
drive for growth) play a substantial role in drawing local government
together with business. Stone suggests this process leads to an affinity
between business and local government, which excludes other actors,
contradicting pluralists models.

In articulating their theory of growth machines, Logan and Molotch
(1987) contrast the exchange value of land (its economic worth) with
its use value (value as living space) to illustrate the conflicting interests
of developer-led growth coalitions focused on exchange value and the

interests of city residents focused on use value. In North America, according to the two authors, exchange regularly trumps use. This fact underlies the development of a growth machine. Growth machines develop in the following manner: place entrepreneurs see the potential for profit from the development and intensification of their property holdings, namely, through the increase in rent. These "rentiers" develop a close relationship with other local business interests. In particular, businesses that rely on the growth of a city to increase their profitability, such as newspapers, are likely to support the interests of developers (ibid., 84).

Developers and their allies, through constant interaction with government, through ample campaign contributions, and through their ability to organize and mobilize, can co-opt local politicians, effectively coercing their involvement in the growth coalition. They supply politicians with the funds necessary to run effective election campaigns. Politicians, in turn, along with local media and other members of the growth coalition, help to perpetuate a link between civic pride and a city's economic and physical growth. This link undermines interest in the use value of land (specifically the use and maintenance of existing areas) as the city focuses increasingly on growth. The focus on growth helps to perpetuate the growth coalition (Logan and Molotch 1987, 60). Molotch argues in a later article that this coalition of growth interests reflected the most common political coalition in American cities, while acknowledging its limited applicability elsewhere. He argues that Americans' acceptance of developers' actions "as the baseline of urban process, rather than as 'disruptions,'" is evidence that Americans take developers' "presence for granted" (Molotch 1993, 32).

Stone (1989) portrays the coalition of business interests and local politicians in a less negative light than the previous authors do. He distinguishes between a traditional social-control model of urban politics, which portrays those directing policy decision making as doing so in a command fashion and a social-production model of urban politics, which he favours. In Stone's social-production model, business does not dictate policy to local government, nor is business capable of doing so. Rather, the social-production model suggests a fit between the political resources of politicians and the economic resources of business, such that a coalition between the two can achieve a level of cooperation in a disparate and fragmented society. Stone argues that the purpose and benefit of regimes (long-lasting informal coalitions) is their ability to carry out public initiatives, something neither business nor local government can achieve alone.

As in the growth machine model, business and politicians are drawn to one another. However, Logan and Molotch argue that business uses its resources in a coercive manner, directing politicians to pursue its particular interests. In contrast, Stone believes that business and politicians share mutual civic interests. Local politicians are concerned with the welfare of the city because it reflects on their performance in government. Businesses, predominantly local in nature, are concerned for the welfare of the city, as the economic welfare will determine the success of their business. The two are attracted to each other's resources because they complement their own. While their motivations may vary regarding any given project, the outcome is usually beneficial to the city. Although, Stone does recognize the potential for other forms of governing regimes, just as earlier regime theorists like Elkin (1985, 1987) do, he, like Logan and Molotch, focuses particularly on the relationship between local politicians and businesses.

More recently, both camps have acknowledged a greater variety of forms of urban politics and governance. In fact, Stone suggests that "for various sectors of the community to come together in a cooperative relationship is far from the usual state of affairs" (2001, 23). More important, both growth machine and urban regime theorists began incorporating other actors into their analysis, specifically middle-class interests. For instance, Logan and Rabrenovic (1990) acknowledge the predominance of middle-class neighbourhood associations as the main opposition to growth machines. Numerous authors, in adopting growth machine theory, also added anti-growth citizen coalitions to the mix. Current analyses adopting the theory now invariably include the neighbourhood-association-led anti-growth coalition as the foil to the developer-led growth coalition. In their analysis of Gainesville, Florida, Vogel and Swanson (1989) describe the city's anti-growth coalition, the main opponent of the local growth machine, as a consortium of "neighbourhood organizations, environmentalists, and watchdogs of elected officials" (71).

In discussing the success of the anti-growth coalition in San Francisco, DeLeon and Powell (1989) suggest that it took a coalition of middle-class and working-class citizens to pass the city's tough anti-growth measures. However, the authors' discussion suggests that the middle class was the protagonist, and won because it was able to co-opt the working class. In a later article, DeLeon (1992b) explicitly makes such an argument. Moreover, he echoes Vogel and Swanson

(1989), suggesting "the neighborhood movement is both an inspiring source and the Achilles' heel of the progressive movement in San Francisco" due to the insular mindset of San Francisco's middle class (De-Leon 1992b, 556). Lastly, Purcell (1997, 2000) also emphasizes the role of the upper-middle class in opposing Los Angeles' growth machine. He argues that a significant contributor to the emergence and growth of the anti- or slow-growth movement in L.A. was the spread of development into wealthy enclaves in the city. According to Purcell (2000), "the upper-middle-class and well-organized homeowners groups ...led the charge" against development (91).

The earliest accounts of urban regimes, particularly the work of Fainstein and Fainstein (1983), who adopt a structuralist perspective more in line with Logan and Molotch (Kantor 1987), portrayed the middle class as part of the governing regime. However, urban regime theory came to recognize the importance of middle-class opposition as well. For instance, Stone (1993, 2001) in later works began to portray them as adversaries in the same vein as the growth machine literature. In fact, Elkin (1985), much earlier, suggested that while the middle classes initially supported the growth machine when it was involved in redevelopment of inner cities, they quickly became opponents when projects such as highway development began to encroach on their own neighbourhoods.

This distinction suggests the importance of temporal factors in the relationships between actors involved in the politics of urban development. More important, it also captures how geography affects actors' interests. Only when development began to encroach on middle- and upper-middle-class neighbourhoods did these groups begin opposing the regime, usually by incorporating and organizing themselves in neighbourhood associations.

Most early writings on growth machines and urban regimes also omitted or failed to develop an understanding of the changing relationship among actors in local politics resulting from economic change. Despite emphasizing the importance of the economy in determining the relationship between political actors, most urban regime theorists focus on the relationship between *local* business and development interests and politicians, and fail to account for future changes in the economy affecting that relationship. Logan and Molotch note the potential impact of globalization on business, as international conglomerates replace local businesses, but do not develop the point. One of the few authors to not make this omission is Paul Kantor (1987; with David 1988), who, writing contemporaneously to Stone and Logan and Molotch, presages both the increased role of citizen groups, in the form of neighbourhood associations, and the effect of a changing economy on the interests of business and its relationship with local government. Kantor argues, from the perspective of urban regime theory, that local government's leverage over business has eroded due to globalization, while citizen-group associations' have increased their access to and influence over local politicians. Kantor states: *"In this type of regime public officials are constrained to reconcile their responsiveness to the citizenry (popular control) with the promotion of their economies (market control). These dual control processes create a tension for government that is inherent in this political economy"* (Kantor with David 1988, 13, emphasis in original).

By the mid- to late 1990s, despite drawing mostly on Logan and Molotch and Stone's respective conceptions of growth machines and urban regimes, a number of authors began recognizing the influence of globalization and economic change on the role and behaviour of business in local politics, much as Kantor depicted it. For instance, Mark Purcell (1997, 2000) suggests that the emergence of international developers, less focused on the Los Angeles market, have significantly weakened the growth machine there. Orr and Stoker (1994) note the declining interest of the big three American car companies in the future of Detroit as they focus increasingly on the success or failure of their multinational operations. Both Gainsborough (2008) and Strom (2008) argue that as globalization erodes the interests of many businesses in local politics, developers have become the main business actor in local politics, because of their continued interests in urban development.

Both the process of globalization and the increasing role of developers as the main protagonists in urban politics are particularly pertinent to Toronto. The city is home to many national, continental, and international headquarters of businesses, including many continental and international developers. However, the city is also the main market for a number of local developers, particularly those involved in the condominium market. The following section outlines the interests and incentives that direct the behaviour of specific political actors as depicted by both growth machine and urban regime literature. It also demonstrates that, despite significant differences, the two theories portray the behaviour and many of the interests of actors in the same fashion.

Developers, Neighbourhood Associations, and Local Politicians

Developers, citizen groups in the form of neighbourhood associations, and local politicians form the triad of political actors that dominate the politics of urban development in American LPE literature. Although Stone lumps developers in a group with all other local businesses, Logan and Molotch conceive of developers as a distinct group: place entrepreneurs. As the term place entrepreneurs suggests, the two authors conceive of developers as land speculators and the main proponents of the growth machine. Most of the later literature on urban regimes (see, for instance, Purcell 1997, 2000) and growth machines (Vogel and Swanson 1989; DeLeon 1992a, 1992b), tends to emphasize the role of developers over other members of the growth coalition. Earlier regime literature (Fainstein and Fainstein 1983; Elkin 1985) also focused more heavily on the role of developers, especially as they were concerned with redevelopment. As Gainsborough (2008) and Strom (2008) suggest, developers have increasingly become the main protagonists in local politics in various American cities.

Like all businesspeople, property owners/developers seek increasing returns on their investments. To achieve increasing returns, developers seek to develop and intensify their holdings. However, to proceed with development, developers require the approval of local government. According to Logan and Molotch (1987), developers enlist the aid of other businesses by enticing them with the purported economic benefits of development. Together, the coalition of businesses and developers uses its resources to ensure the support of local politicians. In contrast, Stone (1989) does not envision the business coalition as buying the support of politicians. Rather, he believes there is a natural synergy that attracts business and politicians to each other. There are a number of incentives luring business into a coalition with politicians. Fainstein and Fainstein (1983) refer to this as a "symbiotic relationship" (250), as both groups benefit. Local government's control over development is one of the primary resources that attract local businesses into coalitions. Thus, Stone's (1989) account suggests, just as the growth machine literature does, that developers, in particular, will lobby and attempt to co-opt local politicians and government.

Although the two theories differ in their emphasis on developers' role in urban politics, both Logan and Molotch and Stone initially treated upper-middle-class neighbourhood associations with similar disinterest, as previously mentioned. According to Logan and Molotch, middle-class citizenry are better able to mobilize than other groups to counter the growth machine; however, the authors never address how the emergence of such opposition would shape urban development politics, nor do they suggest that such a middle class–led movement could govern in lieu of the machine. In fact, in referring to the middle class as the "Vanguard of the Bourgeoisie" (Logan and Molotch 1987, 141), the authors suggest that the middle class, or those aspiring to be middle class, may actually facilitate the destruction of existing low-income communities if the exchange value of the neighbourhoods is right.

The middle class in this instance may be better characterized as the upper middle class. This thesis uses the two terms interchangeably to denote the citizens and homeowners with the resources necessary to organize and mobilize. The typical conception of the "middle class" in much of the urban regime and growth machine literature is of the professional class including lawyers, doctors, and other professions of similar community standing and resources. In his later work on urban regimes, Stone (1993) suggests a progressive middle class could actually form a governing coalition with local politicians. However, he emphasizes that such a regime would still require the monetary resources of local business, necessitating coercion, and is pessimistic about middle-class fortunes in local politics, just as Logan and Molotch are. Despite this pessimism, other authors, before both Stone and Logan and Molotch, argued that, while constituting a small proportion of the population of inner cities, middle-class professional migrants to the downtown core have established themselves as an important foil to developers in many American cities. Mollenkopf (1983) refers to these individuals as "urban pioneers," a group with the organizational skills and political resources unavailable to lower-income residents (181).

Later writings, drawing on both urban regime and growth machine theories, have emphasized the importance of these groups as well. However, many of these accounts suggest such residents have existed within central cities for much longer than Mollenkopf suggests. More important, these writings confirm that such middle-class movements, typically dominated by neighbourhood associations, are usually at odds with developers. Logan and Rabrenovic (1990) and Downs (1981) suggest that opposition to development is one of the primary reasons for the formation of neighbourhood associations, especially in suburbs, and confirm the pre-eminence of middle-class citizens in these institutions. Mesch and Schwirian (1996) suggest that both low-income and middle- or upper-middle-class neighbourhood associations are common in Columbus, Ohio. However, their findings suggest that the socio-economic status of a neighbourhood association is the best indicator of its overall activity and effectiveness. Middle- and upper-middle-class neighbourhoods, according to the authors, are more active, organized, and more effective than lower-income neighbourhoods are.

In arguably the most thorough analysis on the constituents of neighbourhood associations, the primary vehicle for citizen mobilization in most North American cities, Thomas (1986) argues that socio-economic status affects not only the effectiveness of neighbourhood associations, but also their membership levels. He emphasizes that the average income of a specific neighbourhood is not as important as the percentage of professionals living within the area, suggesting "the important consideration is not the *average* level of socioeconomic status as much as the proportions of the *highest* levels of socioeconomic status" (Thomas 1986, 63–4, emphasis in original). Notably, Ley and Mercer (1980) found the same in Vancouver, where professional elites formed the nexus of a movement against developers in the early and mid-1970s.

As the examples given above demonstrate, middle-class neighbourhood associations focus their efforts on electoral mobilization to influence political decision making. Neighbourhood organizations organize and fund campaigns during election time in order to promote their own position, and to actively support or oppose local candidates. As DeLeon (1992b; and DeLeon and Powell 1989) suggests, middle-class anti-growth advocates in San Francisco were able to oppose the growth machine, in part because they were able to mobilise the working black communities. Purcell (2000) and DeLeon (1992b; and DeLeon and Powell 1989) also emphasize the ability of anti-growth forces to mobilize votes for anti-growth candidates – or in favour of referenda curbing growth, where such an option is available, as is commonly the case in California. Thomas (1986) suggests this success stems from a combination of "time, money, and leadership skills" unavailable to other socioeconomic classes (66). Thus, middle-class neighbourhood associations are interested in opposing development in their neighbourhoods, and will mobilize the electorate to sway local politicians in their favour.

Given the interests of both developers and neighbourhood associations, politicians are not lacking in potential suitors. Both growth machine and urban regime literature recognize politicians' need for the economic support of business (and developers), and the support of the electorate. In both Stone's and Logan and Molotch's analyses, politicians will invariably choose the former, because business and developers can mobilize more effectively and, from the perspective of regime theory, have the necessary resources for governing. However, as the discussion of Los Angeles, San Francisco, and Gainesville attest, growth interests' ability to outmanoeuvre the opposition has diminished in the face of increasingly effective middle-class neighbourhood associations that are capable of influencing electoral outcomes. Whereas local politicians require local business to govern effectively, they require the support of the electorate to govern at all.

Both urban regime and growth machine theories recognize electoral success as the fundamental interest of politicians. Winning elections is the main goal or interest of most local politicians. As Stone's (1989) account of Atlanta's governing regime's coalition with black groups attests, politicians will pursue various means, even if they sometimes contradict their own previous position, to maintain electoral support. From a growth machine perspective (Molotch 1993), local politicians often gravitate towards business interests to elicit the resources necessary for running effective campaigns. In the same vein, Stone (1989) and Elkin (1985) suggest that politicians coalesce with business and developers to influence the perceptions of citizens. As a result, where little middle-class opposition exists, politicians will continue to work to varying degrees with developers. However, where the middle class has mobilized against developers, some, if not all, politicians will begin to oppose pro-development interests, and may align themselves in a coalition with middle-class neighbourhood associations. Alternatively, as Vogel and Swanson (1989) and Purcell's (1997, 2000) case studies suggest, such a situation may place local politicians in an untenable situation, and severely hamper the process of governance. DeLeon's (1992b; DeLeon and Powell 1989) account of San Francisco politics in the 1980s demonstrates the type of politics present when tension exists between strong developers and well-organized middle-class neighbourhood associations. The struggle between such forces is not conducive to long-term policy making, as the two sides constantly repeat pitched battles over development policy. Kantor (with David 1988) refers to this tension between developers and neighbourhood associations as "an explosive dilemma" that local governments are tasked with navigating. He further suggests that this dilemma "frustrates the ability of local political authorities to act responsibly" (ibid., 5).

Thus, both developers and neighbourhood associations focus their efforts on influencing local politicians because the latter control decision making on land-use issues. However, the interests of each group are at odds, which often leads to conflict between them. Each group wields resources attractive to local politicians. Developers offer local politicians the money necessary for running elections, and resources for implementing development policies. Neighbourhood associations offer electoral support, a vital commodity for local politicians, whose main goal is re-election. Local politicians, therefore, must choose one group, and risk offending the other.

Limits of Analysis

The depiction of political behaviour above forms the benchmark this book uses for comparison with political behaviour in Toronto. However, while urban regime and growth machine theories provide powerful tools for analysis, many scholars question the applicability of such theories in jurisdictions outside the United States, or even to other jurisdictions within. Since I am not attempting to investigate the existence of either an urban regime or a growth machine in Toronto, criticisms regarding concept-stretching are not applicable.[4] However, a number of authors suggest this American local political economy literature omits important factors or variables from analysis that will influence and shape the behaviour and possibly even the interests of the actors discussed above.

Goldberg and Mercer (1986) are heavily critical of any attempt to transport American theories of local politics to Canada because of the important *cultural* differences that separate the two countries, while Pierre (1999) and DiGaetano and Strom (2003) further emphasize the importance of accounting for cultural differences in cross-country comparisons of urban politics. However, Goldberg and Mercer (1986) do not specifically address the interest formation or behaviour of political actors involved in urban development in Canada. Rather, they suggest that municipalities in Canada have greater control over issues of planning, and are more likely to be interventionist. Keating (1991) confirms this interventionist tendency, as do Reese and Rosenfeld (2004), though the latter suggest that Canadian cities are still growth-oriented. A number of authors have also emphasized the United States' distinctive attitude towards property rights, where, unlike Canada and Europe, the rights to property are constitutionally entrenched.[5] Probably because of this attitude, Leo (1997) notes how Americans rely much more on the courts to settle development disputes, as the Chicago case discussed in the first chapter demontrates. Thus, according to such authors, important cultural distinctions do exist. Goldberg and Mercer do not provide any substantive reason why cultural differences and greater intervention on the part of municipal government into planning would preclude the politics typified by either growth machine or regime theory, however.

Another group of authors argue that urban regime and growth machine literature underestimate the importance of *structural* (economic) differences both between countries and, more importantly, across time in determining local politics and policy decision making.[6] These authors, themselves, fall within the LPE genre. For instance, Jessop, Peck, and Tickell (1999) suggest the fault of growth machine and urban regime theories is that they are both too particularistic, failing to address the convergence of political behaviour and governance of cities across nations, as result of the shift from a Fordist to post-Fordist economy (regulation theory). This shift, however, is exactly what Kantor (1987; with David 1988), who adopts regime theory, focuses on in his work. If anything, such a criticism of local political economy literature suggests the validity of cross-country comparison, and challenges the supposed influence of cultural distinction between countries. Orr and Stoker (1994) and Purcell (2000) suggest that globalization has led to an increase of multinational businesses and developers, who have increasingly distanced themselves from local politics, thus challenging the typical portrayal of businesses' interest in development. However, all three authors still adopt a local political economy approach to their work, and as Gainsborough (2008) and Strom (2008) suggest, developers have often filled the void that other businesses have left.

This trend in the United States actually suggests a convergence towards the Canadian model, where businesses, particularly banks and commercial developers, are significantly less place-specific.[7] For instance, Canadian banks are national (and increasingly international) in scope (Cobban 2003), as opposed to many American banks that often are confined to specific city regions. While such a trend may make cross-country comparison easier, it suggests a potential flaw in the benchmark this book relies on for comparison. Developers in Toronto may not share the same place-specific interests suggested both by Stone and

Logan and Molotch. Moreover, as Imbroscio (2003) and Davies (2002) suggest, changes to the economy affect the structural limitations on local governance and political behaviour, shaping and changing them over time, such that the applicability of a given theory may wax and wane if it does not consider such factors. Both DeLeon's (1992b) and Fainstein's (2001) discussion of the worldwide crash in the office market of the late eighties and early nineties further emphasizes this point, as the vitality of much of the development industry disappeared virtually overnight.[8] This crash had particular ramifications for Toronto.

In addition to these potential economic and cultural differences between jurisdictions, a number of authors focus on specific institutional differences that could affect comparison. Scholars such as Pierre (1999) and DiGaetano and Strom (2003) – in line with the growing influence of new institutionalist approaches to analysis – argue that most accounts of political behaviour fail to address the general influence of institutions on urban politics. In one sense, I make a similar claim, as I attempt, in part, to address the failure of previous literature on the politics of urban development in Toronto to account for the OMB as a possible variable influencing political behaviour in the city. In addition, this book questions the ability of current American LPE theory to cope with differences in planning institutions and law across jurisdictions in Canada and the United States. In the same vein, Garber and Imbroscio (1996) suggest the greater role provincial governments play in municipal government, relative to American states, shifts the emphasis of urban development politics from the local to the provincial.

Both Cobban (2003) and Keating (1991) emphasize the important regulatory differences between the United States and Canada, such that provincial imperatives can alter politics within cities. Cobban argues that such differences prevent the emergence in Canada of the type of business/local government coalitions depicted by Stone, because local politicians are less likely to require the resources of businesses and developers. However, he does not suggest that the interests of actors involved in the politics of urban development in Canada vary significantly from those suggested by Stone. Furthermore, Garber and Imbroscio (1996) and Clark (1985) suggest that in Ontario, the OMB is, in essence, the proxy of the provincial government regarding urban development issues, such that the OMB becomes the focal point of urban development politics. John Chipman (2002), furthermore, makes the compelling argument that the board allows the province to maintain oversight and involvement in municipal affairs, without involving it-self with the complicated processes of appeals. Moreover, the board al-lows the province to avoid direct involvement in politically contentious debates over development.

Despite these criticisms, Harding (1994) believes both urban regime and growth machine theory do account for both structural and institu-tional constraints. He correctly notes that Elkin (1987), Logan and Mo-lotch (1987), and Stone (1989) all recognize on various occasions the specific applicability of their respective theories to the United States, and that they base this knowledge on their understanding of both the structural and institutional constraints specific to local government in the United States. As a result, however, he suggests that these various constraints limit the use of these theories for cross-national studies. Nevertheless, he, like Strom (1996), suggests the theories still provide useful analytical tools for such analyses. I make the same assumption.

Some of the criticisms outlined above suggest some of the limitations to my approach. For one, as many of the authors attest to either ex-plicitly or implicitly, changes to the economy over time, as well as in-stitutional and cultural changes, may limit the explanatory power of an analysis such as this to the specific period of study. Certainly, the role of the OMB presumably would have been far less significant dur-ing the 1990s when large-scale development, particularly in the down-town area of Toronto, was at a standstill. Furthermore, as evidenced by Rose's (1972) account of early citizen opposition to development in the former City of Toronto, neighbourhood associations once viewed the OMB as an ally against the City and developers. The changes to city council during the 1970s (discussed below), from a council supportive of developers' interests to one opposed, altered residents' perceptions of the OMB from saviour of neighbourhoods to tool of developers and scourge of democracy. However, this very change from pro-growth to anti-growth attitude suggests the usefulness of the approach outlined above for comparative purposes. The pattern of political change in To-ronto bears many similarities with changes that occurred in San Fran-cisco and Los Angeles, for example.[9]

For the purpose of this book, it is only necessary to establish that the basic interests of the actors involved in the politics of urban de-velopment in Toronto parallel those as outlined earlier in the chapter. Thus, while I may not be able to generalize the findings of this book to Toronto beyond the period of study, it may prove very useful for future comparative analysis. Not only was the process of change in Toronto similar to that depicted by the likes of Purcell (1997, 2000) and DeLeon (1992a, 1992b), in their respective analyses of Los Angeles and San Francisco, the actors involved were comparable in each instance, as were their interests. The brief account of the politics of urban development and political change in Toronto that follows suggests that the actors I discuss throughout the remainder of this book share many common characteristics and interests with the actors American local political economy literature portrays. Thus, it calls into question the significance of cultural distinctions between the two countries and the importance of other institutional differences.

Urban Development Politics in Toronto: From Metro to Amalgamation

While scholars of Toronto politics have not addressed the influence the OMB has on the politics of urban development in Toronto, they have written detailed accounts on the politics of urban development, especially on the reform movement of the late 1960s and early 1970s. Magnusson (1983) suggests that issues of land-use planning have been of central importance to the City of Toronto for most of its existence, just as such issues dominate the politics of municipalities in the rest of Canada (Lorimer 1972; Sancton 1983). At the beginning of the twentieth century, Toronto's burgeoning population led to the same problems associated with housing demand and growth felt by other growing cities in North America (Rose 1972). Planning for development through spot-zoning and other measures became of paramount importance, while the debate about whether to grow and invest in infrastructure or to conserve and lower spending became one of the pre-eminent political cleavages (Magnusson 1983). Between the 1930s and 1940s, Toronto established itself at the forefront of urban planning in North America (Rose 1972; Magnusson 1983).

Like most North American cities, Toronto began to expand rapidly after the Second World War. The creation of Metropolitan Toronto (Metro) in 1954 was in response to this expansion (Kaplan 1965; Rose 1972). In addition, like many American cities, Toronto began encouraging investment in downtown development, as well as re-zoning areas for high-rise development. While this created some initial tension between citizens and city planners, the conflict had little impact on the progress of development in the city, though citizen anger towards development projects that threatened the integrity of their neighbourhoods became a lasting issue in the city (Magnusson 1983).

Toronto's programs, from slum clearance and housing projects to downtown development, were all on a much smaller scale than those implemented in many American cities. In part, this may have resulted from the creation of Metro Toronto, which spread the development of subsidized housing throughout the entire Metro area, to avoid creating large neighbourhoods of poverty. More important, Toronto lacked the substantial funds from the federal government that the American cities enjoyed. Both Garber and Imbroscio (1996) and Keating (1991) stress the important distinction between the federal government's role in municipalities' affairs in the United States and its role, or lack thereof, in Canada. Toronto did not have the funds to pursue significant development and redevelopment schemes that American cities did. Nonetheless, Toronto did pursue many of the same policies as cities like Atlanta (see Stone 1989) and Dallas (see Elkin 1987). Clearly, other issues, particularly racial conflict in the United States, which played pivotal roles in development and politics in US cities, were lacking in Toronto. Nevertheless, Toronto politicians and developers demonstrated the same support and interest in major development projects as their American counterparts, so much so that conflict between neighbourhood associations and a city council purportedly dominated by developer-friendly councillors increased, particularly as the City's development plans began encroaching on middle- and upper-middle-class neighbourhoods (Lorimer 1972; Filion 1999).

The single most important event signifying the emergence of neighbourhood associations as important political players in Toronto was their successful defeat of Metro's plans for the Spadina Expressway. The expressway was one of many proposed for Metro Toronto, allowing residents from the outer suburbs easier access to the downtown. As with any plans for highways through developed urban areas, the Spadina Expressway required significant destruction of existing housing and neighbourhoods. One of the affected neighbourhoods was the affluent enclave of Forest Hill, a former municipality that merged with Toronto in 1966. The upper-middle-class residents of Forest Hill, along with other wealthy neighbourhoods, formed the geneses of the ad hoc group Stop Spadina, Save Our City Co-ordinating Committee (SSSOCCC). Middle-class residents were able to rally working-class neighbourhoods to their cause, and were able to defeat the construction of the remainder of the expressway (Rose 1972).[10]

Due in part to the success of the SSSOCCC, neighbourhood associations became increasingly militant in the city. Much like their counterparts in Los Angeles, San Francisco, and Gainesville, Toronto's middle- and upper-middle-class neighbourhood associations began opposing developments they believed encroached on their neighbourhoods. In 1968 a number of neighbourhood associations established the Confederation of Residents' and Ratepayers' Associations (CORRA). This confederation allowed neighbourhood associations to coordinate their opposition to development (Magnusson 1983). The use of referenda, such as that employed in San Francisco in opposition to development (DeLeon and Powell 1989), is not readily available to Ontario municipalities. Nevertheless, Toronto's neighbourhood associations and other anti-development groups were able to mobilize the electorate and defeat a number of pro-developer councillors. The success of anti-growth forces resulted in the victory of the new "reformers" in 1972, ostensibly anti-development in character. The council subsequently passed a moratorium on large-scale development in the downtown. While not as stringent as they appeared, these measures angered developers (Caulfield 1974; Magnusson 1983; Kipfer and Keil 2002). Again, the success of the neighbourhood association movement, and the defeat of the pro-growth council, bears remarkable resemblance to events that unfolded in the American cities discussed throughout this chapter.

Despite the continued clashes between residents and developers, and measures to limit development in the city's core, Toronto witnessed a significant construction boom in the downtown, following its recovery from a mild recession in the early eighties. Office buildings built by Toronto-based developers began rising in the city, as they did around the world. All of it came to an abrupt end in the early nineties, however, as a number of the world's largest developers, including the largest, Toronto based Olympia & York, filed for bankruptcy. Years of speculative development took their toll, and the collapse of the office market, particularly in Asia, signified the beginning of a worldwide recession. This recession was the worst Ontario had experienced since the depression (Kipfer and Keil 2002; Frisken 2001; Fainstein 2001). The bust of the real-estate market wrought similar destruction in a number of American cities as well, notably New York (Fainstein 2001) and Los Angeles (Purcell 2000). The scale of the real-estate sector's collapse emphasizes the continued importance of economic factors, and particularly the importance of globalization. Hence, it lends credence to the convergence thesis of regulation theory scholars like Jessop, Peck, and Tickell (1999).

More important, however, the preceding discussion lends significant credence to the notion that actors involved in the politics of urban development in Toronto are similar to those in American cities, and share the same interests. Regardless of institutional or cultural differences, developers in both the United States and Toronto seek to develop land (not surprisingly), while residents of affluent neighbourhoods oppose developments that purportedly encroach on their enjoyment of city living. Finally, local politicians, as a group, are torn between the monetary resources of developers and the electoral support of neighbourhood associations. Whether or not growth machines or urban regimes exist or have previously existed in Toronto, the underlying assumptions regarding actors' interests within local political economy literature appear applicable to the political actors within the city.

3 The OMB and the Politics of Urban Development in Toronto

The LPE approach to studying urban politics focuses on political behaviour, the influence of the economy, and the institutions of government that shape and set the boundaries for the actions and interaction of different actors.[1] Government institutions do not always shape the interests of actors, but they often influence how actors' pursue their interests. They can also affect how resources are distributed among different actors. Theories such as pluralism and urban regime theory rely on this fact (Stone 1993). The Ontario Municipal Board as an institution of municipal planning in Ontario may not shape actors' interests, but likely influences their behaviour given its potential to redistribute resources in the politics of urban development. Although individual theories of local political economy may not be able to account for the influence of institutions such as the board, the overarching approach to the study of local political economy that underlies these theories can.

Planning Institutions and the Politics of Urban Development

Critics of pluralism, regime theory, and various American theories of urban politics often argue that such theories fail to account for differences in socio-economic policies and institutions between countries. For instance, Davies (2003) argues that urban regime theory cannot account for political behaviour in British cities because such cities lack the socio-economic institutions in place in the United States that force local government and business to work together. In the past, the British government has adopted more interventionist measures than the United States, and has had a more direct role in governing and financing municipal government. Despite such criticism, American scholars have explicitly recognized the limits of their theories. As early as the 1960s, Dahl (1961) expressly acknowledged that the institutions and culture of the United States were responsible for pluralism in America. Stone (1993) argues that regime theory assumes the existence of a liberal political economy directed by private investment (2). This study assumes the same when evaluating the politics of urban development in the City of Toronto.

While certain elements of both pluralism and urban regime theory have little applicability beyond the United States, their mutual focus on resource distribution has wide-ranging explanatory power. Among different resources available to political actors, both Stone (1993) and Dahl (1961), though adopting different terminologies, emphasize businesses' wealth and organizational skills, citizen groups' ability to mobilize the electorate, and local politicians' power of decision making (their authority) as central to understanding local politics. However, the LPE literature in both North America and Europe tends to focus on the first of these resources, though increasingly focusing on the second as well. Governance theory, for instance, examines the changing fiscal relationship between central governments and cities, and how central governments' cuts to cities' funding have encouraged a greater reliance of local governments in Europe on the resources of businesses and not-for-profit organizations (John 2001). Urban regime theory is premised, in part, on the fact that municipal governments in the United States have limited sources of revenue, which is why developers and other businesses are attractive allies for local politicians.

LPE literature in the United States, however, does not examine in any detail local politicians' main resource, authority, particularly when applied to planning policy. Such literature assumes local politicians enjoy such authority and does not examine the ways municipal governments utilize it. However, institutional differences across jurisdictions could alter local politicians' power over planning decisions. A change to local politicians' monopoly of planning decision making could significantly alter the dynamics between and behaviour of local politicians and other political actors, even if other pertinent institutions and socio-economic structures are the same.

The potential for lower-level institutional differences to alter or constrain the behaviour of municipal government is integral to Frug and Barron's (2008) critique of theories including Dahl's (1961) pluralism, Peterson's (1981) economic determinism, and Stone's (1989) regime theory. Frug and Barron argue that differences in state law can have a significant (and often stifling) effect on cities' agency. The two authors are less concerned with the ramifications of such differences for political behaviour, but provide a very useful account of planning institutions in Boston to illustrate their point. The Commonwealth of Massachusetts stripped most planning authority from the City of Boston, placing it instead into three unelected bodies: the Zoning Commission, the Zoning Board of Appeal, and the Boston Redevelopment Authority (BRA). While the mayor appoints the members of the Zoning Commission, state law dictates the type of individuals he or she may appoint. The BRA is its own agency, distinct from the municipal government, and has the power to make long-term planning decisions, but also can veto the City's zoning by-laws.

Frug and Barron (2008) focus on how combining both planning and redevelopment roles in one body affects redevelopment in comparison to other jurisdictions that divide the role. However, in addition to affecting redevelopment, the BRA, the Zoning Commission, and the Board of Appeal could also fundamentally alter urban development politics in Boston. By shifting authority over planning away from local politicians in the city, the state removed one of local politicians' most important resources. The lack of authority over planning could diminish the role Boston's local politicians play in the politics of urban development. Boston is an example of how differences in planning institutions might substantially alter the politics of urban development in different jurisdictions. However, current literature on the politics of urban development does not appear to account for such differences. By examining the role the OMB plays in the politics of urban development in Toronto, I hope to address this hole in the LPE literature, while demonstrating how the LPE approach to urban politics can accommodate such differences.

The OMB: Powers, Practices, Procedures, and Experts

Capturing the entire scope of powers and jurisdiction of the Ontario Municipal Board and its history of development is beyond this one chapter. Other authors, namely Adler (1971), Chipman (2002), and Krushelnicki (2007), have devoted entire books to this subject. Fortunately, this book is only concerned with the board in its function as a planning appeals board. As a result, in this chapter I focus solely on the powers, practices, and procedures of the board as they relate to its role as a planning appeals body.

The OMB is a provincially created arm's-length body whose primary role in land-use planning is to hear and pass judgment on planning disputes concerning amendments to zoning by-laws and official plans (Frankena and Scheffman 1980). Planning is often a contentious issue in cities. As Cullingworth suggests, "Planning is not an independent operation: it seeks to adapt the decisions of private interests (which seek their own benefit) to the decisions of public interests (which seek public benefits)" (quoted in Chipman 2002, 26). Such balancing will inevitably lead to tensions between these often-contrasting interests. In addition, private interests are often at odds. The existence of tension within the planning policy, especially when elected officials make the policy, ensures the process is a political one. The OMB's nature places it within this conflict of interests. It is invariably involved in issues that are highly contentious and that elicit strong sentiments from interested parties, as both Krushelnicki (2007) and Clark (1985) note. The board's quasi-judicial status and its focus on natural justice also contribute to the public nature of its proceedings. Not surprisingly, whether the board should exist at all is a major source of debate.[2]

The Ontario Municipal Board falls under the jurisdiction of the Attorney General of Ontario, which is appropriate given its quasi-judicial nature. It currently has between twenty-five and thirty members with varying backgrounds, including lawyers, engineers, accountants, public administrators, former local politicians, planners, and a host of other individuals with backgrounds or experience in municipal government and urban planning (Chipman 2002; Krushelnicki 2007). The Ontario Municipal Board Act, 1990 is the board's main enabling legislation. However, the board's jurisdiction over local government derives from a copious number of provincial statutes and acts (Environmental and Land Tribunals Ontario 2009). The Planning Act, 1990 is the primary source codifying the board's responsibility as an appeals body over planning disputes, while the Statutory Powers Procedures Act, 1990 consolidates many of the regulations, practices, and procedures of the board pertaining to its quasi-judicial role as they have developed over its existence. Despite this legislation, or due to its vagueness, many of the board's powers, procedures, and practices are not codified in law. Likewise, many of the board's powers expressed in these acts are now redundant or rarely used.

This overlapping and vague legislation makes outlining the board's power and procedures a difficult task. Moreover, the legislation enabling the OMB, particularly the Planning Act, has continued to evolve and change over time, as successive governments have amended the legislation to reflect the times, public opinion, and their own policies. I attempt, here, to portray the power, practices, and procedures of the OMB as they were during the period of my analysis, 1 January 2000 to 31 December 2006. During this period the McGuinty government passed the Strong Communities (Planning Amendment) Act, 2004, which, as its title suggests, amended significant portions of the Planning Act, 1990. Some of these changes altered the Ontario Municipal Board's appeals process, and to a much lesser extent the board's powers.[3] However, while the act contains important changes to the OMB's appeals process and the role of provincial policy in the board's decisions, these changes should not significantly affect or alter the influence of the board on the behaviour of the actors involved in the politics of urban development in Toronto.[4]

The OMB: Powers

Krushelnicki (2007) suggests that "a simple review of the *OMBA* would be misleading. Some of the sections granting authority to the Board are no longer relevant and some of the powers listed are used so rarely (if at all), that they no longer form part of its common practice" (51). For instance, while the board has the power to make inquiries into planning issues, or virtually any other issue falling under its auspices, it never makes use of this power. Rather, the board acts in a passive manner, passing judgment on a given issue only when another party appeals to it for a ruling, or applies to it for its opinion (Chipman 2002; Krushelnicki 2007). Nevertheless, in its role as an appeals board, or tribunal, the OMB wields significant power. In its role as a quasi-judicial appeals body, the OMB has the ability to turn down an appeal, overturn the decisions of a municipal government, substitute its own decision for that of the municipality, or, in certain instances, choose not to hear an appeal at all. Furthermore, the avenues of appeal of OMB decisions are very limited. One may appeal to the courts, but only on matters of law (Ontario, Planning Act 1990), or informally petition the provincial government to overturn the board's decision (a rare occurrence, as it would require the government to pass new legislation to undo the board's decision). The OMB has the same powers, rights, and privileges as the Ontario Superior Court of Justice. Furthermore, the board has the power to administer oaths and to award costs. In addition, the board has the ability to make its own rules regulating its practices and procedures

(Ontario, Ontario Municipal Board Act 1990; Ontario, Statutory Powers Procedures Act 1990).

While the board has power over even minor issues relating to land-use planning,[5] I focus my analysis on its powers as they relate to the politics of urban development in Toronto and to the city's development industry. Toronto City staff, in its own report on the OMB, focuses on official plan amendments, zoning by-law amendments, and interim control by-laws (Commissioner of Urban Development Services 2002). While the board's role as an appeal board during the creation of official plans is also important, an appeal of a new official plan is a special type of appeal that can take years to resolve. For instance, the City of Toronto introduced its newest plan on 28 November 2002, and as of February 2009, has yet to receive complete approval from the OMB. Thus, I too focus only on zoning by-law amendments, interim control by-laws, and official plan amendments. While the politics surrounding the Official Plan and its appeal are interesting in themselves, they fall beyond the scope of this book.

An official plan "provides direction for future planning activities and for public and private initiatives aimed at improving the existing environment" (*Citizen's Guide*, no. 2, 1985 [Ontario Ministry of Municipal Affairs 1985b]). Official plan amendments (OPAs), as the name implies, are amendments to a municipality's official plan, subsequent to its passing. A developer, or any other party, will apply for an OPA when a development project it is proposing does not conform to the official plan (ibid.). Any person or public body can appeal a municipality's decision regarding an application for an OPA. Thus, a developer can appeal a municipality's refusal to amend an official plan, or a neighbourhood association can appeal the municipality's decision to pass an amendment.[6] In addition, if a municipality fails to render a decision within a specified length of time, the applicant can appeal to the OMB (Ontario, Planning Act 1990).

The Planning Act, 1990 provides similar avenues of appeal with regard to zoning by-law amendments (ZBLAs) and interim control by-laws (ICBLs). According to Chipman, "Zoning by-laws provide specific regulations for the use of land, governing matters such as the permitted uses, maximum densities, and building heights, [etc.]" (2002, 15). Whereas,

> interim control by-laws are a special variant of zoning by-laws. A council may within a defined area prohibit most types of development, otherwise

permitted under the zoning by-law, for a period of one year, while it conducts studies and determines what the most appropriate development
policies and zoning provisions for that area should be. The life of such by-
laws may be extended for two additional one-year periods. (15–16)

In all instances – OPAs, ZBLAs, and ICBLs – the OMB can accept the
proposed amendment, modify it, or refuse it altogether. The politics
of urban development in the City of Toronto revolves, in part, around
the Official Plan, zoning by-laws, and applications to amend both. This
fact largely derives from the conflict between neighbourhood associations and developers, and from the City's habitual amending of its own
plan and by-laws. Conflict ensures that some actor will regularly be of-
fended with city council's decisions. The habitual amending of the official plan and zoning by-laws significantly increases the likelihood of
such disputes. Thus, the OMB's powers of decision making, and ability to not only allow an appeal, but to substitute its own decision in
place of the municipality's, is of significant importance to the actors
involved in the politics of urban development in Toronto, just as local
politicians' authority over development and planning is significant in
LPE literature.

An additional factor further intensifies the board's power over planning. Section 2 of the Planning Act, 1990 outlines a laundry list of "provincial interests," which the board must "have regard to" (s. 2). For
much of the OMB's existence, these were the only provisions of provincial interest that guided the OMB. However, Chipman (2002) suggests
the board interpreted "have regard to" very loosely, such that the OMB
decided whether to comply with provincial interests or not. Weak provincial guidelines allowed the board significantly greater scope than
is otherwise apparent in the Planning Act. The province provided no
guidelines relating to issues such as high-density development, such
that the OMB determined the policies on its own. As Frankena and
Scheffman (1980) note, "Most issues which reach the OMB cannot ...
be decided simply by the interpretation and application of laws"; thus,
"it is in [these situations] ... that the OMB exercises the greatest degree
of discretion in its decisions and essentially makes provincial land use
policy by default" (41–2).

The McGuinty government, beginning in 2004, introduced legislation
that established provincial interests in planning and development matters (Ontario, Greenbelt Protection Act 2004 and the Places to Grow Act
2005). However, the OMB still determines whether to allow or refuse a

planning amendment based on its own opinion of the suitability of a development. It can ignore the municipality's stance and can override its official plan. Thus, the board's powers are clearly significant.

The OMB: Practices and Procedures

While the OMB has compiled a list of its own "Rules of Practice and Procedure,"[7] most of the board's practices and procedures, especially as they pertain to this study, are not included in any legislation or codified rules. This fact is in keeping with the vagueness and ambiguity of much of the board's powers. The few government publications I refer to in this section that address the board's practices and procedures are simply guides for navigating the appeals process, aimed at the general public (for example, Ontario Ministry of Municipal Affairs 1985a; OMB n.d.). While these guides are useful, they provide only a brief overview of some of the board's practices and procedures, not an in-depth discussion. Much of the literature on the OMB does not adequately address the board's procedures and practices, instead focusing almost exclusively on the powers of the board, especially with regard to policy making.[8] This lack of discussion is surprising given the controversies surrounding some of the board's practices, in particular its practice of hearing every case de novo. The board's procedures shape the interaction of parties to an appeal and are, therefore, integral to understanding the behaviour of political actors. Fortunately, Bruce Krushelnicki (2007), a member of the board from 1991 to 2003, provides a very useful and informed account of such practices and procedures. I rely heavily on his account in following subsections, and on a few sources from an anthology prepared by the Canadian Bar Association (Bermingham 2001; Bowman 2001).

   The OMB, in its role as an appellant body, behaves as a court-like tribunal. As such, many of its procedural requirements derive from procedures in criminal and civil courts (Krushelnicki 2007; Ontario Ministry of Municipal Affairs 1985a). However, though the board functions within the same framework as courts in its role as a quasi-judicial tribunal, it does so "with less formal, less rigid and less technical proceedings" (Krushelnicki 2007, 91). The notion of less formal proceedings, and the more lax procedural requirements of the board relative to the courts, results from the board's interpretation of the principle of natural justice. In most respects, all courts in Canada adhere to the principle of natural justice. The principle of natural justice entails an individual's right to know of any decisions or actions that could affect his or her interests, and affords them an opportunity for a fair hearing to address the individual's concerns, and a means to rectify them (Bermingham 2001; Krushelnicki 2007).

The board has adopted a less formal style of hearing from a typical court. Everyone who deems an issue within their interest is able to participate in the board's proceedings, with or without legal counsel. The appellant(s) in OMB hearings, as well as the respondent(s), are "parties" to the hearing, and have the right to present witnesses and cross-examine their opponent's witnesses, in the same way as parties to court hearings. However, the board also allows for "participants" to a hearing. These participants lack party status, but are interested in the case, and are able to submit their opinion in writing or orally to the board. They are not, however, allowed to call or cross-examine witnesses.

The board's granting of participant status to anyone interested in a specific appeal highlights the more lax atmosphere of its hearings compared to a court of law (Krushelnicki 2007; Ontario Ministry of Municipal Affairs 1985a). Despite the board's practice of convening hearings in an adversarial manner, similar to the courts, the board will hear almost anyone with an interest in the appeal (Krushelnicki 2007). However, involvement in an OMB hearing can be expensive and often less than satisfactory for some parties or participants, a key issue I consider throughout this book. The board's focus on the principle of natural justice and the less formal character of its hearings offers and encourages the participation of neighbourhood associations and other such groups in an adversarial forum with developers and municipal government.

Along with the principle of natural justice, the board's practice of hearing each case de novo, aside from being very contentious in the past, could have significant ramifications for the politics of urban development in Toronto. The term de novo entails treating each case as if it is new, regardless of previous municipal government decisions, or even other board decisions (Krushelnicki 2007; OMB n.d.). This practice effectively allows the OMB to render its own decision with complete disregard for any previous decision of the municipal government. The GTA Task Force (2003) argues that the act of hearing a case de novo undermines a municipality's planning process, and that the OMB should only act as an appeals body in instances where a municipality's decision is "clearly improper or unreasonable ... or deprives the parties of their right to natural justice" (7). Furthermore, some critics of the board believe its practice of treating each case as de novo allows developers to skirt a municipality's planning process altogether. Where a developer feels the OMB will be more receptive to an application for a development than would a municipality, the developer can submit a poorly constructed application to the municipality in question, and focus on preparing a different application for the OMB hearing. Because the hearing is de novo, the original application has no bearing on the board's decisions.[9] The board focuses only on the plans the developer submits to the board at the beginning of the hearing process.[10] However, while the initial application can have little or no bearing on a hearing, the developer can introduce into evidence the opinion of the municipality's planning experts, which can have significant bearing on the board's decision if the municipality rejected City Planning's[11] advice in its decision (Krushelnicki 2007).

The board's practice of hearing cases de novo could significantly influence the relationship between developers and municipal government, because a developer can avoid dealing with a municipality altogether, and can use the municipality's own planning experts against it. This practice, along with the board's broad powers of decision making, could undermine local politicians' appeal to the development industry by removing their main resource: authority over land-use planning. By undermining their role in planning, the OMB may be eliminating an important source of leverage and influence for local politicians.[12] Local politicians' authority over planning decision making is key to LPE theories of urban development politics, as this authority shapes the relationship between local politicians and other actors.

Other Appeal Bodies in Canada and the United States

Appellant bodies responsible for appeals of local planning decisions are common in North America. Many of these boards or commissions share traits with the Ontario Municipal Board. However, despite these similarities, the differences between the OMB and other provincial and state bodies demonstrate just how powerful, comparatively, the board is. Given the number of provinces and states in North America, I focus solely on appeal bodies most similar (in terms of powers and procedures) to the OMB.[13]

Appeal Bodies in the Rest of Canada[14]

The province of Saskatchewan has a Saskatchewan Municipal Board (SMB), whose Planning Appeals Commission (PAC) arm is responsible for hearing appeals of local planning decisions.[15] Like the OMB, PAC hearings are adversarial in nature and court-like, though less formal. However, the PAC's powers are significantly weaker than the OMB's. The PAC, as opposed to the OMB, is the second line of appeal in planning disputes. Most municipalities in Saskatchewan appoint development appeals boards (DABs), which hear and decide appeals of municipal council decisions on planning. Unlike OMB hearings, which are de novo, the PAC can hear only evidence available and presented at the DAB hearing. Neither the PAC nor DABs can hear appeals relating to official plan amendments (or their equivalent). They also cannot nullify zoning by-law amendments, nor can they modify zoning by-laws (Saskatchewan Municipal Board 2003; Saskatchewan, Planning and Development Act, 2007).

Some American states also have local boards, either as the only avenue of appeal before the courts or as a precursor to the state-level appeals body. At best, Saskatchewan's DABs are a check on municipal decisions involving minor variances. Toronto's city council does not render decisions on such planning applications. Instead, it allocates this responsibility to the Committee of Adjustment.[16] Although, the committee is not an appeal body like DABs, individuals can appeal its decisions to the OMB, just as one can appeal the decision of a DAB to the PAC in Saskatchewan. Applications for minor variances, while often responsible for tensions among neighbours, rarely have the same political salience as OPAs or ZBLAs. As a result, the Committee of Adjustment has little influence on the politics of urban development in Toronto. Since both DABs and the PAC are limited to hearing issues on minor variances as well, they too likely have little influence on the politics of urban development in Saskatchewan.

Moving east, the Province of Manitoba employs the Manitoba Municipal Board (MMB) as a planning appeals body. The MMB shares many qualities with the OMB. As with both OMB and PAC hearings, the MMB conducts hearings in an adversarial and court-like manner. The MMB can hear appeals against new official plans before they become law, just as the OMB does. However, the MMB cannot modify such documents once they are in force. In addition, the Manitoba

Municipal Board's function regarding zoning by-law amendments differs from the OMB's, in large part because local planning commissions,
not municipal councils, make the initial decisions regarding Zoning By-
law Amendments (ZBLAs).[17] When a planning commission refuses a
ZBLA, the applicant can appeal to the municipal council. Only when
the council overturns the planning commission's decision can an opponent of the amended by-law appeal to the MMB. In addition, once a
municipality passes a zoning by-law, no one can appeal it (Government
of Manitoba 2008; Manitoba, Planning Act 2005).

These restrictions on appeals relating both to official plan amendments and ZBLAs suggest the MMB is not likely to have the same influence as the OMB on the politics of urban development. Not only is
the MMB unable to modify plans and by-laws, developers cannot appeal decisions to refuse development to the MMB if the planning commission and municipal council agree in refusing the application. The
majority of appeals in Toronto to the OMB derive from city council's
neglect of or refusal to allow a planning application, and developers account for the majority of appeals in Toronto. Given the MMB's inability
to hear such appeals, it is unlikely to share the same influence that the
OMB may command in Ontario, and Toronto specifically.

In the Province of Quebec, the origins of the Commission Municipale Québec (CMQ) are very similar to the transition of the Ontario
Railway and Municipal Board to the OMB. In addition, the CMQ
emerged at the same time, in the early 1930s. As with the OMB, during the Great Depression the CMQ's main responsibility was not planning, but the oversight of municipal finances. Nevertheless, the CMQ
has also acquired powers over planning since its creation. In Quebec,
regional county municipalities constitute the upper tier of municipal
governments (consisting of multiple lower-tier municipalities). These
upper-tier municipalities are responsible for creating and implementing land-use and development plans for the entire county region. Any
plans or by-laws that lower-tier municipalities adopt must conform to
the county region's development plan. The CMQ's main, and apparently only, role in planning is to ensure that the planning of lower-tier
municipalities conform to the upper tiers' plans. As a result, the CMQ
does act as an appellant body. Local voters (a minimum of five) can appeal lower-tier government's planning decisions to the CMQ, based on
whether the lower tier's planning decision or law fails to conform to the
county region plan. However, the commission does not conduct a hearing. Rather, its members compare the lower-tier planning document to

the upper-tier development plan and render their verdict accordingly (*Loi sur l'aménagement et l'urbanisme; Loi sur la commission municipale*).

The CMQ's role in planning is much more constricted relative to the OMB and other such boards in Canada. Given the civil law tradition in Quebec,[18] the fact that planning appeals focus solely on the strict adherence of lower-tier planning decisions to county region development plans is not surprising. This fact all but removes any political role the CMQ could play in the politics of urban development in Quebec.

In the Atlantic Provinces, New Brunswick's Assessment and Planning Appeal Board (APAB) has similar powers as the OMB regarding the type of appeals it can hear: OPAs, ZBLAs, and so on.[19] However, the APAB focuses on and makes its decisions based largely on legal rather than planning grounds. Section 86(2) of the Community Planning Act, 1973 outlines the criteria for a successful appeal. The appellant(s) must demonstrate that the municipal council's action is an unreasonable use of power, is a misapplication of the province's Community Planning Act, or causes unreasonable hardship, or that the council's action or decision is unnecessary to protect the municipality. However, the applicant can also appeal if a council fails to render a decision on a development application in the prescribed time, much as developers can in Ontario (New Brunswick, Community Planning Act 1973; New Brunswick, Assessment and Planning Appeal Board Act 2001).

Undoubtedly, the criteria above allow the board members significant discretion when rendering their decisions, unlike the process in Quebec.[20] However, the APAB is bound to make its decision on legal grounds, rather than planning ones, meaning it functions far more like an appellant court than its counterparts in the rest of Canada. The APAB seems to be more of a special court than an appraiser of planning practices, which is, to some extent, the function of the OMB and planning boards in Saskatchewan and Manitoba.

Finally, Nova Scotia merged a number of boards with responsibilities over municipal issues into one super board (much as Saskatchewan did).[21] The Nova Scotia Utility and Review Board (NSURB) shares a number of traits with the OMB. It decides on appeals from zoning by-law amendments to plans for subdivisions, and the NSURB can modify by-laws (Nova Scotia Utility and Review Board n.d.b). However, the NSURB diverges significantly from the OMB in its inability to hear appeals regarding municipal planning strategies (MPSs), rough equivalents to Ontario's OPAs. MPSs are the litmus test the NSURB must use for evaluating the planning decisions of municipal governments in

Nova Scotia. The NSURB bases its decisions on planning principles, as the OMB does. However, its decisions must comply with a municipality's MPS, as one of the justifications for an appeal to the board focuses on whether the municipal council decision "conforms with the intent of the ... strategy" (Nova Scotia, Municipal Government Act 1998, ss. 250, 251).

The OMB is not bound to the content of a municipality's official plan (OP), as municipalities in Ontario can easily amend their OPs, and do so liberally at times. This fact provides the OMB with significantly more manoeuvrability when deciding appeals, arguably extending its scope, power, and, most importantly, influence. The distinction is significant; however, in Canada, the NSURB's role in planning, its powers, and its appeals process seem most similar to the OMB's, at least in terms of the relevant legislation relating to both boards.

Appeal Bodies in the United States

Cullingworth (1993; and Cullingworth and Caves 2009) provides a useful overview of the typical development application and appeals process in most American states. According to Cullingworth, most states separate legislative and administrative functions with regard to planning. While the municipal council passes zoning ordinances and the like, some form of planning board or commission, separate from the legislative branch, renders decisions on issues such as rezoning applications and variances. Appeals make their way to boards of appeal or adjustment, and then, as in any jurisdiction, to the courts.

However, despite the existence of state-level appeal bodies, state legislation usually places strict limits on a municipality's authority to modify its own planning ordinances and laws. In the United States, "zoning was originally conceived as being virtually 'self-executing'" (Cullingworth 1993, 14). The common practice of amending zoning and official plans in Ontario is not the norm in many American jurisdictions. Once a zoning by-law or plan is in place, cities judge development applications mostly on their conformity to the by-laws and comprehensive plan (CP – the term used commonly in place of official plan). This fact, arguably, explains the existence of administrative planning boards and commissions at the local level.[22] The board or commission allows or refuses an application according to its conformity or failure to conform to municipal zoning by-laws and plans. As a result, the main function of state-level appeals boards is to determine whether the municipal board or commission correctly applied the municipality's zoning and planning regulations.

This fairly rigid form of planning, contrary to the system in Ontario, is indicative of municipalities' limited ability to amend their own comprehensive plans in some states (where such plans exist). For instance, in Georgia, the state ignores modest amendments, but limits major comprehensive plan amendments to one every five years. In Washington State, municipalities, while not limited in the number of amendments, must receive the approval of the State's Department of Community Development for every change (Gale 1992).

This latter example is similar to the former system in Ontario. However, even when the provincial level reviewed such amendments, the OMB, not the provincial government, was responsible. Today, the OMB functions only as an appeals body, and thus the province bears greater resemblance in this regard to Oregon and Maine. Neither state requires state-level approval for comprehensive plan amendments, and both allow municipalities the freedom to make as many amendments as they choose (Gale 1992).

Although Ontario differs significantly from most American jurisdictions in the scope of planning powers it allows municipalities, some state-level appellant bodies exist that resemble the OMB. In Florida, while individuals can appeal zoning by-laws, the main foci of planning appeals are comprehensive plans and comprehensive plan amendments (CPAs). Thus, the Division of Administrative Hearings (DOAH), an omnibus appeals body, shares an important power with the OMB that appeals bodies in most other jurisdictions lack: the power to approve, refuse, or modify official plan amendments (State of Florida 2012).

The major distinction of the DOAH's appeals process is the route by which appeals make their way to a DOAH hearing (as with the OMB, DOAH hearings are adversarial and conducted in a court-like manner). First, applicants may not appeal to the DOAH if a municipality refuses an application (as in Manitoba). Rather, "affected individuals" may appeal the adoption of such by-laws. Nevertheless, such individuals appeal directly to the DOAH, though the DOAH, like many other boards, focuses solely on whether such by-laws conform to the CP. When reviewing CPs and CPAs, however, the DOAH focuses solely on whether the plan or plan amendment complies with the state's Growth Management Act, 1985. This power is similar to the OMB's since the province now requires the board to consider specific legislation (such as the

Places to Grow Act 2005) in its decisions, though whether the DOAH is as flexible in its decision making as the OMB is questionable. However, before making their way to a DOAH hearing, Florida's Department of Community Affairs determines, itself, whether CPs and CPAs conform to the Growth Management Act, 1985. Any individual or group, including the municipality, can appeal the department's decision to the DOAH, whether the department supports the CP or CPA, or rejects it (State of Florida 2012).[23]

The DOAH has similar powers and jurisdiction as the OMB, but the involvement of the Department of Community Affairs, entailing the direct involvement of state government in comprehensive planning, suggests that the influence or effect of the DOAH on the politics of urban development in Florida would diverge from the influence of the OMB in Ontario. Nevertheless, the DOAH offers another example where a planning institution may alter the politics of urban development.

Finally, Oregon's Land Use Board of Appeals (LUBA) arguably bears the closest resemblance to the OMB of any such appeals bodies in either Canada or the United States. According to Leo, the LUBA, along with the Land Conservation and Development Commission (LCDC) and its Department of Land Conservation and Development (DLCD), "have become active participants in local politics" (1998, 371). He also argues that the presence of the LCDC has led to the "'LCDC made me do it' defense" (ibid., 372). Local politicians attempt to appear sympathetic to citizens opposed to particular developments, while arguing that they must allow the development because of the LCDC – a defence very similar to that offered by city councillors in Toronto concerning the OMB.

As in Florida, the process to appeal municipal planning decisions is much more complex than in Ontario, involving the LCDC, the DLCD, and the LUBA. The LCDC is the state's planning agency, responsible for overseeing local planning and enforcing state planning policy. The DLCD is the LCDC's administrative arm, and reviews proposed amendments to local plans, just as the Department of Community Affairs does in Florida. However, while the Department of Community Affairs can prevent a municipality from enacting a comprehensive plan amendment, the DLCD cannot; rather, the Department of Land Conservation and Development must appeal the amendment to the Land Use Board of Appeals if the municipal government chooses not to comply with the Department of Land Conservation and Development's decision. Individuals can also appeal, regardless of the DLCD's position on the proposed amendment (Cullingworth 1993; Cullingworth and Caves 2009). Nevertheless, the agency's presence is likely an important factor in the politics of urban development, a presence absent in Ontario. As in the Florida case, the direct involvement of a department of state in planning could alter the politics of urban development in Oregon.

Several thousand amendments make their way to the DLCD every year, suggesting the practice of amending comprehensive/official plans is as common in Oregon as it is in Ontario (Cullingworth 1993). However, Liberty (1998) suggests appeals to the LUBA are rare, accounting for 1 per cent of all appealable DLCD decisions. Thus, actors in Oregon may not be as litigious as actors in Ontario. Regardless, the LUBA has all the powers of the OMB. It can reject or allow plans or plan amendments, zoning by-laws, and zoning by-law amendments. In addition, the board conducts hearings in a fashion similar to an OMB hearing.

A few important differences between the LUBA and the OMB exist, however. The LUBA does not allow non-parties to participate in hearings (State of Oregon 2008). For instance, a neighbourhood association must be a party to a hearing, and cannot participate in a more limited way as they can in an OMB hearing. This fact suggests the LUBA focuses more heavily on legal issues than the OMB. However, in effect, the LUBA has significant scope when rendering a decision. For instance, it can overturn the decision of a municipality if the municipality "made a decision not supported by substantial evidence in the whole record" (Oregon Land Use Act 1973, 197.835 9(a)(C)). Thus, as the LUBA suggests itself (see State of Oregon 2008), hearings are usually highly technical in a manner reminiscent of the OMB. The LUBA has the potential to be as influential in the politics of urban development in Oregon as the OMB is in Ontario. However, the limited number of appeals in Oregon (as of 1998 at least) would significantly affect the LUBA's influence. Furthermore, the existence and role of the LCDC and DLCD as interveners in the process undoubtedly has a significant effect on the board's role and the politics of urban development in Oregon. After all, until recently, the OMB was the only provincial-level agency focusing on land planning issues in Ontario. Even with the introduction of the Places to Grow Act, 2005 and other similar legislation, the Government of Ontario seems far less involved in local planning than state agencies in Oregon.

The OMB is not as unique as Chipman (2002) and Krushelnicki (2007) suggest. Clearly, such boards are fairly common. In fact, many boards share procedural elements with the OMB. Nevertheless, even the most similar appeals bodies lack certain elements potentially crucial to the OMB's role in the politics of urban development. Moreover, Oregon's LUBA, while probably the closest approximation to the OMB, resides in a significantly different setting, which Ontario and Toronto typify, than that characterized by most American local political economy literature. The State of Oregon is an active participant in local planning, which likely entails important deviations in the behaviour of its local political actors. These facts further illustrate how important institutional differences across jurisdictions can change and shape the politics of urban development. Given the scale and scope of the OMB's powers, it has the potential for significant influence over the politics of urban development in Toronto. The wide variation in planning institutions that exists in both countries and the potential for such institutions to shape the politics of urban development demonstrates the necessity of addressing their role when studying local political economy, a practice currently lacking in the field.

Experts, Developers, Neighbourhood Associations, and Local Politicians

Experts

The first question I raised in the Introduction was whether *the existence of the OMB affects the role Toronto's planning community plays in the politics of urban development*. This question is integral to understanding the influence of the board, as the role of planning experts and other related professions in the OMB's appeals process is substantial. Their importance arises from the OMB's focus and reliance on their expertise, which in turn, along with the board's powers, practices, and procedures, likely influences and shapes the politics of urban development in Toronto.

Bowman remarks that, in contrast to the courts, which are often wary of expert opinion despite its increasing availability, "the leading of expert evidence before the Board represents the rule rather than the exception ... Board hearings often represent a contest among duelling experts" (2001, 3). The process of city planning itself is highly reliant on expertise, such that the subset of professionals that are involved in planning and development are commonly referred to as the "planning community." Chipman suggests that the board relies on the opinion of this community when determining what constitutes "good planning," which is one of the major tests the OMB applies when making decisions (2002, 33). He is not alone in emphasizing the role of expertise in OMB hearings.

According to Bowman, an appellant or respondent that "does not retain the appropriate expert at a Board proceeding runs the risk that the Board will not have the evidence that it requires in order to make the decision that the party is seeking" (2001, 4). This quote emphasizes one of the main criticisms that citizen groups, such as neighbourhood associations, level at the board's appeals process. The cost of hiring experts, not only to testify but to conduct the required testing and research to testify, can be high. Municipalities, particularly large ones like the City of Toronto, have their own expert staff, and can afford to hire additional experts when needed. The same can be said for most major developers. Neighbourhood associations, by contrast, often lack the funds necessary to hire such expert witnesses, and, as a result, feel that the process "stacks the deck" against them (Krushelnicki 2007). The costs associated with an appeal, arising from the use of experts, could significantly influence the behaviour of neighbourhood associations, particularly in their approach towards both developers and especially politicians.

Krushelnicki (2007) makes a compelling argument about expertise in land-use planning in Ontario, one which Bowman (2001) echoes to some extent. They suggest that a city's planning expert, despite being in the employ of a municipality, will, nonetheless, stick to his or her opinion regarding a particular development, even if that opinion conflicts with the decision of the municipal council. As with any witness in a court proceeding, planners or other experts are sworn to tell the truth when presenting evidence or expert opinion to the board. A developer can introduce an expert's earlier opinion into evidence at a hearing, which would undermine the expert's testimony if he or she were to change it (Krushelnicki 2007). The board increasingly scrutinizes the research and tests of planning experts, such that an expert who conducts his or her testing and research rigorously and professionally would have little ability to deviate from his or her results when testifying (Bowman 2001; Krushelnicki 2007).

Krushelnicki argues that a planning expert has every incentive to conduct his or her work in the most professional manner given that any planning report or opinion forwarded to municipal council from a planning expert could eventually make its way into an OMB hearing. He suggests that "all of this provides a very real incentive to give honest, defensible advice at all times, whether under appeal or not"

(Krushelnicki 2007, 354), as failure to do so could undermine the expert's legitimacy and, as a result, employability. Tom Keefe (Keefe interview 2008), Toronto's director of community planning for Etobicoke York District (formerly North York), echoes this sentiment. Furthermore, Krushelnicki (2007) suggests that this emphasis on professionalism applies to any planning expert hired on retainer by a party to an OMB hearing.

Given the board's presence and emphasis on planning rationale when rendering its decisions, planning experts in Toronto should play a more important and arguably central role in the politics of urban development in the city. At a minimum, they are crucial to OMB hearings, but they may also be responsible for directing the entire application process.

Developers

The second question I asked is whether *the existence of the OMB affects the behaviour of developers in Toronto*. Before exploring this question, it is important to note one significant difference that exists between the realities of Toronto's development community and the development industry in the United States, particularly as local political economy theorists depict it. While local developers in many American cities give way to international developers, many of Toronto's local developers have become international, while maintaining their headquarters in the city. For instance, Purcell (2000) notes the increasing internationalization of the development industry in the Los Angeles area. He argues that this change has diminished or altered the role of developers in that city's politics. In contrast, Olympia & York, the largest office developer in the world before its collapse in the early 1990s, with major holdings in cities such as New York and London, was a company founded and based in Toronto (Magnusson 1990; Fainstein 2001; Charney 2005). Today, other Toronto-based companies such as Brookfield and Cadillac Fairview have become international developers.[24] In one sense, because these developers are Toronto-based, they may have a greater interest in or loyalty to the city than they would with such important markets as Los Angeles or San Francisco. Given their significant involvement in Toronto's current construction boom,[25] this may be the case. However, as Orr and Stoker's (1994) discussion of the auto industry in Detroit suggests, a transnational corporation's loyalties may not lie with their home city.

In fact, the reality of transnational developers' presence and involvement in Toronto may be more similar to the role of office-building developers/owners in San Francisco, as portrayed by DeLeon (1992b). DeLeon suggests that a split developed in San Francisco between property developers and landlords, particularly in the office market. He notes that office-building owners supported many proposals to reduce significant office development in San Francisco's downtown, to avoid any increase in competition. Developers such as Cadillac Fairview and Brookfield are both developers and property owners/managers. Charney (2005) argues that these developers jealously protect their investments in the downtowns of all of Canada's major cities. Furthermore, the increased rents from greater demand would appeal to them. Thus, the interests of Toronto's transnational developers are ambiguous at best, and possibly contradictory; as a result, the account I offer of their involvement in the politics of urban development in Toronto is limited.

Regardless of the interests of major office developers in the city, the interests of condominium developers in Toronto closely parallel urban regime and growth machine theories' depictions of businesses' and developers' interests. Toronto's condominium developers have a vested interest in the Toronto market, as they are predominantly local in character and focus, with a few exceptions. Furthermore, condominium developers are not landlords, and so lack the conflicting interests of the large office developers. They also abound in Toronto, largely as a result of the sustained boom in condominium demand through much of the first decade of the millennium (Policy and Research 2007). The majority of Toronto's condominium developers, such as Tridel, Context, Canderel Stoneridge, Menkes, and Daniels are based within the city itself, build exclusively within the city-region, and have a major stake in the continued growth of the city. Some companies, like Minto, an Ottawa-based developer, and Concord Adex, a Vancouver-based developer, have invested heavily in new development in the city. Thus, despite being outsiders, they too have a major stake in the city's continued growth and development.[26] In these respects, Toronto's condominium developers are little different than the developers both Logan and Molotch (1987) and Stone (1989) depict in their respective books, and are focused exclusively on the exchange value of land and on encouraging growth. As such, their interests and behaviour should be similar.

According to the local political economy literature, developers in Toronto should actively seek a close and favourable relationship with local politicians and city council, as doing otherwise would place their interests in jeopardy. Certainly, there is little for a developer to lose in cozying up to local politicians, as the latter control land-use planning in the city. However, though city politicians have such power, the Ontario Municipal Board has the power to overturn the decisions of city council, and to replace those decisions with its own. Furthermore, the practice of hearing each case de novo may allow developers to sidestep city council altogether. Given the board's heavy reliance on expert testimony to inform its decisions, a savvy developer need only ensure that its development proposal meets the rigorous demands of what the OMB considers good planning, avoiding issues that could arise with local neighbourhood associations. Because developers can appeal the decision of council to the OMB, the need to work with local politicians to ensure development could diminish. Furthermore, the structure of the city's government, as well as citizen activism, may limit the opportunities for developers to co-opt politicians.

Developers in Toronto may have little reason to lobby local politicians. They also have far less incentive to contribute to election campaigns, in contrast to developers in other cities, who are often leading sources of funding for council candidates. Lastly, given the board's role as final decision-maker, developers in Toronto have far less reason to negotiate with the City towards a compromise on controversial development proposals.

Neighbourhood Associations

My third question asks whether *the existence of the OMB affects the behaviour of neighbourhood associations in Toronto.* Toronto's neighbourhood associations have a long history and are important and active players in city politics. They also have demonstrated an anti-growth attitude on many occasions. In the late 1960s, these groups successfully mobilized to defeat major development projects in the city. The most celebrated accomplishment of these groups during that time was their success in halting construction on the proposed Spadina Expressway. The same coalition of neighbourhood associations and other citizen groups also managed to mobilize the electorate and defeat the pro-development council that dominated politics in the city at the time. Ever since this period, neighbourhood associations in Toronto have established themselves as a permanent and important fixture in the city (Lorimer 1970, Magnusson 1983), just as similar organizations have in American cities such as Los Angeles (Purcell 2000) and San Francisco (DeLeon and Powell 1989; DeLeon 1992b).

The neighbourhood associations in Toronto share a socially progressive outlook with their counterparts in LA and San Francisco. Also, while such organizations are becoming increasingly diverse, they remain dominated by the white upper-middle class, as do their American counterparts (Kipfer and Keil 2002).[27] The terms most often used to refer to these groups in Toronto, ratepayers' or residents' associations (most of these groups self-identify as such), are indicative of the interests of such groups. These associations are composed primarily of home owners (as opposed to renters), whose interests, in the terminology of growth machine theory, lie both in the use and exchange value of their own property. A brief survey of neighbourhood associations' opposition to development in the city suggests that they are the major source of citizen activism and anti-development sentiment in the city.[28] Their recent fights with developers demonstrate that they remain active participants in the politics of urban development in Toronto, and continue to oppose development (Hiller 2002; Boyle 2005; Macdonald 2007). Toronto's neighbourhood associations closely parallel Thomas (1986) and Mesch and Schwirian's (1996) depictions of such organizations in American cities. Most authors writing from the LPE approach in the United States now recognize the potential of such groups to mobilize public opinion and influence the behaviour of politicians. Purcell (2000), DeLeon (1992b), Vogel and Swanson (1989), and Thomas's (1986) accounts of neighbourhood associations in the United States suggest very little differentiates Toronto's neighbourhood associations from their American counterparts.

In many American and Canadian jurisdictions, if neighbourhood associations are unable to sway local politicians, they have few avenues of appeal, aside from the courts. In Toronto, neighbourhood associations can appeal to the Ontario Municipal Board. Rose (1972) suggests that at one point during the 1960s, neighbourhood associations perceived the OMB as an ally in their disputes with developers and city council. The board's appeals process and its interpretation of the principle of natural justice enable such groups to challenge a council decision they oppose. However, a number of factors make appealing to the OMB untenable for many neighbourhood associations. As I mentioned earlier, most of these factors derive from the board's emphasis on expert testimony. First, the cost associated with retaining such experts is high, and may be prohibitive. In addition, Chipman notes that, where a developer and a municipality agree on a proposed development, the OMB will support the tandem 79 to 80 per cent of the time (2002, table 2.3, 55). At best, according to Chipman's statistics, a neighbourhood association will win one time out of five after enduring an often exceedingly expensive and long process.

These facts suggest the importance of local politicians and city council to neighbourhood associations. Even though the OMB can overturn the decisions of Toronto's city council, the city has the means and the expert staff to successfully counter a developer's appeal. As a result, the actual behaviour of neighbourhood associations in Toronto is unlikely to deviate significantly from the behaviour that local political economy scholars predict. In fact, Toronto's neighbourhood associations' reliance on local politicians could exceed that of American groups, as they can only appeal an OMB decision to the courts if they can demonstrate that the board made an error in law, such as deciding on an issue outside of its jurisdiction. Though a neighbourhood association can be supportive, neutral, or combative towards a development, Kipfer and Keil's (2002) case studies suggest that their relationship is often the latter. The only time neighbourhood associations have an incentive to work with developers is when other options have failed, or they see no other alternative. The ability of neighbourhood associations to mobilize voters' support, especially at election time, is their main resource.

While the OMB may offer an avenue of appeal when city council decides against them, neighbourhood associations fair poorly at board hearings, negating the promise of such recourse. Neighbourhood associations in Toronto retain their ability to mobilize the electorate and influence elections, and thus they likely adopt the same approach as their contemporaries in other cities when battling development. Despite the existence of the board, neighbourhood associations in Toronto should continue to focus their efforts on winning the support of local politicians.

Local Politicians

Lastly, my fourth question addresses the relationship between the OMB and local politicians in Toronto, asking whether *the existence of the OMB affects local politicians' decision making and behaviour towards other actors.* Like any other politician in a democratic system, local politicians in Toronto want their constituencies to re-elect them. Toronto's weak mayor system and ward-based elections are not common in the United States (especially the former, see Sancton 1983). However, Purcell's (1997, 2000) description of Los Angeles suggests Toronto shares similar legislative and executive institutions. Furthermore, there is a long history of conflict between neighbourhood associations and developers in Los Angeles, as in Toronto. Thus, local politicians in Toronto, like their Los Angeles counterparts, may find themselves conflicted over the need to secure the fiscal resources of developers versus securing the support of neighbourhood associations during election time, or facing what Kantor (with David 1988) describes as an "explosive dilemma." In fact, Sancton (1983) suggests that, while issues of race or differences in ethnicity are often the most important cleavages in American local politics, the most salient division in Canadian cities is that between pro- and anti-growth forces. If anything, this fact bolsters the importance of development issues in local politics in Toronto, and increases the turmoil for local politicians.

However, as Cullingworth (1987) notes, the powers and practices of the OMB allow local politicians to avoid making difficult planning decisions. Politicians in Toronto need not worry about hampering economic development and growth in the city by opposing developers' wishes, as the OMB can overrule council's decisions, just as local politicians in Oregon can rely on the LCDC. Thus, as Gillespie (2007), a local journalist suggests, "councillors [in Toronto] have been known to vote against a development that fits the City's official plan but that local residents don't want just so they can get re-elected, knowing the OMB will later approve the project" (F4). Former city councillor Paul Sutherland echoes this sentiment, suggesting that "many councillors have complained about the OMB, even though when they have finished complaining, they are wink-winking: 'Thank God, it was there'" (quoted in Rusk 2005). While such accounts are anecdotal, they suggest that local politicians are cognizant of the role the OMB plays in local politics. This role derives not only from the OMB's decision-making powers, but also from its practice of treating every hearing de novo. Although Krushelnicki insists that the board does consider a municipality's decision, the board's decision is not premised on the validity of such decisions, nor does the board bear any responsibility "to make a finding that the [municipality] ... erred or failed procedurally" in rendering its decision (2007, 82).

The anecdotes above suggest the board allows local politicians in Toronto to avoid the political quagmire that is the politics of urban development. At the very least, the OMB is a useful scapegoat for politicians looking to avoid blame for unpopular planning decisions. Because of its presence, most local politicians in Toronto should avoid taking responsibility for planning decisions.

Summary

In summary, without the board's presence, the politics of urban development in the City of Toronto would unfold, presumably, in a manner similar to that in American cities such as Los Angeles or San Francisco, as the interests of the actors involved in urban politics in Toronto are basically the same as for their American counterparts. However, the powers of the OMB to uphold, reject, modify, or substitute city council's decisions on development, along with the practical implications of its use of the principle of natural justice, de novo hearings, and focus and reliance on expert testimony, could influence and shape the behaviour of these political actors, such that they deviate, in some instances significantly, from those in American cities. The following four questions provide the foundation for the ensuing analysis of the OMB's influence on the politics of urban development in Toronto:

Question 1: Does the existence of the OMB affect the role Toronto's planning community plays in the politics of urban development?

Question 2: Does the existence of the OMB affect the behaviour of developers in Toronto?

Question 3: Does the existence of the OMB affect the behaviour of neighbourhood associations in Toronto?

Question 4: Does the existence of the OMB affect local politicians' decision making and behaviour towards other actors?

4 OMB Appeals in Toronto from 2000 through 2006

From 2003 through 2006,[1] the City of Toronto received over 392 applications for official plan amendments (OPAs) and rezoning changes (Policy and Research 2006; City Planning 2005, 2004); of these applications, roughly 200 (or 51 per cent) resulted in an OMB appeal.[2] That such a high percentage of applications make their way to the Ontario Municipal Board accentuates its importance to planning in Toronto. However, aside from Chipman (2002) and the City's (Commissioner of Urban Development Services 2002) limited analysis of board appeals and decisions, very little information concerning the actual pattern of appeals and decisions in either Toronto or the Province of Ontario exists. The lack of a general conception of the board's role in city planning and of actors' behaviour leading to and during an appeal is a significant barrier to research. This obstacle emerged early on during my research for this analysis. Selecting cases for study was problematic because there was no way to determine the typical behaviour of political actors in the planning and appeals process. Although the media cover a number of the more contentious development proposals the board deals with each year, these are but a small portion of the total number of applications for zoning and OPAs. In addition, they represent only highly contentious proposals, which, as a result, are unlikely to represent the typical unfolding of planning politics in the city. For instance, devoting an entire chapter of analysis to the role of neighbourhood associations in the politics of urban development would be a useless endeavour if such associations were involved in few cases. Without a broader understanding of the board's role in city planning, little can be extrapolated from in-depth case studies about its influence on the politics of urban development in Toronto. To overcome this barrier, I conducted a quantitative analysis of over three hundred appeals regarding official plan amendments, zoning by-laws, zoning by-law amendments, and interim control by-laws, from 2000 through 2006. The results of this analysis provide the background for the case studies in later chapters.

General Findings

As chart 4.1 suggests, there have been some fluctuations in the number of OMB decisions and settlements over the time span of this analysis. The chart includes OMB decisions, settlements between parties to appeals, and withdrawn appeals. The chart demonstrates the consistent and significant involvement of the OMB in the city's planning and development during the seven years of my analysis. The number of decisions and settlements in 2000 was drastically lower than in later years (28 versus 36 in the second lowest year, 2002); this fact likely reflects both the absence and undercount of withdrawn appeals.[3] In addition, the tremendous surge in the housing market Toronto experienced during this decade had just begun at the time. However, following 2000, the board decided, or the City settled, an average of 44 appeals each year. Only 2002 and 2004 deviated significantly from that average.

Chart 4.2 examines the reasons for appeals over this same time span, to determine whether there have been any significant changes in the types of appeals being made to the board over time. The first column in each group represents the number of appeals emerging from city council's rejection of a proposal in each given year; the middle captures appeals due to neglect; and the right column, appeals of the City's approval of a proposal. As the chart indicates, reasons for appeals have fluctuated significantly over the seven years. Appeals resulting from city council's neglect to render a decision usually account for a plurality of cases in each year. However, in 2001, appeals against council's decision to approve a development proposal accounted for a significantly higher proportion of the total number of appeals for that year; in addition, appeals from neglect are much lower. While this fact is interesting, given the number of appeals made each year, the fluctuation likely does not reflect any important changes to the politics of urban development in the city over this time. Alternatively, if something significant occurred in 2001, it did not have a continued impact beyond that year.[4] Appeals to the OMB due to council's neglect or rejection of a proposal account for a majority of all appeals in every year – from a low of 50 per

Chart 4.1. Number of OMB decisions/settlements

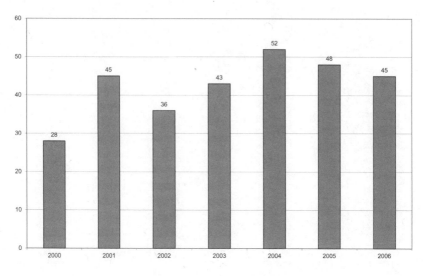

Chart 4.2. Reason for appeal by year

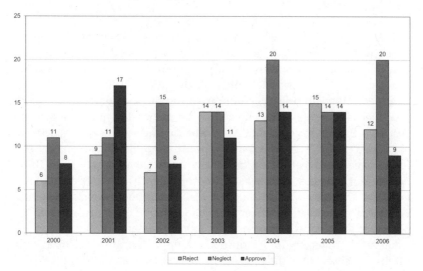

Chart 4.3. Frequency of appellant type

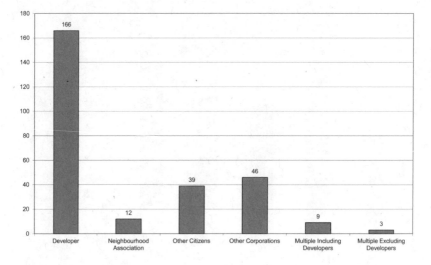

cent in 2001 to a high of 74 per cent in 2006. Thus, the fact that developers are the appellant in over 60 per cent of appeals to the OMB, as indicated in the following chart, is not surprising.

Chart 4.3 captures the number of appeals made by each appellant type (from the left: developers, neighbourhood associations, individual citizens or small unorganized groups, corporations other than developers, multiple types of appellants including developers, multiple types of appellants excluding developers) during the span of this analysis. As indicated above, developers account for the vast majority of appeals. Appeals by other corporations (both for and against development) come in a distant second, while appeals by individual citizens or small groups of citizens (four or five individuals at most) come in third.[5] Neighbourhood associations account for slightly above 1 per cent of all appeals. The few appeals originating from neighbourhood associations is notable given their involvement in 38 per cent of all cases during the period of this analysis (see chart 4.10 for more details).

Given the overwhelming number of appeals from developers, one might conclude that developers prefer their chances at the OMB to dealing with the City, while other appellants are less inclined towards

Chart 4.4. OMB decisions by reason for appeal

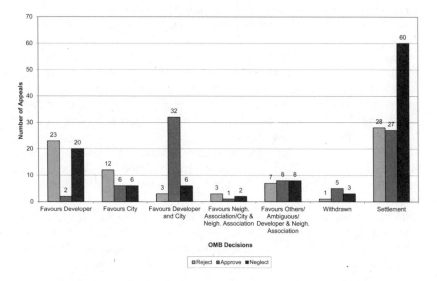

the board. However, both Chipman (2002) and city staff (Commissioner of Urban Development Services 2002) claim that the board does not favour developers in its decisions. To assess this claim, chart 4.4 indicates whom the board decided in favour of sorted by the reason for appeal. The data in chart 4.4 suggest that the OMB does favour developers more often than any other parties to a hearing, at least statistically. In almost a third of the appeals arising from council's rejection of a proposal (the first column from the left), the board favoured developers. In over a third of the cases, developers either withdrew their appeal or settled with the City or other appellant. Thus, developers were victorious in almost half of the cases that resulted in an OMB decision. In cases of neglect (the third column in each group), the City fared even worse when compared to developers. While well over half of all such appeals resulted in settlements (final column from the left), OMB decisions favoured the developers 3 to 1 over the City. Not surprisingly, when developers and the City supported one another during an appeal (third set of columns from the left), the OMB decided in favour of the two over 80 per cent of the time.[6] Whether or not this apparent bias in OMB decision making is reflective of a bias in the institutional processes or in the board's decision making, the board undoubtedly influences the politics of urban development in Toronto. However, these data do not convey conclusive evidence of the reason for such bias in favour of developers.

The clearest finding to this point is the sheer number of appeals that result in settlements. Table (4.1) examines whether the proportion of settlements and whom the OMB favours remains constant across the seven years under study. The table provides both the number of decisions, withdrawals, and settlements as well as their percentage of the total for each year (in parentheses).

City council resolves differences between parties before the OMB rendering a decision (the final column from the left) in 43 per cent of appeals, or 122 of 285 (though this number fluctuates significantly from year to year, from a high of 65% in 2000 to a low of 31% in 2003). The data also demonstrate a significant jump in decisions favouring developers in 2006 (12), and a notable lack of decisions favouring developers in 2000 (1). For 2000, the significantly greater number of settlements may account for the lower number of victorious developers. That year is also notable as the only one where the board favoured the City more often than developers. This fact suggests that 2006 was a far more combative year for urban development politics, even though almost 38 per cent of appeals resulted in settlements.

Despite these fluctuations, the data suggest significant cooperation and discussion among actors in urban development politics in Toronto, given the number of appeals the City is able to settle before a board hearing. This cooperation may exclude other actors beyond the City and developers, or could indicate, simply, that both the City and developers wish to avoid the OMB. In either scenario, this remains an important finding. The politics of urban development in Toronto may not be particularly combative, unlike similarly situated cities like San Francisco and Los Angeles, where infighting between anti-growth and pro-growth forces has undermined constructive dialogue (DeLeon and Powell 1989; Purcell 1997, 2000). Conversely, it may be an indication of the weakness of one side relative to the other.

Planning Experts

Local political economy literature does not address the role of planning experts in the politics of urban development.[7] Presumably, the literature overlooks the role of planning experts because, while they are

Table 4.1. OMB decision by year

OMB decision by year	Favours developer	Favours City	Favours developer and City	Neigh. associations with/w/o City	Favours others/developer & neigh./ ambiguous	Withdrawn	Settlement
2000	1 (3.8)	2 (7.7)	2 (7.7)	1 (3.8)	2 (7.7)	1 (03.8)	17 (65.4)
2001	5 (12.5)	3 (7.5)	6 (15.0)	2 (5.0)	10 (25.0)	1 (2.5)	13 (32.5)
2002	4 (12.9)	3 (9.7)	5 (16.1)	0 (0.0)	1 (3.2)	2 (6.5)	16 (51.6)
2003	8 (19.0)	5 (11.9)	11 (26.2)	1 (2.4)	0 (0.0)	4 (9.5)	13 (31.0)
2004	9 (17.3)	4 (7.7)	6 (11.5)	1 (1.9)	4 (7.7)	3 (5.8)	25 (48.1)
2005	8 (16.7)	3 (6.3)	7 (14.6)	1 (2.1)	3 (6.3)	5 (10.4)	21 (43.8)
2006	12 (26.7)	4 (8.9)	5 (11.1)	1 (2.2)	5 (11.1)	2 (4.4)	17 (37.8)
Total (Mean)	47 (16.5)	24 (8.4)	42 (14.7)	7 (2.5)	25 (8.8)	18 (6.3)	122 (42.8)

involved heavily in planning, their involvement in the politics of urban development is as an adviser on policy, both for the public and private sector. Planning experts act in the same fashion in Toronto. While they are responsible for judging planning applications, for creating the official plan and zoning by-laws, they function as an arm of the municipality, which the local politicians control. However, Bowman (2001), Chipman (2002), and Krushelnicki (2007) all suggest that planning experts' role in OMB appeals is different. In fact, all three authors emphasize the pivotal role planning experts' testimony plays in the board's decision making. The board's emphasis on planning expertise could alter the importance planning experts have to the politics of urban development.

The data below address the three authors' claims. First, chart 4.5 examines how often the OMB refers to expert testimony as a deciding factor in its decisions versus the number of times it did not by whom the board favoured in its decision.

The columns to the left in each group indicate how often the board did not cite planning experts, while the columns to the right indicate when it did cite them. In total, the OMB referred to expert testimony in almost 70 per cent of all cases.[8] Even in instances where the City and appellant(s) reached a settlement, the OMB still referred to experts' testimony and opinion 61 per cent of the time, despite not needing to justify its position in these cases.[9] In fact, in all categories, excluding withdrawn cases, the board cited expert testimony in at least 60 per cent of the cases. Clearly, planning experts' opinions matter to the board when it makes decisions. What is even more intriguing is the board's use of expert testimony to justify its decisions that solely favour developers. In such cases, the board cited expert testimony almost 90 per cent of the time (the first two columns from the left). Decisions against the City are liable to generate more media coverage than any other decisions, media coverage that is often negative towards the OMB. Given this fact, perhaps board members feel obligated to justify their decisions as best they can.

The above findings are consistent with Bowman, Chipman, and Krushelnicki's assessment of the board's focus on expertise. They also suggest the possibility that the presence of the OMB has increased planning experts' influence on the politics of urban development in Toronto. By focusing so heavily on expert testimony, the OMB seems to have increased the influence of experts in the city. The OMB decides appeals based in large part on the strength of parties' experts' testimony.

Chart 4.5. Expert cited in OMB decisions by OMB decisions

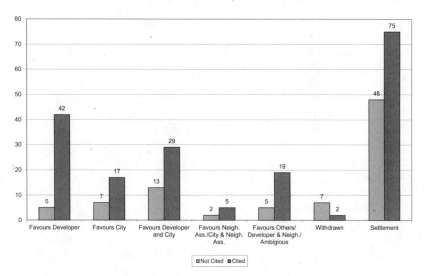

Bowman's (2001) statement that "Board hearings often represent a contest among duelling experts" (3) appears to reflect accurately the hearing process.

Given the importance the board places on planning experts' testimony, City Planning's opinion of a proposed development should influence the City's success (or failure) at the board, depending how city council responds to City Planning's recommendations. Chart 4.6 examines who the board favoured in each appeal by City Planning's opinion of the development application. Each group of columns represents one of four stances City Planning may take towards a development proposal (from left to right: outright support, hesitant support, provisional rejection, and outright rejection). The columns within each group represent whom the board favours in its decision.

The data suggest that, while the outright rejection of a proposal by city planners by no means assures victory for the City during an OMB hearing, it does substantially improve the City's chances of winning an appeal. The data in the table also suggest that when city planners support a proposal outright, city council is more likely to settle an appeal or side with the developer. This fact suggests council relies heavily on the

Chart 4.6. OMB decisions by city planner opinion

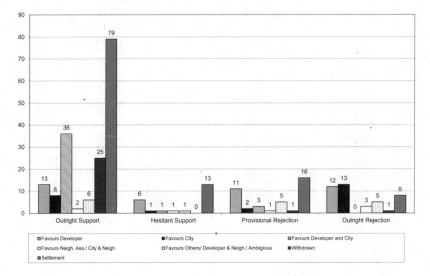

opinion of its planners, though it does not clarify whether this results from the OMB's existence or not. While the results for provisional support may seem counter-intuitive compared to the rest of the findings, in such instances, City Planning is confident that it can reach a settlement with the developer, thus not necessarily indicating its disapproval of the proposal. The high proportion of settlements in this category supports such a contention, while the high proportion of decisions favouring developers may reflect council's decision to cease negotiations altogether with the developer despite City Planning's recommendations.

The number of cases where city planners supported a developer's proposal outright is another important finding. In 169 of 296 cases, or 57 per cent of all appeals, city planners supported developers' proposals. With this fact in mind, chart 4.7 examines the reason for appeals by City Planning's opinion of development proposals to determine how often city council sided with City Planning. As with the previous chart, each group of columns represent the variety of recommendations emanating from City Planning. The columns, from left to right, reflect council's rejection of a proposal, neglect or failure to render a decision in the prescribed amount of time, and approval of a proposal.

Chart 4.7. Reason for appeal by city planner opinion

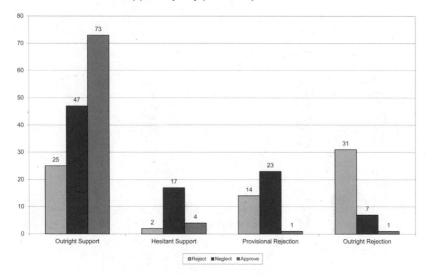

Roughly half of the instances where city planners supported an application that went to the OMB (third column from the left) resulted from council's approval of the application; thus, developers were not the appellants. An additional 30 per cent resulted from council's failure to render a decision (second column from the left), and less than 20 per cent involved the City refusing an application.[10] These findings suggest that city council will usually adopt City Planning's recommendations. Toronto's City Council appears to place great weight on City Planning's opinion. Council's reliance on planning expertise, along with the board's reliance on the same, suggests planning experts can play a significant role in shaping planning policy, both at the municipal level and at the OMB.

The data from chart 4.8 and chart 4.9 in the following section suggest some of the ramifications of planning experts' importance to city council and board decision making. Chart 4.8 examines City Planning's opinion regarding development proposals against the type of developer the proposal emanates from. For the most part, the type of developer making the application does not seem to affect city planners' opinion of the development application. The one exception is small-time

Chart 4.8. City planner opinion by developer type

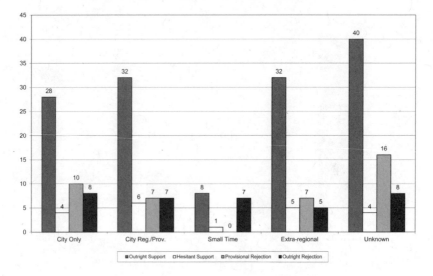

Chart 4.9. OMB decisions by developer type

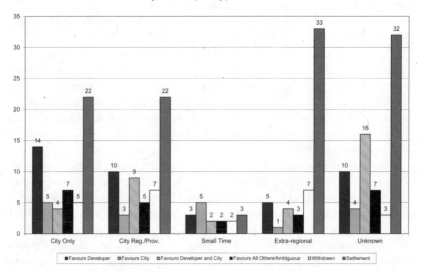

developers. Only slightly more than half of such developers received approval from City Planning. In fact, City Planning rejected the proposals of small-time developers as often as other types of developers, even though small-timers account for significantly fewer applications. As chart 4.9 suggests, small-time developers fare poorly at the OMB relative to other types of developers. Their lack of success with City Planning appears to translate directly into a lack of success at the OMB.

Keefe (interview, 2008) stated that city planners tend to reject poorly composed development applications, regardless of the nature of the planned development, and also suggested that many small-time developers had difficulty meeting the requirements of city planners. Given the OMB's focus on planning rationale, small-time developers' limited means would undoubtedly hamper them. However, small-timers' plight also suggests the importance of winning over City Planning. Developers who do win city planners' support seem to fare better at the OMB. These findings indicate that planning experts play an important role in the politics of urban development in Toronto. However, they offer little insight into whether the OMB's existence is responsible for this importance, and so no answer to my first question: *Does the existence of the OMB affect the role Toronto's planning community plays in the politics of urban development?*

Developers

Given that certain developers (namely, large commercial-office developers) are not present in the data set, any information drawn from the data is limited to those developers primarily involved in residential, mixed-use residential, and retail development.[11] This fact is not a significant handicap to this analysis, however, since the residential market dominated the development industry in Toronto during the period of this analysis. This section examines how developers fare at OMB hearings, and provides a general overview of developers' participation in board appeals.

Chart 4.9 compares whom the OMB favours in its decision with the type of developer involved in the appeal, to determine whether developer type influences success at the OMB. The individual columns represent the number of decisions favouring different actors, starting with developers from the left, and ending with settlements. Each group of columns represents a different type of developer (from left to right: developers operating only in the city proper; ones operating in the greater

city region and the province; small-time developers, with limited resources and experience in development; transnational, continental, and
nationally focused developers, as well as foreign ones; and developers
that could not be categorized due to limited information). The data in
chart 4.9 are intriguing when considered against the data from the previous section.

There is more deviation regarding developers' success at the OMB
than with City Planning. Extra-regional developers settle far more
often than either local or city-region developers. Extra-regional developers settled in 33 instances, or in 62 per cent of all appeals they were
involved in. Both local and regional developers settled in fewer than
40 per cent of cases. Local developers were the most successful at the
OMB, winning 25 per cent of their appeals on their own (or 50 per cent
not resulting in a settlement), and an additional 7 per cent with the
support of the City. Despite these variations, the data in chart 4.9 do
not suggest the OMB is biased in favour of any one type of developer.
Instead, the data confirm developers' proclivity to settle with the City.

This data suggests that a functional working relationship exists between developers and the City. City council will occasionally oppose
development proposals, but is more likely to settle with developers before an appeal results in an OMB hearing. This fact may indicate that developers are willing to work with the City, suggesting local politicians
may still be important to developers. However, developers are responsible for initiating an overwhelming majority of appeals (60 per cent).
By settling so often, the City may be trying to avoid OMB hearings.
Developers may still find the OMB a more useful avenue for securing
the approval of their developments, regardless of whether they actually
end up at a hearing or not. The threat of a hearing could be enough to
convince city council to settle, especially if City Planning is supportive
of the application. If such is the case, then the OMB does influence developers' behaviour, at a minimum, offering them additional means to
influence local politicians (essentially through coercion). Such findings
suggest a tentative, affirmative response to my second question: *Does
the existence of the OMB affect the behaviour of developers in Toronto?*

Neighbourhood Associations and Local Politicians

Neighbourhood associations were actively involved in at least 38 per
cent of all OMB appeals. Chart 4.10 documents their participation in
development disputes from 2000 through 2006. The left columns reflect

Chart 4.10. Neighbourhood association involvement by year

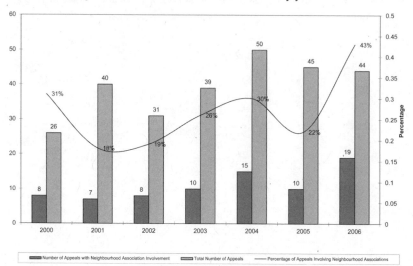

the number of appeals neighbourhood association were involved in, while the right indicates the total number of appeals for each year. The line captures fluctuations in neighbourhood associations' involvement over the seven-year span. The chart demonstrates that neighbourhood association involvement in the politics of urban development is a constant factor in Toronto. However, it also indicates an upward trend in their involvement in appeals. This trend may be an indication of increased militancy among neighbourhood associations, except for 2005, where their involvement dipped to earlier levels.

Chart 4.11 juxtaposes this trend of neighbourhood association engagement against developers' increasing success at the OMB and the possible decline of cooperation between developers and the City at OMB hearings. The solid line captures the percentage of appeals won by developers over the seven years. The dotted line reflects the line from the previous chart, while the segmented line reflects the percentage of appeals won by developers and the City when working together. Whereas the percentage of neighbourhood association involvement is based on the total number of OMB appeals, the percentage of OMB decisions favouring developers and city/developers exclude settlements and withdrawals; thus, there exists some potential for error in comparing the three. Nevertheless, both neighbourhood association

Chart 4.11. Developer success at the OMB and neighbourhood association involvement

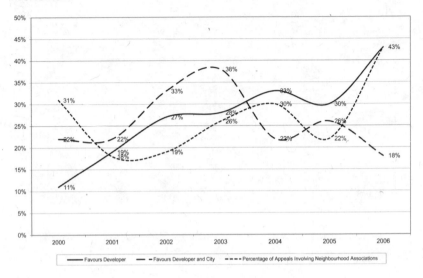

involvement and developers' success at the OMB appear to increase from 2001 onward.

Table 4.1 indicated a disproportionate number of settlements between the City and appellants in 2000 and 2001. This fact may account for the lower number of decisions favouring developers and the City in these years. Thus, City and developer cooperation could be in relative decline at the same time as neighbourhood association participation in appeals is increasing. These conclusions are very tentative, but are, nonetheless, compelling. While neighbourhood associations increasingly involve themselves in OMB appeals, local politicians may be less inclined to join forces against anti-development interests at an OMB hearing. If this is the case, the changing trend may offer some insight into my fourth question: *Does the existence of the OMB affect local politicians' decision making and behaviour towards other actors?* It appears that the OMB allows local politicians to avoid offending neighbourhood associations' interests. Absent neighbourhood association involvement, the City appears far more inclined to work towards an agreement with developers. These data do not, however, offer any definitive correlation between these factors.

Table 4.2. Neighbourhood associations' involvement and OMB decisions

N = 276	Value of Φ
Favours developer	.124[b]
Favours City	−.110
Favours developer and City	.032
Favours neighbourhood association and City (and neighbourhood association alone)	.197[a]
Favours neighbourhood association and developers	.139[b]
Settlements	−.194[a]

[a] Approximate significance at the 0.01 level (2-tailed)
[b] Approximate significance at the 0.05 level (2-tailed)

As chart 4.3 indicated, neighbourhood associations are rarely the appellant in OMB appeals, but as the previous two charts suggest, neighbourhood associations are willing to engage developers at the OMB. However, neighbourhood associations fare poorly at the board. Excluding two anomalous cases where a developer and a neighbourhood association allied with each other, neighbourhood associations won favourable decisions from the OMB in only 14 per cent of the cases they engaged in, excluding withdrawn cases and ones resulting in settlements. Given how few appeals neighbourhood associations initiated (4 per cent), it is unlikely that they perceived the board as an ideal means to oppose development.

As a further indication of how poorly neighbourhood associations fare at the OMB, and of their relationship with other actors (especially city council), table 4.2 reports the Phi coefficient for neighbourhood association involvement in OMB appeals against the outcome of the appeals. In addition to the negative relationship between settlement and neighbourhood association involvement (the last row), there exists a significant, though weak, relationship between neighbourhood association involvement and decisions favouring developers (the first row). Both findings indicate that neighbourhood associations continue to seek out the support of local politicians, as the LPE literature suggests, offering a tentative answer to my third question: *Does the existence of the OMB affect the behaviour of neighbourhood associations in Toronto.* On its own, the negative relationship between settlement and neighbourhood association involvement could simply indicate neighbourhood associations' intransigency. However, the positive relationship with developers' victory at the OMB may indicate city council's decisions to support the neighbourhood association against the developer. Presumably, city council ignores city planners' support for projects (as discussed in earlier in this chapter) in large part because of neighbourhood association opposition. The City is unlikely to win an appeal when its own planners support the proposal.

Conclusion

While none of these findings is conclusive, some provide an indication of the behaviour of actors and the overall structure of the politics of urban development in the city. One of the most important findings from the data relates to my focus on four actor groups to the exclusion of any others. The American local political economy literature focuses on local politicians, developers (and local businesses), and, increasingly, neighbourhood associations. My analysis focuses on these three actors as well, in large part because of the formative literature in the United States and in Canada. However, I also place more emphasis on the role of developers than other businesses, a focus supported by recent evidence from the United States emphasizing the pre-eminence of their role in urban politics above other businesses (Strom 2008; Gainsborough 2008). In addition, I include planning experts in my analysis, a group of actors the LPE literature usually omits. While planning experts are not political actors in the same vein as developers, politicians, or neighbourhood associations, the data analysis above suggests they play a significant role in the politics of development in the city and in the OMB's appeals process.

The data set did not exclude other actors. It includes the larger business community, other citizen groups, and individual citizens. These other actors are involved in the disputes of planning and development. However, they play a relatively minor role, at least in the OMB appeals process. Given both Logan and Molotch (1987) and Stone's (1989) belief that the larger business community would support development in most instances, its absence from the appeals process may not indicate its absence from development politics. Local businesses are unlikely to actively intervene in favour of a developer's project at the OMB, as involvement costs money. If local businesses have a role, it is likely a passive one, unless the business is opposed to a development or city by-law, at which point local businesses are more likely to become engaged. In contrast, individual and small groups of citizens often engage actively in the appeals process, accounting for over three times more appeals of council's decisions than neighbourhood associations (39 to 12). They fare very poorly, and usually lack the support of the important actors involved.

The data provide significant evidence of the important role planning experts play in the politics of urban development in Toronto, both in the initial application phase and during OMB appeals. Both the OMB and city council rely heavily on planning experts. While the OMB does decide on occasion in favour of developers despite city planners' objections, the City fares much better when opposing developments city planners reject. In addition, the City fares horribly when city planners support a development it opposes. With regards to the planning community in general, one cannot overstate the important role it plays in the OMB appeals process and, as a result, in the politics of urban development in the city. Without the aid of experts, any appellant or opponent to a development will likely fail in front of the board. This fact explains the poor showing of individual citizens and small-time developers.

The data are contradictory concerning developers. One of the most striking findings of the analysis is, first, how many development applications result in an OMB appeal, and, more important, how often the City and developers successfully negotiate a settlement before the board can render a decision. This apparent cooperation, despite the significant presence of predominantly anti-development neighbourhood associations in the city, contrasts sharply with the situations Purcell (1997, 2000) and DeLeon (1992b; and DeLeon and Powell 1989) depict in Los Angeles and San Francisco respectively. These cities reflect the dilemma facing modern governments as Kantor (1987; with David 1988) portrays it. Local politicians have lost their leverage over business, while citizens' ability to influence policy making grows. In these cities, confrontation between anti-growth and pro-growth forces produces an atmosphere not conducive to the cooperation apparent in Toronto. Contrarily, city council's sporadic support for neighbourhood associations conflicts with the situation in Atlanta, as Stone (1989) depicted, or as in Logan and Molotch's (1987) example of the growth machine. In both theories, local politicians shun neighbourhood associations and other citizens for the support of developers and other businesses.

The City's willingness to settle with developers contrasts with local politicians' and city council's apparent support for neighbourhood associations opposing development. City council appears willing to oppose developments supported by city planners if neighbourhood associations resist them. The analysis does not indicate how neighbourhood associations acquire the support of city council, but does suggest that neighbourhood associations are adept at winning that support, and trends suggest they may be increasingly so. Over the seven years of this analysis, the City seems increasingly unwilling to support developers during an OMB hearing, while developer victories and neighbourhood association involvement creep up.

The analysis in this chapter provides context for the eight case studies to follow. There exist elements of conflict and cooperation in the politics of urban development in Toronto. Local politicians will support neighbourhood associations against developers, often ignoring the advice of city planners and opposing developers even when the likelihood of victory is low. However, they appear to defer to city planners otherwise, and, on some occasions, city council will support unpopular development proposals. This pattern of behaviour suggests that local politicians are conscientious and considerate of the potential benefits and pitfalls of choosing to support or oppose a development. Thus, they seem cognizant of the dilemma referred to by Kantor (1987; with David 1988). The data cannot reveal local politicians' actual process of decision making, however. Nevertheless, the data analysis in this chapter reveals a pattern of urban development politics in Toronto notably divergent from the politics of urban development that American local political economy literature depicts. Assuming that literature is not flawed in its depiction of actors' interests, this analysis suggests that some factor, presumably the Ontario Municipal Board, is influencing the politics of urban development in Toronto.

5 Experts and the Planning Community in Toronto

In a scathing article focusing on the approval of a new Four Seasons Hotel in Toronto's tony Yorkville district, journalist Eric Reguly noted how council's support for the project was especially fortuitous given that "far smaller proposed developments in Yorkville were given the bum's rush by city planners and councillors" (Reguly 2006). Reguly specifically focuses on then ward councillor Kyle Rae's support for the project, in light of his and city council's rejection of another developer's project. Other journalists focused less on council's perceived bias than on the substantial sum of money the City would receive through section 37 of the planning act and as a concession from the developers to a neighbouring school (Gray 2006; Scrivener 2007). Although Reguly noted City Planning's support for the development in passing, the target of his wrath was clearly local politicians. Likewise, other journalists focused on the lure of money as driving council's planning decisions. Toronto's news media did not address City Planning's rationale for supporting the development, nor did they approach planners with questions regarding the differing treatments of development proposals in the area. However, City Planning was heavily supportive of the development (City Clerk 2006a). City planners also worked alongside neighbourhood associations, developers, and Councillor Rae when amending the proposal to address residents concerns. More important, the support of the City's planning expert played an important role in persuading the Ontario Municipal Board to support the proposal.

This neglect of planning experts' role in the politics of urban development is not specific to Toronto's news media. Academic literature on the subject, and even literature focusing on the place of planning experts in urban development politics, downplays their importance to the process. Local political economy literature is not immune to making this omission. Though LPE literature in the United States emerged, in part, as a critique of economic determinist and pluralist theory, it has much in common with both. Specifically, it shares with pluralism a focus on the actions and relationships between political actors in local politics. Although LPE literature conceives of government as more than a mediator between interests, recent literature on the politics of urban development focuses on the competition of interests for the support of local politicians, much as pluralist theory does. When the salient issue is development, developers and neighbourhood associations are the two main contenders for the support of city councillors. This model of the politics of urban development suggests that the conflict between pro-growth and anti-growth advocates, and local politicians' decision to support one or the other, drives city planning. However, as the preceding chapter suggests, in most instances, local politicians in Toronto will rely on City Planning's advice when rendering decisions on planning policy. This fact suggests that the bureaucracy, in the form of planning experts, plays a significant role in the politics of urban development in Toronto.

Unlike many authors working from the LPE approach, Elkin (1987) believes bureaucrats in municipal government are important players in city politics. He also argues that, in attempting to expand their autonomy, they often hinder the relationship between local businesses and local politicians. Despite his observations, LPE literature does not address, for the most part, the role of planning bureaucrats in the politics of urban development. While Mollenkopf (1983) devotes some time to city planners in *The Contested City*, he focuses mostly on the role they played in stigmatizing and uprooting neighbourhoods in Boston and San Francisco (173–9), rather than on their overall role in the politics of urban development. However, in their respective works on the Ontario Municipal Board, Bowman (2001), Chipman (2002), and Krushelnicki (2007) all emphasize the importance of planning experts to the OMB, and the previous chapter suggests planning experts' role in urban development politics may be even greater. Given how crucial their role is to the appeals process, omitting them from analysis of the politics of urban development would be a grave oversight, even if LPE literature often does so.

Additional evidence supporting the importance of planning experts to the politics of urban development in Toronto could reveal two important omissions in local political economy literature: first, the importance of planning experts to the politics of urban development; and second, the potential importance of variations in planning institutions to the politics of urban development in North American cities. This chapter examines planning experts' roles during both the application stage of the development process and during the OMB's appeals process (including the hearing). By examining their role throughout the entire planning process, I hope to answer my first question: *Does the existence of the OMB affect the role Toronto's planning community plays in the politics of urban development?* With this goal in mind, this chapter examines two cases of proposed development in Toronto, the Four Seasons Hotel and Aldergreen Estates. The two case studies examine not only the role of city planners, but also the role of the entire planning community, of which city planners are central players.

Toronto's Planning Community

The term "planning experts" encompasses a variety of professionals involved in city planning and urban design. "Planning community" expands the concept of "planning experts" to include lawyers practising planning and tribunal law in and for the City of Toronto. Both terms include professionals from both the public sector (City Planning) and private sector. City planners preside at the centre of the planning community in Toronto (Paton interview 2008). Although one city councillor derisively called city planners "trained gatekeepers" (Rae interview 2008), the term "gatekeeper" is not an inappropriate description of city planners' role in city planning. In jurisdictions with less flexible rules and laws regarding OPAs and Zoning By-law Amendments than Ontario, city planners' main role is as gatekeepers of the official plan and municipal zoning by-laws. In such cities, when a developer applies to develop land, city planners examine whether the proposal conforms to the municipal by-laws and official plan. Non-conformance results in a refusal, conformance results in approval. In some jurisdictions, city planners are the final decision-makers because of this rigid interpretation of planning laws.

In Toronto, city planners are among a number of planning experts that make up the City Planning Division (City Planning). Toronto's city planners' role is more robust than that of many of their counterparts in other municipalities, and was especially so during the period of this analysis (2000 through 2006). During this period, they grappled with the antiquated plans and by-laws of the six former municipalities of

Metro Toronto, and the City's new official plan, enacted in 2002 but yet to come into complete effect. The city planners spend a significant amount of time considering and interpreting the City's official plan, zoning by-laws, and provincial policy statements. The flexibility the City has in amending the official plan and zoning by-laws requires more of city planners than simply testing development proposals against existing laws.[1] City planners, under the auspices of Community Planning, a subdivision of City Planning, also compose the final staff reports for the community and city councils, and play an important role in facilitating discussions between communities (and neighbourhood associations) and developers (Paton interview 2008). In essence, city planners steer development proposals through the application process. They are responsible for ensuring that every individual who is required to or interested in seeing and commenting on a proposal has the opportunity to do so, and for processing the proposal within the mandated period (Keefe interview 2008).

Despite the primacy of their role in the planning process, city planners are not alone in influencing planning policy and decisions. Depending on the size and type of proposal, a number of other planning experts and different types of planners take part in the development application process. For instance, some of the City's planning experts specialize in urban design. These specialists focus on the architecture and built form of a proposal in comparison to the existing built form of the surrounding buildings and neighbourhood (Paton interview 2008; Rae interview 2008). Professionals in traffic, parking, forestry, and landscaping, as well as experts in the City's heritage division, and even the Toronto Regional Conservation Authority, can play a part in the process, and are among the "planning experts" that form the City Planning Division (Paton interview 2008).

In the private sphere, developers will either employ their own experts or hire external consultants to prepare and plan their development proposals. In addition to architects, developers employ equivalent experts for each type of expert the City employs. In cases where city council chooses to ignore or dismiss the recommendations of City Planning, the City will also employ external consultants from the private sector (Paton interview 2008). Each of these types of experts plays a role, even if marginal in some instances, in shaping the form of development, and, as a result, the built form of the city of Toronto. Finally, planning and tribunal lawyers practising in the city or in the employ of the City are important to the application process, and are especially important when development proposals make their way to the Ontario Municipal Board. Planning and tribunal lawyers are often responsible for marshalling planning experts before the board. All of these professionals, both from the private and public realm, constitute the "planning community."

According to John Paton (interview 2008), the City's director of planning and administrative tribunal law, the planning community in Toronto is fairly small. Despite the thousands of lawyers in Toronto, only a few practise land-use planning law, and even fewer practise in Toronto. City lawyers and private-sector lawyers involved in the application process and in OMB appeals are usually very familiar with each other. Likewise, Keefe (interview 2008), the head of community planning in Etobicoke York, notes that most of the city's planning experts, both from the public and private sector, have attended the same schools or worked with each other in the past. Given the familiarity among lawyers and planning experts, Paton (interview 2008) suggests that private-sector lawyers only get one chance to mislead or dupe the city. Constant contact ensures disreputable professionals are weeded out of the process. Familiarity forces a level of honesty between fellow professionals.

The Planning Community's Influence in Toronto

That the planning community plays a role in the development of Toronto is undeniable. Whether the importance or influence of that role is intensified under the auspices of the Ontario Municipal Board is the main focus of this chapter. Chipman (2002), Bowman (2001), and Krushelnicki (2007) all speak of the primacy of planning experts to the OMB appeals process, and the data from the previous chapter support this claim, but none speaks of the role of planning experts in the application processes, nor of their behaviour. Given that LPE literature does not offer a direct account of planning experts' role or behaviour, the following analysis is more conjectural than the analysis in the following three chapters. However, the general model of urban development politics in the LPE approach and the conspicuous absence of planning experts offer a limited means of comparison.

In cities like Chicago, city council can pass any by-law, regardless of the planning justification, so long as the by-law or decision is within the municipality's power. According to LPE literature, council should base its decision in such instances largely on the relative strength of the pro-growth and anti-growth advocates in the city. As a result, planning experts' arguments in favour or against a development should be of little consequence. In addition, while planning experts are never absent from discussions of planning issues, they should play a minor role in the politics of urban development, and should not have significant influence on policy decision making or on the behaviour of other actors. Given that LPE literature does not address the role of planning experts in the politics of urban development, the preceding depiction of their role and influence in said politics is somewhat speculative. However, it does suggest that in absence of the OMB planning experts would have little influence on the behaviour and decision making of other actors in the politics of urban development.

In Toronto, city council's fiat is not enough to ensure the passing or rejection of a by-law or planning amendment before the Ontario Municipal Board, even if completely within the prescribed powers of the City. Without an appellant, a proposal can go forward even without the backing of planning experts. However, the possibility of an appeal requires that any settlement or agreement among interested parties pass the litmus test of good planning, whatever that may be,[2] to gain acceptance at the board. This fact suggests that planning experts play a central role in the decision-making process. Both public- and private-sector planning experts must be involved in the application process from the beginning and be more attentive to detail because of the threat or possibility of appeals, as the strength of their work plays a substantial role in winning a favourable decision from the board. In addition, planning expert opinion should be paramount in obtaining settlements between City, neighbourhood associations, and developers. This account of planning experts' role in the politics of urban development in Toronto suggests that the city's planning experts direct the entire application process, and, as a result, play a central role in the politics of urban development in Toronto.

The analysis in the remainder of this chapter focuses on both the application process and appeals process. The applications process begins when a developer approaches the city, either formally or informally,[3] with a development proposal, and concludes once city council renders its decision (or fails to render a decision, resulting in an appeal). The appeals process begins with the formal appeal to the OMB, and ends when the City and other actors reach a settlement, the appellant withdraws the appeal, or the OMB renders its decision.

Both city staff and private-sector planners alike echo the belief that experts are paramount in front of the board. Neither group dismisses the role of city councillors or neighbourhood associations, but they are unequivocal regarding experts' importance to the appeals process (Smith interview 2008; Paton interview 2008). In addition, they believe that the possibility an application will make its way before the board influences both public- and private-sector experts' work, as it ensure its integrity. During the application process, developers, neighbourhood associations, local politicians, and even other planning experts may scrutinize and criticize the findings and advice of planning experts, offering evidence of the strength and quality of planning experts' work. Board hearings result in even more scrutiny, and even demand it, reinforcing the need for planning experts to be attentive to detail in their work.

Question 1 asks whether the existence of the OMB, along with its procedures, increases the influence of planning experts in the politics of urban development. That they seem attentive to their work and its role in board decisions suggests they perceive themselves as important to the appeals process, but does not indicate the role they may play in the application process or the politics of urban development as a whole. The board of directors of the Markland Homes Association suggest planning experts can play an important role in the application process. They recounted a story of a consultant facilitating cooperation between the MHA and a developer (Board of Directors interview 2009).[4] In addition, employees from the City confirmed the findings from the previous chapter. City council will typically listen to City Planning (Paton interview 2008; Keefe interview 2008).

Despite these findings, Peter Smith (2008), a private-sector planning consultant, suggests that external professional consultants have no bearing on policy decisions during the application process. He also notes that city councillors will ignore City Planning's advice. Chart 4.7 in the previous chapter supports this latter claim, but only in a minority of cases. In most cases, the City follows its planning experts' advice. Nevertheless, on twenty-five occasions from 2000 through 2006, city council did ignore City Planning's outright support when rejecting development proposals. That the City fared poorly in such instances is evidence of city planners' importance in OMB hearings. However, the data offer little insight into the broader role of planning experts in the politics of urban development.

If the board affects the role of planning experts in Toronto, their role and influence on other actors should be apparent during both the application and appeals process. There should be evidence of the centrality of their role in negotiations between the City, developer, and neighbourhood associations. In addition, developers and neighbourhood associations should be actively courting the support of City Planning.

The Four Seasons Hotel

On 28 July 2005, Bay-Yorkville Developments Ltd. submitted an application to the City for a fifty-five-storey combination hotel and condominium building and a thirty-storey condominium building. Bay-Yorkville Developments is a partnership between Menkes Development Ltd. and Lifetime Homes (Diamond 2005a). Menkes is an all-purpose builder (low-rise and high-rise housing, commercial, and industrial) operating in the Greater Toronto Area, though most of the company's developments are high-rise condominiums located in the city proper.[5] Lifetime Homes (Lifetime Urban Development Group) exclusively builds condominium high-rises in the former City of Toronto. Four Seasons Hotels joined the partnership of Bay-Yorkville Developments as the operator and owner of the hotel portion of the larger proposed building (Diamond 2005a). Not only is Four Seasons Hotels one of the largest hotel chains in the world, it was also founded, and maintains its headquarters, in Toronto. The new hotel was one of four five-star hotels proposed or under construction in the city at that time (Won 2005). Given that its headquarters is in Toronto, Four Seasons sought to "protect its turf" (ibid., B3) against other hotel operators in the city, such as Ritz-Carlton, Trump, and Shangri-La, each of which planned their own five-star hotel.[6]

Bay-Yorkville Developments and Four Seasons proposed the development for the upscale Bloor-Yorkville neighbourhood on the northern limits of the downtown, not far from Four Seasons' existing four-star hotel. The size of the larger building was unprecedented for the area, originally proposed at 205 metres, a height more representative of the financial district to the south (City Clerk 2006a). The City convened an open house meeting for neighbourhood residents to express their thoughts on the proposed development. Following the open house, Kyle Rae, the ward councillor, proposed the establishment of a "Working Group consisting of various representatives from the Yorkville community, the applicant's team and City staff" (City Clerk 2006a), and himself. The working group included a number of representatives from neighbouring condominium developments, a number of neighbour-hood associations (ABC Residents' Association, Yonge-Bay-Bloor Association, Greater Yorkville Residents Association), the local business improvement association, a representative from the neighbouring Jesse Ketchum Public School, and a representative from SAVE Yorkville Heritage Association (SYHA), an activist association formed to protect the integrity of Yorkville (Four Seasons Working Committee [FSWC] 2005c).

While the local businesses and condominium residents supported the proposal for the most part, SYHA, the ABC Residents' Association, and the parents' council from Jesse Ketchum, among others, were less than impressed with the size of the building. Minutes from the working committee's meetings suggest that the architect for the development, Peter Clewes, played a significant role in the discussion with neighbour-hood residents and attempted to accommodate many of their wishes. City planners, on the other hand, were either silent through much of the process, or were absent from the proceedings (FSWC 2005a, 2005b, 2005c). Eventually, the working committee submitted an application to the City that proposed a significant reduction in the size of the larger building, from 205 metres to 179, and a more modest reduction for the smaller building, from 125 metres to 110 (City Clerk 2006a).

In its initial commentary on the proposal, the Toronto District School Board (TDSB) did not oppose the development. It did not foresee any negative impacts on local schools, including Jesse Ketchum Public School, which neighbours the site, as they could accommodate new residents (and new pupils) in the area (Silva 2005). However, the TDSB later decided the buildings would cast too great a shadow on the yard of the elementary school, depriving its students of sunlight (ibid.). As a result, the developer agreed to pay the TDSB $2 million to overcome its opposition. The TDSB claimed the agreement came with support from the Jesse Ketchum Parents' Council (Gray 2006). However, the parents' council maintained their opposition to the development throughout the working group process, and would not support the proposal unless the developer addressed the issue of shadows. Both SYHA and the ABC Residents' Association proved unyielding in their opposition to the de-velopment (FSWC 2005a). Despite the continued opposition of a few members from the working committee, City Planning recommended approval of the amended application to city council (City Clerk 2006a). City council enacted two by-laws approving the development on 27 April 2006 (By-law no. 330-2006;[7] By-law no. 331-2006).

Much enthusiasm existed for the proposed development among some neighbourhood residents, local businesses, and the ward councillor, Kyle Rae. In addition, despite the significant size of the development, city planners supported the development, as did a majority of city councillors and the mayor (Toronto Star 2006). Perhaps because of its support for the development, City Planning appears to have had little influence on the application process, aside from its usual role in vetting the proposal. Given Councillor Rae's enthusiastic support for the development, the application may have succeeded at council without City Planning's support. Thus, this case does not provide much evidence of the City's planning experts' influence on council's decision making. The one planning expert who appears to have influenced the development the most was the developer's architect, Peter Clewes, who worked with area residents on the design of the building. While he did not achieve unanimous support, he appears to have played a pivotal role in the negotiations, along with Councillor Rae.

The Appeal

Following council's passing of By-laws no. 330-2006 and 331-2006, a number of the remaining opponents of the development submitted appeals to the OMB. The SAVE Yorkville Heritage Association listed ten reasons the board should overturn council's decision. The SYHA focused on, among other things, the density and the height of the building, the shadows that the two towers would cast, and even the structure of the working committee, which the SYHA claimed resulted in "inadequate discussion" (SYHA 2006). Along with the SYHA, the ABC Residents' Association (ABC) filed a similar notice of appeal complaining of the height, shadows, increased traffic, and lack of public parking (ABC Residents' Association 2006). The Jesse Ketchum Public School Parents' Council also appealed council's decision. While it echoed aspects of both the SYHA and ABC's appeal, the main focus of its appeal was the impact of the development on the school (Makuch 2006). Finally, a number of nearby residents appealed the decision (see, for instance, Donald and Chu 2006).

The appeal of city council's decision in the Four Seasons case is one rare instance where a neighbourhood association, ABC, chose to appeal a decision of council.[8] The other two neighbourhood associations for the area, the Greater Yorkville Residents Association and the Yonge-Bay-Bloor Association, chose not to appeal the decision. The lack of a united front among area residents probably undermined the positions of the four appellants from the onset of the appeals process. Before the second OMB prehearing, ABC, the parents' council, and the individual residents, settled with the City and developer (*Save Yorkville Heritage Association v. Toronto (City)* [2006]). The settlement agreed upon by the City, developer, and appellants involved the increase in size of the larger tower from 179 metres to 195 metres in height, and the reduction in size of the smaller tower from 110 metres to 89 metres. In addition, Menkes and Lifetime offered additional funds for the improvement of a local park and street. The reduction of the smaller building reduced the shadows cast on Jesse Ketchum Public School, meeting the concerns of the school's parents' council. In the OMB's final decision, the board noted ABC's support for the settlement (*Toronto (City) Official Plan Amendment no. 361 (Re)* [2007]). However, in its submission to the board, the SYHA claimed that ABC did not support the development, but could no longer afford to continue fighting it. In fact, the SYHA claimed that ABC's lawyer, Stanley Makuch, was not even party to the negotiated settlement (SYHA 2007).

Following the withdrawal of the other appellants, the SYHA was the sole party in active opposition to the development. A number of the appellants, including ABC and the parents' council, had hired the law firm of Cassels Brock (a firm with significant experience at the OMB) to represent them during the appeals process and potential hearing. The SYHA had initially retained its own legal counsel, but, for whatever reason, eventually joined forces with the other appellants. When ABC and the other appellants dropped their appeals, the SYHA no longer had legal counsel (*Save Yorkville Heritage Association v. Toronto (City)*; Latham 2006; Brown 2006). On 28 February 2007, over the remaining objections of the SYHA, the Ontario Municipal Board dismissed the appeals and authorized the settlement between the City, developer, and other appellants.[9] Not surprisingly, in light of the data from the previous chapter, the OMB drew heavily on expert opinion from both city staff and the developers' staff and external consultants (*Toronto (City) Official Plan Amendment no. 361 (Re)*). The submission from the SYHA and the board's comments regarding the SYHA's participation in the hearing substantiate the importance of planning experts' role in the appeals process. The SYHA's tactic at the board hearing was to draw upon the expert testimony and reports of both the City and developers' planning experts to demonstrate the inappropriateness of the design. It also drew upon one shadow study it commissioned from the IBI Group.

In addition, the association emphasized the important and famous Canadians who opposed the development. The SYHA circulated a list of names that included, among others, author Margaret Atwood, singer Catherine McKinnon, and, most important, planning guru Jane Jacobs (SYHA 2007).[10] Councillor Kyle Rae derisively referred to these individuals as "celebrity planners" in addition to referring to the SYHA as "the lunatic fringe" (Rae interview 2008).

The board noted early in its short decision that although the SYHA had not "settled its appeal, it [had] chosen not to call any expert evidence" during the hearing (*Toronto (City) Official Plan Amendment no. 361 (Re)*, para. 2). Following this comment, it repeatedly referred to evidence given by the developer's planner, Peter Smith. In addition, the board openly recognized,

> some frustration voiced by area residents as they endeavoured to dispute the interpretation of the applicant's planner and City staff report that supported the proposal. That frustration was, of course, compounded by the settlement by other appellant parties representing area residents and a resident's group originally to be represented by counsel and planning expertise. (*Toronto (City) Official Plan Amendment no. 361 (Re)*, para. 15)

This recognition did little to aid the SYHA's case, however, as the board noted the group's failure to provide any expert evidence that contradicted the City or developer's planning experts (*Toronto (City) Official Plan Amendment no. 361 (Re)*).

The SYHA acknowledged its own lack of expertise in its submission to the board, but emphasized that its members were educated and informed residents (SYHA 2007). However, the lack of expert witnesses and trained legal counsel obviously undermined the SYHA's bid to have the City's decision overturned. The SYHA's representatives at the OMB hearing even failed to submit their written presentation to the board at the appropriate time during the hearing (Latham 2007). All of the planning experts involved in the OMB hearing, whether from the public or private sector, appear to have supported the development. The OMB relied on the planning experts' testimony and reports throughout.

Aldergreen Estates

The site proposed for Aldergreen Estates, 121 Avenue Rd., has a long and convoluted history. It was once the location of St Paul's Methodist

Church. The church, over a hundred years old, burned down due to arson in 1995. The Litwin family owned the church and an office building across the street. The fire at St Paul's was the third to strike a Litwin property in six years. According to an article in the *Globe and Mail* (Barber 2006), Mark Litwin was behind the plans for a seven-storey, 26.6-metre, mixed-use office/residential building that Colson Investment first proposed for the site on 16 November 2004 – the focus of this case study (Barber 2006; Aldergreen Estates 2005). At some point in the proceedings, Colson Investment became Aldergreen Estates Inc.[11]

Following the demise of the church, city council of the former City of Toronto enacted ICBL no. 1995-0509 to provide planners an opportunity to review the land-use policies for the site, to determine an appropriate replacement for the church. Most of the site had remained unoccupied since. However, the 2004 proposal was not the first. A proposal for twenty-nine residential units met its end due to council's passing of new by-laws for the site. Council felt the proposal involved excessive intensification. While the developer initially appealed the by-laws to the OMB, it sold the land to another developer, who settled with the City. The new developer proposed to build four detached homes and a one-storey commercial development on the site. However, the developer sold the land before anything was built. The new owner proposed seven three-storey town homes for the back half of the lot. The developer built the seven town homes, and proposed a three-storey office building for the remainder of the site, but again sold the remainder of the lot before anything was built, this time to Colson Investments/Aldergreen Estates Inc. Colson Investments/Aldergreen Estates Inc. subsequently proposed the seven-storey, 26.6-metre mixed-use building (Community Planning 2004a).[12]

The settlement between the City and the second owner of the site allowed for a 14 metre building on the remainder of the lot. City Planning felt the 26.6 metre proposal was inappropriate for the site, and recommended city council refuse the development application. In addition, residents from the neighbouring retirement home to the south of the site, and at least one of the residents from the seven town homes built on the site, vehemently opposed the development. City council accepted both the advice of City Planning and the few opponents of the development, and refused the development application on 7 December 2005 (City Clerk 2005a). Aldergreen Estates Inc. had already appealed the decision to the OMB on 28 July 2005 due to city council's neglect (Devine 2005).

Despite recommending the refusal of the development application, City Planning was not opposed to greater intensification for the site than the by-law allowed. At the initial community meeting held by city staff, roughly thirty neighbouring residents attended. Most attendees were opposed to the development. The owners of the town homes, much like the opponents of the Four Seasons Hotel, feared the shadows a larger building would cast on their backyards. In a submission to the community council, one owner of a townhouse on the back end of the site meticulously detailed the amount of money he and his wife spent on the house ($1.4 million to purchase the house, an additional $300,000 on the interior, and $90,000 on the landscaping of the backyard), and his abhorrence in discovering a few months after the purchase and renovations were complete that the new owner had a proposed a development higher than zoning by-laws permitted for the site (Kubbernus 2005).[13] Residents of the retirement home, which was, in fact, taller than the proposed building, feared the loss of their view of St Clair Hill and Casa Loma, and the potential loss of sunlight (though the proposed building was situated north of the home) (Heisey 2005). City Planning, the developer's planning experts, the owner and residents of Hazelton Place Retirement Residence to the south, and representatives from the town homes on the site met on a number of occasions over seven months to discuss the development. The staff report provides little indication of who directed or led these meetings, but City Planning eventually proposed its own compromise (City Clerk 2005a).

City Planning forwarded its recommendation to the Toronto and East York community council. It suggested that it work with the city solicitor to oppose the appeal, while supporting a six-storey, 21.1-metre development at the OMB. However, city council chose to amend City Planning's suggestions and proposal for the site. At the behest of Councillor Rae and the Toronto and East York Community Council, city council decided to exclude city planners from the OMB appeals process, instead hiring private-sector experts. In addition, city council proposed a five-storey, 19-metre building for the site, which would fall within the parameters of the existing height and density limits for the site (City Clerk's Office 2005a).

Despite their involvement in discussions with the developer and neighbourhood residents, the city's planning experts appear to have had little influence on council's decision. The developer's planning experts appeared to have played a minor role as well. The OMB decision suggests that neighbourhood residents did not care for City Planning's proposal. The only participant who paid heed to the City's planning experts was the developer, whose revised proposal, according to the OMB, did not deviate significantly from City Planning's (*Aldergreen Estates Inc. v. Toronto (City)*). Given Councillor Kyle Rae's open disdain for anti-growth activists (Rae interview 2008), council's decision to ignore City Planning's advice is surprising. The City's poor showing at the OMB when lacking city staff's support obviously did not deter city council. City Planning and planning experts in general appear to have played a minor role in the proceedings, with one important exception. They clearly influenced the developer, as it would later adopt many of their suggestions.

The Appeal

The Aldergreen Estates appeal varies significantly from the Four Seasons appeal in a number of ways. The appellant was the developer, not one of multiple opponents to the development. City council opposed the development, and Aldergreen Estates Inc. and the City appeared unable to reach a satisfactory settlement before the hearing. Given the difference between city council and City Planning, this fact is not surprising. Aldergreen Estates Inc. would have known beforehand that its revised proposal did not deviate significantly from that proposed by City Planning, which would lend additional support to its case. Though not as large a group as the neighbourhood associations that opposed the Four Seasons Hotel, neighbouring residents opposed to Aldergreen Estates maintained a united front and managed to retain an experienced law firm to represent them.[14] In fact, the firm of Papazian, Heisey, and Myers was the same that initially represented one of the appellants in the Four Seasons appeal (Heisey 2005, 2006). Also, the town homes and retirement home residents, bolstered by the owner and operator of the retirement home, Diversicare, were able to retain their own planning expert (*Aldergreen Estates Inc. v. Toronto (City)*).

The board began its decision by noting that it "was provided with three competing visions for the site: the applicant's proposal, as revised; the City's proposal; and a variation of the City's proposal, recommended by Diversicare/Webster Residents." In addition a "variation of the Aldergreen proposal, recommended by City staff but rejected by Council when the application was refused, was also addressed in the evidence" (*Aldergreen Estates Inc. v. Toronto (City)*, para. 2). Aldergreen Estates' revised proposal did not vary in height from the original (26.6

metres), but did vary in the number and height of setbacks incorporated into the building,[15] a requirement of city staff. City Planning's
proposal, while ostensibly only 21.2 metres in height, would have been
26.2 metres high if including the standard 5-metre mechanical penthouse. The main variation between the two proposals was the location and height of the setbacks. City council supported a building no
taller than that suggested in the development guidelines for the area,
14 metres with a 5-metre mechanical penthouse (19 metres in total). The
board also considered issues relating to the location of the retail component of the building and access from the street in its decision (*Aldergreen
Estates Inc. v. Toronto (City)*).

The board relied heavily on the testimony of all the experts, regardless of whom they represented, but, for the most part, they appeared to
side with experts representing Aldergreen Estates (though the board
sided with residents and the City concerning the retail component of
the development). However, the board repeatedly referred back to the
development proposal City Planning had recommended to the community council. In addition, when suggesting its preference for the testimony of the developer's experts, the board repeatedly noted that the
developer's revised proposal did not deviate significantly from that of
City Planning. The OMB in the end allowed the appeal, in part. It modified the developer's proposal with recommendations from City Planning's report (*Aldergreen Estates Inc. v. Toronto (City)*).

In the closing comments of its decision, the board noted that it had
adopted a number of recommendations from City Planning's report to
council. The board remarked:

> While staff's recommendations were rejected by Council ..., with the ben-
> efit of expert evidence and argument, the Board concludes that the devel-
> opment guidelines set out below form an appropriate basis to approve the
> application and balance the competing goals of developing a vacant site
> and minimizing impact to adjacent landowners. (*Aldergreen Estates Inc. v.
> Toronto (City)*, para. 46)

The board's closing remarks capture the importance of planning experts to the appeals process, even when – as in the case of City Planning
– the expert does not partake in the proceedings.

All three parties to the appeal, Aldergreen Estates, the City, and the
neighbouring residents, relied on their own experts to support their
respective position. Residents did not invoke celebrities or their own

education to sway the board. However, a number did express their own dissatisfaction with the development proposal directly to the board. The developer presented more expert opinions to the board than the City and residents combined, however. Aldergreen Estates marshalled an urban design planner, an architect, traffic expert, and land-use planner. The City could only muster an architect with expertise in urban design and a land-use planner, while residents employed their own planner as well (*Aldergreen Estates Inc. v. Toronto (City)*). Had the City sided with City Planning, it presumably would have had more expert representation to support its position before the board.

The board, while favouring the testimony of the developer's experts, clearly relied heavily on City Planning's report to council. This case confirms the findings from the previous chapter. Although the City hired additional planning consultants, the fact that the City's own planning experts supported a proposal considerably larger than that which council favoured clearly undermined the City's position at the hearing. That all parties to the hearing had experts changed the dynamics of the appeals process relative to the Four Seasons case. However, both the City and residents' experts argued in favour of a development proposed by non-experts (Toronto and East York Community Council and the neighbouring residents themselves).

This case suggests that the City's planning experts have a relative advantage at the board. City council's proposal to the board did not deviate from the proposal it articulated when amending City Planning's report. This proposal did not originate from contrary expert opinion, but from city councillors themselves. Thus, experts representing the City were articulating a proposal they did not originate; as was the neighbouring residents' expert. The City's planning experts are the only experts involved in the process not bound directly to the whims of other actors (even the developer's planning experts must conform in some degree to the wishes of their employer). They are, therefore, better positioned to render an opinion based entirely or mostly on their expertise. In the absence of the board, City Planning, while still initially acting in an advisory capacity to city council, would invariably have to adjust its opinion on a proposal to conform to that of council, or if not actually support it, then implement council's vision. However, a board hearing would reveal any significant change in city planners' opinion, which would likely work against the City when the board renders its decision. Thus, the City's planning experts not only enjoy an increased level of autonomy, but require such autonomy to function within a system where the possibility of appeal to the board exists.

The combination of City Planning's opinion and a revised proposal from the developer incorporating some of City Planning's suggestions assured the weight of expert testimony tipped towards the developer. Despite their absence from the appeal and hearing process, the City's planning experts significantly influenced the decision of the OMB, and the final built form of the development. As in the previous case, the board did not openly criticize any of the work or testimony of the various experts, mentioning only whose testimony and work it preferred.

The community council and city council's rejection of City Planning's recommendations suggests the limits of planning experts' influence. City council did not adopt any of City Planning's recommendations regarding an alternative proposal for the site. City council and neighbouring residents' unwillingness to compromise with the developer emphasizes the weak influence planning experts exerted over local politicians and citizens when both are aligned during this application process. However, City Planning did sway the developer and its own experts in this instance.

Summary of Findings

This chapter addresses my first question: *Does the existence of the OMB affect the role Toronto's planning community plays in the politics of urban development?* Any evidence suggesting the City's planning experts do not affect the decision of city council, developers, or neighbourhood residents would indicate that the board does not increase their level of influence. Evidence that planning experts affect the decisions and actions of actors involved in the politics of urban development would indicate the board's influence. Both cases presented here substantiate the findings from the previous chapter, as well as Bowman (2001), Chipman (2002), and Krushelnicki's (2007) claims. Planning experts are vital to OMB hearings. Not only the lack of expertise, but the lack of proper counsel undid the SYHA's efforts to prevent the construction of the Four Seasons Hotel. Nonetheless, in this case, planning experts' role seems limited to the appeals process, aside from Clewes's role in the working group. The board's decision in the Aldergreen Estates case was far longer and more detailed than its decisions regarding the Four Seasons, despite the fact that Aldergreen Estates is a much smaller and less conspicuous development. The detailed decision evidences the involvement of expert testimony from all parties to the hearing. The board weighed the arguments of the residents in the Aldergreen Estates case far more heavily than the SYHA's arguments in the Four Seasons case.

The evidence suggests that for planning experts to sway the board, they must ensure a high level of attentiveness to detail in their work. Board hearings usually involve heavy scrutiny of the planning rationale for and against a specific proposal. While the cases offer little evidence that planning experts' work receives the same scrutiny during the application process, Keefe (interview 2008) suggests city planners could not ignore the possibility of an OMB hearing. According to Keefe, city planners do their best to serve the interests of their employers (city council), but recognize that any recommendation to council must be defensible in front of the OMB: "You may like to say different things to city council, because it would be easier, but in the end, you have to be able to stand up and say it is good planning. The thing you may want to say to council may not cut it. So, in the end, you give your best advice in all cases" (Keefe interview 2008).

Both Smith (interview 2008) and Blazevski (interview 2008) echo Keefe's sentiments. Thus, these findings and comments further emphasize the necessity of City Planning's autonomy from city council in the planning process.

In a small number of OMB decisions, the board has openly chastised city experts due to the weakness of their testimony. In a 2006 decision the board referred repeatedly to the City's lack of credibility, and also referred to the City's lack of planning rationale as "troubling" (*Davenport Three Develco Inc. v. Toronto (City)*, para. 82). In this instance, the City's planning experts, not outside help, represented the interests of the City. In a 2005 decision, the board was even more critical of City Planning. It accused city planners of having failed to review a number of reports on the proposed development from other city departments, and having failed to review thoroughly the developer's application (*Toronto (City) Official Plan Redesignate Land Amendment (Re)* [2005] O.M.B.D. no. 1059). These cases do not necessarily reflect City Planning's support of a council position on a development, despite initial differences, but the failure of City Planning to conduct a thorough investigation of a proposal. However, they are indicative of what would happen in a board hearing should the City's planning experts ignore their own professional opinion, and try, instead, to represent that of council.

This finding appears to be the most important drawn from these cases. It offers an explanation of Smith's (interview 2008) belief that the board will usually find a way to support City Planning. The board's existence allows the City's planning experts greater autonomy than their private-sector counterparts, which in turn provides them with an advantage during an OMB hearing. Although local politicians may intervene early in discussions between city staff and developer, the possibility of a board hearing counters any weight that a council member or citizen group can bring to bear on a city planning expert. Their jobs are not dependent on their support of city council's position, especially as they act in an advisory capacity. Even if the work is poor, the board expects planning experts to give honest testimony during a hearing regarding a development proposal. Keefe (2008) states that City Planning may wish simply to accept the will of councillors and vocal critics of a proposal, but cannot given potential for a board hearing. This fact exposes the City's planning experts to criticism from neighbourhood associations, sympathetic politicians, and sometimes the media. However, because private-sector planning experts must support the position of their employers, their work is more likely to result in weaker planning rationale. Thus, *ceteris paribus*, the board would be more apt to accept the testimony of the City's planning experts over that of private-sector planning experts.

That the board does not always side with City Planning is, perhaps, evidence of Smith's (interview 2008) belief that the City's planning experts and legal counsel lack the same experience as their private-sector counterparts, thus compromising the City during board hearings (Smith interview 2008). Both Smith and Councillor Rae note how poorly prepared the City's planning experts were in the West Queen West Triangle case, a prominent case that resulted in a controversial board decision. Councillor Rae (interview 2008) also refers to the City's planning experts during this case as "baby planners" due to their youth and lack of experience, while Keefe (2008) notes the high turnover rate among planners at the City, as they moved from the public sector to the private during the boom in development. These elements hamper what is otherwise a process that favours the City's planning experts.

These findings, though unexpected, suggest the board influences the behaviour of the City's planning experts so that it differs from the behaviour of planning experts in other jurisdictions. The lack of direct comparisons limits the strength of this finding. However, while planning experts in other North American cities likely enjoy the same type of job security as those in Toronto, they may be more open to pressure from local politicians and other interests. City councils with final decision-making power over planning can ignore the advice of a city's planning experts without the same repercussions that the City of Toronto could face at an OMB hearing. Without the incentive the board provides the City's planning experts to present honest advice on a proposal, they may be more willing to give in to demands of council or other interests.

Of course, such findings, while of significant importance to any understanding of planning in the City of Toronto, do not indicate the role of planning experts before OMB hearings (during the application process), though the City's planning experts clearly do not act solely as gatekeepers, and play a role beyond that of adviser to council. The Four Seasons case offers mixed evidence regarding experts' role in the politics of urban development. Peter Clewes played an important role during the working group, but City Planning appeared absent from much of the process. There is no evidence that City Planning's support for the development swayed city council, particularly as the councillor for the ward, Kyle Rae, enthusiastically supported the proposal from the beginning (Rae interview 2008). The Aldergreen Estates case offered equally mixed evidence. Planning experts, whether city employees or otherwise, appear to have had no influence on the decision of council or the position of neighbouring residents. However, the developer clearly listened to the advice of City Planning, adopting many of its suggestions for the site in the revised proposal it presented to the board. This finding suggests that developers are aware of planning experts' influence on OMB decisions and, in particular, of the board's bias in favour of City Planning. This suggests that the board does increase the importance and influence of planning experts towards some political actors, but does not indicate an overwhelming influence.

Even without a clear method of comparison in this case, the evidence from the two case studies above provides a tentative answer to *Question 1*. Planning experts are key to board hearings. The findings from chapter 4 suggest that council will usually rely on City Planning, but are less likely to do so when a specific proposal develops salience and opposition within a community. Nevertheless, the City's planning experts seem to have more influence over city council in Toronto than their counterparts in other cities. They can play an important role in negotiations among groups, but they do not appear to sway the opinion or behaviour of neighbourhood associations in particular. However, the Aldergreen Estates case suggests the City's planning experts can influence developers significantly. The analysis of Pulse Condominium

in the following chapter provides even greater evidence of this influence on developers. The influence City's planning experts have at the
OMB is likely the main cause of this influence, suggesting the board
does increase the influence of planning experts in the politics of urban
development.

That the OMB is the cause of this increased role is evidence that a
variation in planning institutions can affect the politics of urban development and the actors involved in it. Evidence of this fact suggests the
LPE literature may be omitting an important element and actor when
studying the behaviour of and relationships between actors in the politics of urban development. The board places an important resource in
the hands of planning experts, legitimacy. To win a board hearing, participants must make a legitimate argument for or against a proposal,
and planning experts are the means to establish such legitimacy.

In effect, the board not only shapes the role and influence of certain actors (in these cases planning experts), but determines the language that permeates discourse over development. The language of
the politics of urban development in Toronto is the language of land-
use planning. Planning experts become the focal point of board hearings because they are the masters of this language. Even in the Four
Seasons case, where the SYHA lacked any expert witnesses during the
hearing, the association tried to adopt the language of land-use planning to argue against the proposal. This finding is important, because
it suggests that the board diminishes the importance of the language of
exchange and use value that often dominates development discourse
in other jurisdictions in North America. For instance, in the anecdote
concerning Philadelphia from chapter 1, proponents of the proposed
skyscraper spoke of its future effect on the city's economy to justify approving the proposal, while opponents argued that it would destroy
the fabric of the neighbourhood it was proposed for. Such arguments
are not absent in Toronto. However, the board ensures that they do not
determine the fate of a development proposal in the city. Proposals live
or die at the board depending on the strength of the planning rationale
supporting them. Thus, instead of arguments pertaining to the effect of
a development on the community, on the tranquillity of a neighbourhood, or on housing value, board hearings focus on shadows, traffic,
access to transportation, and density. Both exchange value and use
value are implicit in such discussions, but the language used is very
different, and often inaccessible to laypersons.

The following chapters continue to examine how planning institutions can affect the distributions of resources in urban politics, and how important these institutions can be when studying the politics of urban development. This chapter and the evidence from the previous chapter suggest that any account of the politics of urban development in Toronto would be remiss if it were to ignore the presence of planning experts in the process. Given their omission in local political economy literature, one could assume that such experts exert little or no influence and play a minor role in planning and policy making in American cities. Clearly planning experts play some role in Toronto, however. Studying their role, even if it is minor, and their relationship with other actors, could illuminate more of the politics of urban development in other cities. In addition, the cases studied in this chapter suggest the board limits dialogue, at least during its hearings, to issues of use value, rather than exchange value. This fact is very important because the conflict between the two often permeates the discussion in other jurisdictions. Exchange value is never absent from the minds of developers and other actors in Toronto, but the appeal process diminishes its role in determining planning policy.

6 The Politics of Toronto's Development Industry

In early summer 2001, Peter Ellis, an architect from the prestigious Chicago firm Skidmore, Owings and Merrill, presented his vision for two high-rise condominiums at the southeast corner of Yonge and Eglinton. The two buildings would soar fifty-four and forty-seven storeys high and marked one of Ottawa-based Minto Development's earliest sojourns into Toronto's emerging condominium market. According to reporters at the scene, local residents booed and heckled Mr Ellis for most of the presentation (Saunders 2001). At the time, Minto's proposal far exceeded in height all other condominium developments proposed for the city. The two buildings would tower over the existing office buildings and low-rise residential neighbourhoods that surrounded the site. Almost two years passed from the time Minto submitted its proposal to City Planning to the final settlement between the developer and the City. Minto's victory reflected the developer's determination to push for development in spite of significant opposition, and its ability to outlast its opponents. The fight over "Minto Midtown" also heralded the arrival of condominium developers as major players in the politics of urban development in Toronto, and their tumultuous relationship with local politicians and neighbourhood residents.

Developers, as their name suggests, are of vital importance to urban development. An understanding of their interests, behaviour, and relationship with other actors is also vital to the local political economy approach to urban politics and, not surprisingly, to the study of the politics of urban development. Toronto may lack the regimes or growth coalitions typified in much of the American LPE literature; regardless, developers still play a large role and are the major protagonists in the politics of urban development in the city. This chapter examines the behaviour of the development industry in Toronto. In addition, it addresses the strategies developers adopt in pursuing their business in the city, focusing on their interaction with local politicians, City Planning, and neighbourhood associations. Understanding the strategies developers adopt, and their behaviour towards other actors will allow me to address my second question: *Does the existence of the OMB affect the behaviour of developers in Toronto?* In addition to probing two cases of proposed development in the city, Minto Midtown and Pulse Condominiums, this chapter examines local politicians' campaign contributions for the 2006 municipal elections to further explain developers' involvement in Toronto politics. The two case studies examine the behaviour of the developers involved in each case and consider this behaviour against the traditional portrayal in local political economy literature.

The Development Industry in Toronto

Toronto is home to most of Canada's, and some of the world's, largest office developers, owners, and managers, including Cadillac Fairview, Brookfield, and Oxford Properties Group (formerly of Edmonton).[1] Despite their size and importance to the city as major property owners and managers, none of these developers constructed a building in the City of Toronto from 2000 to 2006, in large part because of the long-term impact from the collapse of the development industry in the early 1990s (see Fainstein 2001; and Charney 2005).[2] While both Brookfield and Cadillac Fairview recently completed large office buildings in Toronto's downtown core,[3] neither played a significant role in the politics of urban development during the period of this analysis. Cadillac Fairview's ventures into the condominium market are fairly recent and have been largely uncontroversial due in large part to the locations of the developments (adjacent to the central business district, and on derelict railway lands).[4]

Condominium developers were the most important developers involved in the politics of urban development during the seven years this analysis covers, as the condominium market dominated development in Toronto during this time. However, retail developers, such as SmartCentres, played an important role as well. According to Keefe (2008), a small number of Toronto or regionally based developers account for most condominium development from 2000 through 2006. For instance, Tridel Corporation, the city's largest condominium developer, built over twenty condominium buildings in the city during the period of this analysis. Other larger companies, such as Menkes, H&R Development, and Daniels Corporation, each built approximately ten. Keefe (interview 2008) also notes that a number of foreign developers have ventured into the city's market, though often in partnership with a local developer. For instance, Taylor Wimpey PLC, the second largest builder of homes in the world, acquired Monarch Corporation, one of the city's oldest housing developers (founded in 1917).[5] Monarch moved into the condominium market in 2003 and had built nine condominium buildings by the end of 2006. Otherwise, many small-time developers have emerged and vanished over time, though some have found success and grown. Other types of developers, including low-rise residential developers from the suburbs surrounding Toronto, have also ventured into the city, with mixed results (Keefe interview 2008).[6]

From 2003 through 2006, developers in Toronto applied for 219 condominium approvals. After construction, the developer submits an application to turn the new building into a condominium, so individuals who purchase units can begin to occupy the buildings; thus, the number of applications for condominium approval provides a good reflection of the number of condominium buildings completing construction in a given year. Eight developers accounted for roughly 32 per cent of the condominium developments completed from 2003 through 2006, while a host of medium to small firms were responsible for the rest.[7] As chart 6.1 illustrates, such residential developments account for the vast majority of OMB appeals, whether from neglect, refusal, or council approval. Each column in the chart portrays the type of developments involved in an appeal by the reason for the appeal. Appeals involving residential developments accounted for 74 per cent of appeals of council's rejection (the first column from the left), 66 per cent of appeals from neglect (the middle column), and 54 per cent of appeals of approval (the final column). Thus, much of the politics of urban development in Toronto from 2000 through 2006 is about condominium development, as the plurality of cases appearing before the OMB focus on such development.

While some firms, such as Minto, Concord Pacific, and Monarch, are either based in another city or owned by outside interests, the majority of condominium developers in the city are highly reliant on the Toronto and Greater Toronto Area market for their livelihood. As a result, these developers share many of the interests and traits of developers in other North American cities. However, in most jurisdictions outside of Ontario, developers are unable to appeal city planning decisions to such

Chart 6.1. Development type by reason for appeal

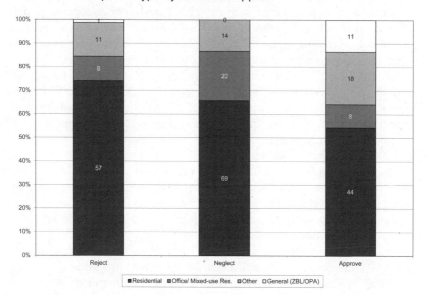

a powerful body as the Ontario Municipal Board. LPE literature suggests local politicians' attractiveness to developers derives from council's final power over planning policy and decision making. Although local politicians in Toronto do render decisions on development, they do not have the final say in matters of planning and development – the OMB does. In addition, whereas political issues beyond the planning justifications for a development (such as community sentiment) may factor into local politicians' decisions, the OMB bases its decisions largely on planning grounds. These facts suggest the relevance of my second question: *Does the existence of the OMB affect the behaviour of developers in Toronto?* The following section begins by examining the role and behaviour of developers in LPE literature and considers how the OMB may influence both.

LPE Literature and Toronto's Development Industry

David Harvey (1983) echoes Logan and Molotch's (1987) term "place-entrepreneurs" in his characterization of the "speculator-developer," arguing that such developers are central to the functioning of a capitalist system. According to Harvey, "Since the urbanization process relates to economic growth in general, the speculator-developer who is, in effect, the promoter of urbanization, plays a vital role in promoting economic growth" (256). Although not all scholars of LPE adopt a Marxian standpoint as Harvey does, his characterization of developers captures the vital role they play in urban development and the politics surrounding it. They not only influence local politicians through campaign financing, but are important contributors to economic growth in many cities. Harvey argues that developers must ensure that the necessary institutions are in place for them to make a profit. In the United States, they do this "through the manipulation of zoning decisions" (ibid., 257). A necessary corollary of this is their need to influence or manipulate local politicians, who control zoning and planning in cities. Harvey's depiction of developers' role and behaviour in the politics of urban development reflects the broader assumptions inherent in the LPE literature.

As seen in the previous chapter, in Toronto, and the rest of Ontario, often all a developer needs to ensure development proceeds is a strong planning rationale that can sway the Ontario Municipal Board. Local politicians, therefore, may not be as enticing to developers given that the OMB will make a final decision if municipal council and the developer cannot agree. In jurisdictions lacking such a board, developers may finance the campaigns of local politicians, directly lobby them (Logan and Molotch 1987), and be willing to negotiate with less accommodating municipal councils where necessary. In Toronto, the OMB's existence may well remove any incentive for developers to pursue such relationships with local politicians and city council. In particular, they would be less prone than Logan and Molotch's place entrepreneurs to finance local politicians' electoral campaigns. They would also expend less effort in lobbying local politicians and be less inclined to negotiate with the City. Given that 45 per cent of OMB appeals result in settlements (see chapter 4, chart 4.4) the final statement may appear week. However, city council, possibly, may be approaching developers with concessions leading to settlements to avoid losing any section 37 contributions from developers should the OMB decide in their favour. In such a scenario, developers still need not pursue an active relationship with local politicians. If city council wishes to avoid an OMB hearing, they can instruct city planners and the city solicitor to concede to the developer's wishes before the appeal.

Campaign Financing in Toronto

Both Stone (1989) and Logan and Molotch (1987) recognize campaign financing as an important means for developers and other businesses to influence local politicians. While briefly criticizing Nelson Polsby's conception of pluralism, Stone notes, "When the business elite constitutes the principal source of campaign funds, it is a direct and significant factor in the electoral sphere" (1989, 186). Logan and Molotch suggest that campaign funding is a major source of leverage for developers with local politicians. The threat of losing such funding makes local politicians beholden to their developer patrons. In many American jurisdictions, local developers, and their growth-machine allies, can outspend their opponents to ensure the election of a candidate favourable to development (1987, 230–6).

In Ontario, the Municipal Election Act, 1996 forbids donations to council candidates greater than $750 (s. 71(1)). The legislation also explicitly forbids businesses from donating above the limit through subsidiary companies (s. 72). This limit to funding could significantly hamper a particular developer's attempt to influence an election (or a local politician), but a group of developers could support and influence a particular candidate (this could include explicit cooperation among developers, or involve uncoordinated support for the candidate most sympathetic to development). Developers could still influence council candidates and policy decision making in the city despite these limits to campaign financing. However, because the OMB has the final say on issues of development, developers may direct their attention towards the board, primarily by relying on planning experts to plead their case, rather than involve themselves in elections or in funding election campaigns.

Even a brief survey of municipal election financing in Toronto demonstrates that developers in Toronto do fund the campaigns of council candidates. In the 2006 municipal election, Menkes donated $4500 in total to six candidates running in the election. MintoUrban, the Toronto-based condominium arm of Ottawa-based Minto Development Inc., contributed $4000 to eleven council candidates. Mid-size developers Goldman Group and Verdiroc contributed $5450 and $6350 respectively to city council candidates. Finally, Castlepoint, one of the three companies involved in a major residential tower in the city's downtown core, and a relative newcomer to the city, contributed $12,750 to nineteen candidates. Numerous developers made more modest campaign contributions, ranging from a few hundred dollars to a few thousand. For the larger developers, such contributions would likely not be a significant investment, but they are investments nonetheless. These campaign contributions can be significant to the candidates.

In most instances, developers contribute to the campaigns of the incumbents. Menkes donated to six candidates' campaigns in 2006. Of the six, four were incumbents. Of the other two one was a former councillor, Peter Li Preti, who had lost his seat in 2003, and Michelle Bernardinetti (discussed below), who was running to replace the retired incumbent. Of all eleven candidates Minto donated funds to, only Bernardinetti was not an incumbent. In ridings where anti-growth candidates were the incumbents – Michael Walker (see the Minto Midtown case below) in ward 22 and Mark Grimes (see the One Sherway case in chapter 6) in ward 6 – developers did not donate to any candidate, an important fact as it indicates that developers in the city are not actively campaigning against an anti-growth candidate. This scenario contrasts sharply with Vogel and Swanson's (1989) depiction of pro-growth forces in Gainesville, Florida, where such groups actively oppose "candidates or incumbents who question growth or whose support is not ensured" (71). The relatively modest spending of developers on local politicians' campaigns may represent only an attempt on developers' behalf to remain in good standing with politicians favourable or open to development in their wards. If so, developers are not focusing as intently on influencing local politicians (and indirectly the electorate), as the LPE approach suggests. While developers are donating to election campaigns, that they do not engage in electoral battles with anti-growth incumbent councillors suggests their main focus may not be on local politicians. The effort and cost necessary to defeat an anti-growth incumbent may be greater than the expected benefit, as developers may also rely on appeals to the OMB.

In one ward in the 2006 municipal election, developers did focus on securing the election of a specific candidate, though whether they coordinated their support is unclear. Close to a dozen developers donated over $5000 combined to Michelle Bernardinetti, wife of MPP Lorenzo Bernardinetti (Vincent 2008), in her bid to replace retired councillor Gerry Altobello in ward 35. In addition, other corporate donors provided an additional $10,000 (approx.)[8] in donations to her campaign. Ward 35 is diverse, composed of mostly lower- and middle-income households, but also including many households with income in excess of $100,000 (Urban Development Services 2003). The ward also includes former industrial lands that are among the last areas in the city available for low-rise residential development (Harvey 2008), which makes it an important area in the city for the development industry. The development industry and local businesses clearly identified Michelle Bernardinetti as the ideal choice for councillor of the ward. However, despite outspending her main rival, Adrian Heaps, Bernardinetti lost by eighty-nine votes, though she would later defeat Councillor Heaps by over two thousand votes in the 2010 election.

Developers' inability to secure Bernardinetti's victory in 2006 may reflect why they are unwilling to support pro-growth candidates against anti-growth incumbents like Walker or Grimes. Adrian Heaps, despite meagre contributions from corporate donors ($900 in total), was able to raise five-sixths of Bernardinetti's contributions ($25,000 to $30,000) entirely on the basis of individual contributions. Campaign finance limitations could severely erode developers' ability to influence municipal elections if candidates can access equal funding from wealthy individual donors. Campaign financing limits undermine one of the main sources of leverage developers enjoy over local politicians. Absent the OMB, developers would need to secure the support of city council for development projects. With the existence of the OMB, however, the imperative to secure local politicians' support diminishes. Developers continue to offer token donations to councillors who have been favourable to development in the past, and to councillors in wards they wish to build in, but, otherwise, they do not engage as actively in opposition to anti-growth councillors as their counterparts in the LPE literature.

That developers do finance local politicians' campaigns suggests they have not abandoned the politics of urban development entirely. However, they appear more selective in their involvement than the LPE literature otherwise suggests. Local political economy literature maintains that developers' involvement in the politics of urban development should be pervasive. This study of electoral campaign financing indicates that it is not. The following two cases studies examine developers' behaviour and role in the broader politics of urban development in light of this finding.

Minto Midtown

In March 2000, Minto Development Inc., an Ottawa-based condominium developer, bought a parcel of land located at the Yonge and

Eglinton intersection in midtown Toronto. Minto selected the design of Skidmore, Owings and Merrill, a prestigious Chicago architecture firm, following a competition to design two condominium towers for the site (Diamond 2001a). On 22 December 2000, Minto submitted to the City an application for both an official plan amendment and a zoning by-law amendment ("Exhibit A" 2000). The proposal involved the demolition of an existing ten-storey government office building and the erection of two condominium point towers, fifty-four and forty-seven storeys in height (*Minto YE Inc. v. Toronto (City)* [2002] O.M.B.D. no. 703). At about the same time, representatives from Minto approached the local ward councillor Michael Walker with their proposal. Councillor Walker promptly threw the representatives out of his office (Rae interview 2008, Walker interview 2008).

The proposed towers were significantly in excess of the height and density limits set out in the by-law and former City of Toronto's official plan, which was still in effect at the time. However, in preparation for work on a new official plan for the amalgamated city, Paul Bedford, the City's chief planner, had identified the area as a part of the city intended for intensification (Blazevski interview 2008; Dill and Bedford 2000). Thus, planning for the Yonge-Eglinton area was in flux at the time. The proposed development fell within the jurisdiction of the Midtown Community Council.[9] Most council members, led by Councillor Anne Johnston, from the neighbouring ward, appeared to back the proposal. However, Michael Walker, supported by a bevy of neighbourhood associations, vehemently opposed the development (Levy 2001).

In early 2001, a coalition of existing area neighbourhood associations formed the Federation of North Toronto Residents Associations (FoNTRA) to coordinate their opposition to the existing planning process in Toronto. In a letter to Mayor Mel Lastman, the members of FoNTRA complained that City Planning, and specifically chief planner Paul Bedford, already tacitly supported the Minto proposal. The associations supported Councillor Walker's bid to have council reject the proposal outright without further process. FoNTRA threatened to pursue its fight through the media and political arena if necessary. Finally, the association noted that City Planning was ignoring the "millions in property taxes paid by ... home and condominium owners directly and by tenants indirectly" as well as neighbourhood residents' contributions and support for local schools and charities (Francoz and Freel 2001).

On 2 April 2001, Councillor Walker sent a letter to his fellow members of the Midtown Community Council (MCC), noting his outrage that city planners would even consider such a proposal. He further suggested that the content of City Planning's initial report would "serve to create a program of negotiation where residents will be co-opted to bargain for 'benefits' from such a proposed development," and would "ultimately serve to hurt them [neighbourhood associations] at the Ontario Municipal Board" (Walker 2001b). Councillor Walker and local residents were particularly upset that City Planning's report on the development was appended to the next day's community council meeting without any notice to local residents or the councillor (Walker 2001b).

On 3 April 2001, the MCC considered the report, Councillor Walker's motion to defer the proceedings having failed. The MCC, led by Councillor Johnston and Councillor Flint, adopted City Planning's recommendations for a focused review of the Yonge-Eglinton Secondary Plan,[10] which would include neighbouring residents, Councillor Walker, City Planning, and Minto. The motion passed four to two (City Clerk's Division 2001b). According to one reporter covering one of the meetings between the developer and local residents, some residents "booed and heckled as Chicago architect Peter Ellis" described his vision for the towers (Saunders 2001).

Having failed in its bid to have the project rejected outright, FoNTRA continued to press local councillors to oppose the development. A month after the 3 April council meeting, FoNTRA complained that the focused review remained a "design-based review in too many areas rather than an in-depth, comprehensive impact assessment" (FoNTRA 2001b). Presumably, the association felt it was not having success in reducing the size and scope of the development. Minto subsequently sent a letter to the MCC opposing any changes to the focused review's terms of reference, noting that the developer had had no input into the original terms (Diamond 2001b). In a presentation to the MCC on 12 June 2001, FoNTRA continued its attack on the development and the developer, noting the lack of discussion regarding a section 37 contribution from the developer.[11] FoNTRA argued that Minto did not expect to contribute anything to the City. As with many of the cases in this book, FoNTRA complained of the shadows the buildings would cast on neighbourhood houses and buildings.[12] The association also feared that the increased traffic from the development would lead to gridlock, and that the building would contribute to existing overcrowding on the Eglinton subway station platform (Tyacke 2001).

The Midtown Community Council considered FoNTRA's presentation and the request for changes to the terms of the focused review at its 12 June 2001 meeting. Councillor Walker failed in his bid to have the terms amended to consider only the existing official plan and not Paul Bedford's "Toronto at the Crossroads." The MCC appeared to have made no substantive changes to the terms of reference (City Clerk's Division 2001a). On 3 October 2001, City Planning updated the MCC regarding the status of the focused review, providing a rough deadline of the first quarter 2002 for the review's final report, and suggesting the review had been, and continued to be, a useful exercise (Community Planning 2001).

However, by late October 2001, the relationship between Minto, Councillor Walker, and the neighbourhood associations appears to have completely deteriorated. Robert Blazevski, representing Minto, wrote Councillor Walker a letter asking him to cease the distribution of what Blazevski considered misleading flyers entitled "Oh No Minto," which Councillor Walker's office had prepared. In his reply, Councillor Walker did not concede any relationship between the distribution of the flyers and the following day's meeting of the MCC. In addition, the councillor advised Blazevski that he "had no intention of terminating the distribution of this flyer, nor any other materials that indicate my determined opposition to your proposed development" (Walker 2001a). At the following day's community council meeting, on 23 October 2001, FoNTRA again stated its opposition to the development, requesting the reduction of the buildings to no more than twenty storeys high. The association continued to articulate its disapproval of the focused review's structure. They noted that a city planner stated, as did a number of councillors, that the City could not reject the proposal because of the OMB. If council rejected the application, Minto would appeal to the board, at which point, the City might lose any possible concessions it could gain from settling with the developer. Chapter 8 discusses local politicians' purported reliance on this refrain to justify their support of development in the face of neighbourhood opposition. FoNTRA suggested that by allowing the Minto development, the City was undermining its own position at the OMB in future appeals by allowing such a deviation from the official plan (FoNTRA 2001a).[13]

Almost a year following the submission of its initial application for development, Minto appealed to the Ontario Municipal Board, citing council's failure to render a decision within the ninety days mandated by the Planning Act. In Minto's notice of appeal, Stephen Diamond, the company's lawyer and partner of the law firm McCarthy Tetrault, outlined a number of reasons for the appeal that went far beyond the

City's neglect to render a decision. Diamond noted Minto's cooperation in working with the City, but also noted that the developer had become increasingly frustrated at the number of extensions made to the review process, such that the final date of city council's decision was increasingly uncertain. Diamond also cited the campaign launched by Councillor Walker and area neighbourhood associations against the project, which Diamond suggested was misleading. He argued that Minto had addressed the bulk of issues raised by neighbourhood residents, and that the neighbourhood associations had failed to demonstrate any significant impacts arising from the development. Finally, Diamond noted that even if the City approved the development, the area neighbourhood associations would likely appeal City Council's decision (Diamond 2001a).

Despite the appeal, or perhaps as a step leading to the OMB hearing, Minto submitted a revised proposal for the site in later January of 2002. The proposal maintained the height and density of the taller north tower, but reduced the height and density of the smaller south tower from forty-seven storeys (162 metres) to thirty-nine storeys (137 metres) (City Clerk 2002d). Four days following Minto's submission of the revised proposal, Councillor Walker submitted a communication to the MCC seeking council's approval to send a representative to the OMB hearing. In his letter, Councillor Walker asked that council hire an independent planning expert if necessary[14] to oppose the development at the OMB in support of the current official plan of the former City of Toronto. Walker claimed that Minto had not addressed any of the issues that planning staff had raised in their preliminary report to council, nor those concerns area residents raised. In addition, Councillor Walker asked for an adjournment of the hearing as city council had not had an opportunity to consider the appeal. Finally, he asked that Mayor Lastman send, on behalf of city council, "a letter to the Minister of Municipal Affairs and Housing requesting that the Province abolish the Ontario Municipal Board or make substantive change … [to the board] to reflect the democratic underpinnings" of society (Walker 2002).

On the same day that Councillor Walker submitted his letter to the MCC, City Planning informed council it would submit, on 25 February 2002, the final report of the focused review. This date was two days before the scheduled OMB pre-hearing. City Planning also noted the report would recommend refusal of the Minto development proposal. In mid-February, city council adopted Councillor Walker's request for an adjournment (City Clerk 2002d). City Planning had actually submitted its final report on the focused review and Minto Midtown on 11 February 2002. Nevertheless, the MCC did not consider the report until its 25 February meeting (City Clerk's Department 2002). The OMB rejected the request for adjournment. At the 27 February pre-hearing, the board did allow for an additional pre-hearing, however, which would allow city council to consider the proposal (presumably with the revisions) (*Minto YE Inc. v. Toronto (City)* [2002] O.M.B.D. no. 291).

In mid-April 2002, city council finally reached a decision. Rather than refuse the proposal outright (which was the stance taken by the Midtown Community Council), council asked that the city solicitor work towards a compromise with the developer before the commencement of the OMB hearing. Council set a number of guidelines for negotiations. First, Minto must reduce the buildings' heights to minimize the shadows they would cast, as City Planning had advised. Second, Minto must provide a $1 million contribution towards affordable rental housing for seniors. Third, Minto must ensure the courtyard was publicly accessible. Fourth, Minto must provide below-ground access to surrounding buildings and the Eglinton subway station. Finally, Minto must contribute $200,000 towards the constructing of a pedestrian walkway to Eglinton station (City Clerk 2002d).

Minto initially approached Councillor Walker when it first proposed the development. However, the company's relationship with the councillor deteriorated rather quickly. According to Blazevski (interview 2008), Minto was able to win the support of Anne Johnston, councillor for the neighbouring ward. As with the case of campaign financing, the developer maintained a relationship with local politicians. However, at a certain point (roughly a year following the submission of their initial application) Minto grew too frustrated with the prolonged process, and appealed to the OMB in a bid to either expedite the application process or avoid continued dealings with the City. As with campaign financing, there existed a limit to Minto's involvement with city council. The OMB offered the developer an exit strategy and, as a result, the developer in this instance lacked the same incentive to lobby local politicians, contrary to the LPE literature's depiction of developer behaviour.

The Settlement and Hearing

On 30 April 2002, John Paton, the City's solicitor for the case, faxed the OMB the details of a settlement between the City and Minto. Minto agreed to reduce the height of both towers, from 187 metres to 160 metres for the north building, and from 162 metres to 118 metres for the south building. Minto also agreed to all the terms set forth by city council in its mid-April decision, including the $1.2 million in contributions (Paton 2008). Councillor Walker reacted quickly to this unforeseen development, demanding information from the City's chief administration officer regarding the negotiated settlement (which the CAO suggested Councillor Walker already had in his possession) (Council Minutes 2002). Blazevski (interview 2008) suggests Councillor Walker and the area neighbourhood associations thought the development was dead.

Councillor Walker also submitted a communication to city council entitled "2195 Yonge Street – City Council's 10 Million Dollar Boondoggle" on 6 May 2002. In it Walker lambasted his fellow councillors for refusing to listen to the people who elected them. Furthermore, he suggested the amended motion before council in mid-April had been misleading. According to Councillor Walker, "While seemingly approving a defence at the Ontario Municipal Board," the motion "was ... an agreement to be entered into by the City Solicitor. That deal was to be signed by the City Solicitor in isolation from local residents, their representatives or the City's experts in the Urban Planning Division" (City Clerk 2002a, 2). He also took specific aim at Anne Johnston, the councillor for the neighbouring ward, who had proposed the "11th hour motion" outlining the criteria for a settlement. He noted that many of the benefits that Johnston proposed in the outline for a settlement were in fact part of Minto's revised proposal from January. Finally, Councillor Walker argued that the City was due somewhere between six and ten million dollars in section 37 benefits, well beyond the sum of $1.2 million agreed to in the settlement (City Clerk 2002a). The attempt of some city councillors to reopen the file failed (City Clerk 2002b). The city solicitor attended the final OMB hearing on 18 September 2002 in support of the development. Three neighbourhood associations (representing FoNTRA) attended the hearing as parties to oppose city council's approval of the development. According to Councillor Walker, the community raised $120,000 for the hearing (Walker interview 2008).

The neighbourhood associations did not fare well in front of the board. The City did not introduce its own witnesses and planning experts at the hearing, instead relying on Minto's – City Planning having recommended refusal of the development (Paton interview 2008). The neighbourhood associations hired their own experts and summoned the City's planning experts to testify at the hearing. The board repeatedly noted in its decision that both the associations' experts and City Planning contradicted the position of the associations and often corroborated Minto's experts' testimony. Early in its decision the board noted that "one extremely remarkable feature" of the hearing was "the amount of evidence called on behalf of the Associations, under summons to the witnesses, which actually was supportive of the proposed development" (*Minto YE Inc. v. Toronto (City)* [2002] O.M.B.D. no. 703, para. 14). In the final part of its decision, the OMB suggested that the City had accurately reflected council's position regarding the appeal, and noted that council had the opportunity to re-examine the proposal before the board hearing, but chose not to. The OMB allowed the appeal based on the terms of the settlement between the City and Minto (*Minto YE Inc. v. Toronto (City)* [2002] O.M.B.D. no. 703).

In the following municipal election, Anne Johnston, who had championed the proposal and aided in its final approval, lost. Councillor Walker claims her loss was in large part due to her support for Minto Midtown (Walker interview 2008). Councillor Rae (interview 2008) suggested otherwise. He suggests that after a long tenure as councillor for the area, Councillor Johnston had lost much of the energy needed to engage residents in her ward. Following her departure in 2004, City Council passed two by-laws allowing for the development of the two residential towers at the intersection of Yonge and Eglinton (By-laws no. 247-2004 (OMB) and 248-2004 (OMB)).

In appealing to the OMB, Minto indicated its dissatisfaction with the City and the application process. However, Minto actively participated in the focused review for the Yonge-Eglinton Centre, and waited well beyond the ninety-day period before appealing to the OMB. The developer also submitted revised plans reducing the size of the buildings and made some effort to accommodate the City's demands. Finally, Minto was willing to settle with the City before the board hearing. This behaviour suggests active cooperation between Minto and the City. Notably, following Anne Johnston's "11 hour" intervention, Minto worked with City Planning and the city solicitor, not local politicians.

The Minto Midtown case is distinct from many of the clashes over high-rise condominiums that followed. Toronto has allowed numerous developments far in excess of the Minto buildings, as has the OMB (although most are in the city's downtown). When Minto proposed the development, it was, as planners noted (City Clerk 2002d), far in excess of anything ever proposed for that area in the city, and at the time, it was by far the tallest and largest proposed building in the city since the end of the office boom in the early 1990s. Minto may have felt the need to secure the City's support for its proposal at the time, because there existed few recent examples of the OMB allowing such a significant development in the city. In contrast, when Menkes and the Four Seasons proposed their development in 2005, the City and the OMB had already allowed a significant number of buildings well in excess of existing by-laws and official plan requirements (and far larger than the Minto proposal).

Minto did not ignore local politicians and did not eschew working towards a compromise with the City. In addition, the developer continued to work with the City for almost two years before the final board hearing on the matter. Rather than nullifying the developer's interest in local politicians and city staff, the OMB acted as an additional path or means towards an end: the development of Minto Midtown. The OMB did not replace council.

Pulse Condominium

In the first half of 2002, Pemberton Group, a medium-sized Toronto-based developer, applied for a permit to build two thirty-two-storey condominium towers along Yonge Street, to the south of Finch Avenue, in the former City of North York (Community Planning 2002a). The condominium directly to the west of the proposed site, Symphony Square, had faced significant opposition from the local neighbourhood association, the Edithvale-Yonge Community Association (EYCA) as well other opponents such as the Metropolitan Separate School Board (MSSB). The EYCA opposed the development for many of the same reasons as opponents of Minto Midtown and the Four Seasons Hotel. They noted potential traffic problems, lack of open spaces, the size and number of units, local school overcrowding, and the built form as issues the developer needed to address (DeBacker 1996). The MSSB, on behalf of St Cyril Catholic School, opposed the development due in large part to the disturbances from construction (Director of Education 1995). The City of North York eventually allowed the tower, and the EYCA did not appeal council's decision to the OMB. However, following the construction of the condominium, the City won an OMB decision to force the developer to remove some aboveground parking spots and replace them with parkland as outlined in the initial by-law (*Symphony Square Ltd. v. Toronto (City) Committee of Adjustment* 1999; Condominium Application n.d.).

Pulse Condominiums, the Pemberton Group's proposal for the adjacent site on Yonge Street, did not encroach on low-density residences or local schools. In fact, the site was situated between Symphony and Yonge Street, Toronto's main street. Nevertheless, residents, including the EYCA, did not initially support the development. The North York Community Council (NYCC) first considered the proposal on 18 September 2002 (City Clerk's Division 2003). On 20 November 2002, the City held its first community consultation on the development. Sixty neighbourhood residents attended the meeting. Residents and City Planning staff raised two main issues regarding the proposal: that the building would increase traffic in an area that was already dealing with high levels, and that the buildings were too close to the adjacent condominiums on Lorraine Drive (Symphony being one of them) (Community Planning 2003a).

Regina Ip, a resident in Symphony Square, was particularly opposed to the development. Whether Ms Ip attended the meeting is unclear; however, on 11 December 2002, she wrote Tom Keefe, then acting director of planning for the North District, and the North District's senior planner, Dennis Glasgow. In her letter she complained of the short notice given for the community consultation meeting (seven days). In addition, she detailed a list of issues with the proposed development. As with the residents that attended the 20 November meeting, Ms Ip took exception to the closeness of the proposed towers to her own building, citing issues of privacy and safety. She also questioned whether the construction would do damage to the adjacent buildings and parking lot, and noted that the towers would block sunlight from entering her building. This fact would deprive senior citizens in the building of their only exposure to sunlight in the winter months (Ip 2002).

Discussion with Pemberton, the City, and local residents continued throughout the beginning of 2003. City Planning submitted its final report on 26 May 2003. In its report, City Planning indicated its continued concern about increased traffic in the area, but also noted that most residents accepted the construction of a new westbound service road to the south of the site as an acceptable solution to the problem. Pemberton would have to agree to donate the land to the City to allow for its construction. Otherwise, City Planning's report cites a number of changes Pemberton made to the proposal to accommodate the City and local residents' concerns. To address the issue of the proximity of the building to adjacent condominiums, Pemberton moved the development closer to Yonge and away from the other buildings, and rotated both towers 45 degrees to provide greater privacy to the residents in the adjacent buildings, and to provide a greater view area to those building's

residents. The developer's own experts considered the shadow cast by
the building to be excessive, so the developer took additional measures
to reduce the effect, including lowering the height of the buildings
(from thirty-two storeys each to twenty-seven and twenty-six storeys).
Overall, City Planning considered the proposed development a "considerable improvement over the existing large parking lot and grocery
store" (Community Planning 2003a, 7).

In its 11 June 2003 decision, the NYCC considered twelve submissions from area residents and businesses, including one from the residents of 23 Lorraine (Symphony Square) and the EYCA. In addition,
a representative from another association, the Yonge Corridor Condominium Association, appeared before the community council. John
Filion, councillor for the Ward, moved that the NYCC adopt City Planning's recommendation. The motion carried (City Clerk's Division
2003). City council adopted the same in its 24–26 June 2003 meeting
(City Clerk 2003a). Whether local neighbourhood associations were
entirely satisfied with city council's decision is unclear; however, no
media reports exist suggesting continued ire among local residents. In
addition, neither the EYCA nor the Yonge Corridor Condominium Association participated in the ensuing OMB hearing that Regina Ip initiated (in fact, no additional residents from her building appeared to be
involved either).

The Appeal

Despite the apparent lack of opposition among her fellow neighbours,
and the consensus among developer, City Planning, and City Council,
Ms Ip (who appeared to have hired legal counsel), chose to appeal council's decision on 4 November 2003. In her appeal, Ms Ip highlighted a
number of issues she felt neither the developer nor the City had yet
addressed. She raised many of the same issues she had outlined in her
original letter to Tom Keefe and Dennis Glasgow: the proposal did not
address the issue of traffic or the safety of pedestrians in the area; the
proposal continued to encroach on her building resulting in issues of
privacy, safety, and health for her building's residents; the buildings
would cause severe winds and noise problems; and, lastly, the City had
not accounted for the consequence of the development on neighbouring parks, schools, public recreation centres, and hospitals (Ip 2003).

Following the receipt of the appeal, Pemberton's solicitor responded
to Ms Ip, noting that City Planning had already raised all the issues she

outlined in her appeal, and expressing the view that Pemberton had addressed all of them. Pemberton's solicitor also noted that the new by-law Ms Ip opposed affected a number of developments in the area, but that she had taken issue only with Pemberton. The solicitor informed Ms Ip of Pemberton's intention to ask the OMB to dismiss her appeal without a full hearing (Horosko 2003b). On 3 December 2003, Pemberton's solicitor informed Ms Ip, who appeared no longer to have legal representation, that the company had filed a motion to dismiss, and the OMB had set a date to hear the motion for 16 December 2003 (Horosko 2003a).

The OMB threw out the appeal on 16 December 2003. In its brief decision, the board noted that one of Ms Ip's claims was that the development did not conform to North York's existing official plan, or the North York Centre secondary plan. Affidavits from both a city planner and Pemberton's planner stated that the proposal was in full conformity with both, however (*Toronto (City) Zoning By-law no. 944-2003 (Re)*). In its preliminary report to council, City Planning had only noted that the development did not comply with the zoning by-law for the area (Community Planning 2002a). In its closing comments, the board noted that "no promise of contrary sustainable evidence [was] … likely to be produced, should her [Ms Ip's] appeal go forward for a hearing" (*Toronto (City) Zoning By-law no. 944-2003 (Re)*, para. 5).

Though the proposal did result in initial opposition or apprehension among local residents and neighbourhood associations, it clearly did not generate the same type of opposition as any of the other three cases discussed in this and the previous chapter. Councillor Filion appears to have been involved throughout the application process. However, there is little evidence of a sustained relationship between Pemberton and Councillor Filion or any other politician in the area. Without significant neighbourhood association mobilization against the development, Pemberton may have not needed to lobby local politicians. Instead, Pemberton focused most of its attention on winning the support of City Planning and other planning experts in the City's employ. Though actively engaged in negotiations with the City, local politicians were not Pemberton's main target. The developer instead focused on the City's planning experts, and made significant changes to its proposal to win their approval.

That Pemberton's initial proposal did not deviate significantly from that already permitted by the existing official plan may well have aided Pemberton in its endeavour. Pemberton did not rely on the spectre of the OMB either as a means to encourage the City to settle, or to avoid the City altogether. However, that it focused most of its effort on engaging the City's planning experts is an important finding, indicative of the OMB's role. The previous chapter concluded that planning experts play a significant role during OMB hearings, and the Aldergreen Estates case suggested developers might be very sensitive to the role planning experts play. This case confirms that conclusion. Working with and coming to an acceptable compromise with City Planning was more important to the developer than engaging with the councillor for the ward.

Summary of Findings

This chapter focuses on the behaviour of developers in Toronto and their relationship with other actors involved in the politics of urban development. In addition, it addresses my second question: *Does the existence of the OMB affect the behaviour of developers in Toronto?* Given the existence of the OMB, developers in Toronto should have significantly less interest in local politicians than their counterparts elsewhere. Any evidence to the contrary would indicate that the OMB does not influence developers' behaviour to any significant extent.

The analysis of campaign financing in the 2006 election shows developers actively funding candidates in the election, a tactic developers in other North American jurisdiction often use either to co-opt or solicit support from local politicians. However, in Toronto, developers typically only contribute to the campaigns of the incumbents. Where the incumbent is clearly anti-growth, developers do not participate in that specific ward. In addition, the sums developers donate to candidates are small compared to the contributions made to campaigns in similarly sized American cities. Logan and Molotch (1987), for instance, speak of the millions of dollars developers spend on elections in Los Angeles. The Province of Ontario limits how much any company or individual can donate to candidates in a municipal election. This constraint accounts for the limited spending of developers, but does not explain their limited interest in waging campaigns against anti-growth candidates in elections. The board's presence is a plausible and likely explanation, however.

Maintaining good relationships with local politicians favourable to development remains important to developers as such relationships can expedite the application process. However, Toronto developers do

not seem to believe that fighting, and potentially losing, electoral battles is a good investment of their resources.[15] Given that they can appeal any decision of city council to the OMB, the potential of a council
favourable to anti-growth interests is not as great of a threat to developers' interests as it would be in other jurisdictions in the United States
and Canada.

The Minto Midtown and Pulse Condominium cases suggest that developers in Toronto are neither engaged in persistent efforts to influence local politicians nor completely absent from the political realm. In
the Minto Midtown case, the developer approached the ward councillor, and when rebuffed, approached the councillor of a neighbouring
ward for support. This account of a developer's behaviour suggests a
similarity between Toronto's developers and developers the LPE literature depicts. In the Pulse Condominium case, the developer appeared
more interested in engaging the City's planning experts, suggesting a
more limited relationship between developer and local politician. Despite the apparent contradictory evidence, however, both cases actually
confirm the findings of the campaign financing analysis.

The divergent contexts of the two cases account for the varied approaches the two developers adopted when approaching the City. In
fact, Minto began the application process in the same manner as Pemberton; it approached City Planning. Pemberton likely approached
Councillor Filion initially, as Minto did Councillor Walker. The varied
responses from local politicians, City Planning, and neighbourhood associations account for the divergent behaviour of the two developers
later in the application process, and demonstrate how the OMB influences developers' behaviour. Initially, both developers received tentative approval from City Planning. In fact, the City's planning experts
appeared more supportive of Minto's proposal than Pemberton's.
However, the developers received different receptions from the ward
councillor and local neighbourhood associations.

The EYCA had some initial misgivings regarding Pemberton's proposal, but these misgivings were not substantive enough for the association to openly oppose the development, and Pemberton appears to
have mitigated many of the association's issues with the development
(that the association's issue with the proposal mirrored many of City
Planning's likely contributed to Pemberton's willingness to compromise). Councillor Filion seemed willing to allow the developer, neighbourhood association (and other residents), and City Planning to work
out their differences, and did not actively intervene, and Pemberton

eventually was able to win the support of City Planning and the quiescence of all but one neighbourhood resident.

In contrast, Minto was unable to win the support of either Councillor Walker or of FoNTRA, and the two appear to have affected the City's planning experts' position on the development (at least until the hearing). Minto's move to win the support of Councillor Johnston appears driven by these factors, and the possibility that it could actually lose at the OMB. After all, projects of that scale outside of the central business district were unheard of at the time. Nevertheless, Minto clearly saw the OMB as an alternative if it failed to win over the rest of council; had it not, the developer would have fought a pitched battle against the anti-growth forces. Although Minto worked closely with Anne Johnston, the developer eventually succumbed to frustration with the application process, and chose to try its hand at the OMB.

The two cases demonstrate that developers will work with the City towards a settlement. The Minto case, along with the analysis of campaign financing, demonstrate that developers will also attempt to influence local politicians. However, developers do not devote the same effort and resources to securing the support and aid of local politicians as their counterparts in other Canadian and American cities. These findings offer an answer to *Question 2: Does the existence of the OMB affect the behaviour of developers in Toronto?* The board does indeed lessen Toronto developers' efforts to engage and influence local politicians. However, the board's existence does not entirely remove the attraction of local politicians for developers.

The most important finding of this analysis goes beyond this specific question, however, and relates directly to the findings of the previous chapter. Both Minto and Pemberton, the latter especially, appeared well aware of the role planning experts play in board hearings. Although Minto eventually appealed the City's failure to render a decision to the OMB, Minto worked with City Planning for over a year in a bid to win its approval. Likewise, Pemberton devoted the bulk of its resources and effort towards winning the support of City Planning. In the cities LPE literature analyses, there exist few incentives for developers to pursue the support of cities' planning experts. Their support will not ensure the support of city councils, as the support of city councils trumps the refusal of a city's planning experts.

As Blazevski (2008) suggests, no one likes to go to the OMB. The application process in Toronto is long, and an appeal to the OMB does not necessarily shorten its length, as the Minto Midtown case demonstrates.

Developers still have a strong incentive to work with the City (Paton interview 2008). However, the board provides developers more options. Paton suggests that developers adopt a "multi-front operation," working with local politicians, City Planning, and even neighbourhood associations when they are well organized. Peter Smith provides an account of such a "multi-front" approach. If a developer wins the support of council, but not City Planning, the developer benefits even if area neighbourhood associations appeal, because the City will not send anyone to fight the developer at the OMB (Smith interview 2008). The Minto Midtown case is an important example of such a phenomenon, even though City Planning appears to have altered its opinion when summoned. However, if a developer can win both the support of the ward councillor and area neighbourhood association or residents, despite City Planning's rejection of a proposal, it removes the possibility of an OMB appeal altogether (ibid.). Having the support of both City Planning and city council can still result in an OMB appeal, as the Four Seasons case in the previous chapter attests, but the likelihood of the appellant winning is slim.

The board's focus on expert testimony offers a very important alternative to support from local politicians. City Planning's support for a development is an important asset for a developer in all instances, because City Council tends to rely on City Planning's opinion when rendering its decision. In addition, City Planning's support increases the likelihood of a developer's victory at the OMB if council decides to refuse the development under pressure from neighbourhood associations. Chart 4.7 in chapter 4 illustrates how the City fares at the OMB when city council sides with neighbourhood associations against the developer and City Planning.

The board's existence not only lessens developers' focus on local politicians, but also significantly intensifies developers' interest in securing the support of City Planning. City Planning's relative autonomy from local politicians (see the previous chapter), makes them an enticing and important partner for developers to pursue when seeking to develop land. Both the Four Seasons and Aldergreen Estates cases, particularly the latter, further testify to this fact. Developers do not abandon their relationship with local politicians due to the OMB's existence, but the board's presence diminishes their interest in local politicians, and result in greater emphasis on City Planning.

7 Neighbourhood Mobilization in Toronto

In exclaiming "Don't let them shove another highrise up our Annex," Don Harron, formerly of the CBC, was expressing his opposition to a proposal for two condominium towers in Yorkville (Deverell 2003). "Our Annex" refers to a neighbourhood adjacent to Yorkville that was once a suburb of Toronto. The City had long since annexed the territory, hence the neighbourhood's name. The Annex Residents' Association is one of Toronto's oldest neighbourhood associations. Its members would ally themselves with residents from Yorkville proper and other Torontonians to prevent the destruction of what Professor Sheila Latham from York University called "the lovely oasis of Yorkville" (Levy 2003). Since the beginning of the long condominium boom in Toronto, neighbourhood associations from some of Toronto's most affluent neighbourhoods have led the charge against what they perceive as an attack on the richness and history of their communities.

Whereas developers and local politicians are always major components of LPE theories of urban politics, authors such as Logan and Molotch (1987) and Stone (1989) did not initially place significant emphasis on the role of neighbourhood associations. Nevertheless, other authors working within the LPE approach have emphasized the importance of their role, especially in the politics of urban development. In his own work on urban regimes, Elkin (1987) noted the changing role of the middle and upper-middle class in the politics of urban development in the United States. These groups, once supportive of growth policies and development, became their fiercest opponents as plans for highway expansion and the like jeopardized their neighbourhoods (ibid.). According to Logan and Rabrenovic (1990), neighbourhood associations are the main means by which such interests "learn about problems, formulate opinions, and seek to intervene in the political process to protect their local interests" (69). The two authors define a neighbourhood association as "a civic organization oriented toward maintaining or improving the quality of life in a geographical setting" (68).

In American cities during the 1960s and 1970s, as in Toronto, neighbourhoods organized and upset the relationship between developers and local politicians. Ever since, the neighbourhood associations that emerged have remained important players in urban politics in many cities, even as their influence waxes and wanes. Because of their role, neighbourhood associations are now among the triad of actors, along with local politicians and developers, central to the LPE approach.

This chapter examines both the role of Toronto's neighbourhood associations in the politics of urban development in the city and their relationship with local politicians, developers, and planning experts, and attempts to answer my third question: *Does the existence of the OMB affect the behaviour of neighbourhood associations in Toronto?* After examining the socio-demographics of Toronto's neighbourhoods and related associations, the chapter considers two cases where neighbourhood associations actively participated in the development process, and in one case, an OMB appeal: 100 Yorkville at Bellair Condominiums (100 Yorkville) and a small townhouse development in the city's west end (Bloor & Mill). These two case studies compare and contrast the neighbourhood associations' behaviour with the behaviour of such associations in the local political economy literature, particularly in the work of authors such as DeLeon (1992b; DeLeon and Powell 1989) and Purcell (1997, 2000).

The Socio-demography of Toronto's Neighbourhood Associations

When conducting research for the data set I utilized for the quantitative analysis of OMB decisions, the names of roughly seventy neighbourhood associations, both incorporated and unincorporated, that were active participants in application processes and OMB appeals emerged. Given that these names came solely from city staff reports and OMB decisions, the number of such associations involved in the politics of urban development in Toronto could be greater.[1] A few of the names appear similar enough that they may be different incarnations of the same group. The City of Toronto lists 315 such organizations on its website as stakeholders in its Zoning By-Law Project.[2] Some of these associations are well organized groups with a long history and many members. For instance, according to the Annex Residents' Association (ARA) website, the association has existed for over 80 years,[3] while the Bayview Village Association (BVA) claims 50 per cent of the residents in the village are paid members of the association.[4]

Other associations appear less organized, and limited in their existence. The Neighbours of St Alban's Park is a splinter group of the ARA, formed solely, it appears, to combat the planned expansion of Royal St George's College, an Anglican boys' choir school. While the ARA appears to have supported the plans, a limited number of neighbouring residents opposed them (*Toronto (City) Official Plan Site-Specific Exemption Amendment (Re)*). The emergence of St Alban's is evidence that not all associations are equal, and that established neighbourhood associations do not always enjoy the support of their residents.

While middle- and upper-middle-class associations are the main focus of many important contributions to the local political economy literature (Thomas 1986; Purcell 1997, 2000; Vogel and Swanson 1989), Toronto has a number of associations in lower-income areas of the city, such as the Parkdale Residents Association. According to the City of Toronto's neighbourhood profile of South Parkdale (based on the 2001 census), roughly 45 per cent of households in the area had yearly incomes of less than $20,000, though the percentage had declined since the 1996 census, while the percentage of households with incomes of $100,000 or more rose (Community and Neighbourhood Services 2004ć, 3), suggesting increasing gentrification in the neighbourhood.

Mesch and Schwirian (1996) identified a number of such lower-income neighbourhood associations in their study of Columbus, Ohio, along with the middle- and upper-middle-income associations. However, they suggested the socio-economic status of the associations and their respective neighbourhoods reflected their effectiveness and level of activity: the wealthier the neighbourhood, the more organized and more effective the association. Thomas's (1986) thorough analysis of neighbourhood associations in Cincinnati supports this fact. According to the author, "The neighbourhoods most involved with City Council are those with the most to protect; that is those in areas with higher median incomes ..., higher homes values ..., and higher proportions of professionals" (Thomas 1986, 109). Downs (1981) echoes this statement. In his account of such organizations, residents with the greatest investments in the area, whether financial or emotional, are the most active participants in such organizations, and enforce a conservative stance towards neighbourhood change (Downs 1981, 174).

Establishing the socio-economic make-up of all or a majority of neighbourhood associations in Toronto is a difficult task. The map presented here (Map 7.1) cannot provide positive proof of the socio-economic make-up of the neighbourhood associations involved in each case. However, it offers the best alternative in the absence of definitive data, depicting the location of OMB cases involving neighbourhood associations in the city and the socio-economic make-up of the city's "neighbourhoods."[5] The shading reflects the number of households with annual incomes of $100,000 or more as a percentage of total households in each neighbourhood. The number of such households provides a strong indication of the presence and strength of upper-middle-class residents in each neighbourhood.[6] Each dot represents one of the seventy-seven OMB cases that neighbourhood associations were involved in from 2000 through 2006.[7]

Map 7.1 indicates that the majority of OMB cases involving neighbourhood associations arose in neighbourhoods with significant numbers of upper-middle-income households. Fifty-seven per cent of the cases are in neighbourhoods where 22.5 per cent or more of the households have incomes of $100,000 or greater.[8] Eighty per cent take place in neighbourhoods with 15 per cent earning $100,000 or more. In addition, many of the cases in neighbourhoods with smaller proportions of high-income households are directly adjacent to wealthy neighbourhoods. The map corroborates Mesch and Schwirian's (1996), Thomas's (1986), and Ley and Mercer's (1980) findings for Columbus, Cincinnati, and Vancouver respectively. The number of upper-middle-class residents in a given neighbourhood relates directly to the presence of active neighbourhood associations. The neighbourhood associations most involved in the politics of urban development in Toronto are comparable, therefore, to the associations that local political economy literature depicts.

However, the City of Toronto lacks the power over development and planning that many municipal governments beyond Ontario enjoy. Despite being close approximations of neighbourhood associations in the United States, associations in Toronto may not share their American counterparts' focus on local politicians, because ultimately the Ontario Municipal Board, not city council, has the final say on any development proposed for the city. In addition, developers in Toronto cannot appeal the board's decisions, while developers from other jurisdictions can return to city council with the same proposal repeatedly until they get a favourable decision. The OMB offers an element of finality not available in many other jurisdictions in North America. However, given the

Map 7.1. Locations of OMB cases involving neighbourhood associations

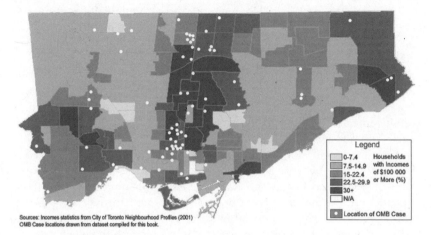

Legend

☐ 0-7.4   Households
☐ 7.5-14.9   with Incomes
■ 15-22.4   of $100 000
■ 22.5-29.9   or More (%)
■ 30+
☐ N/A

⬛ Location of OMB Case

Sources: Incomes statistics from City of Toronto Neighbourhood Profiles (2001)
OMB Case locations drawn from dataset compiled for this book.

cost of an OMB hearing, and their poor track record at the board, Toronto's neighbourhood associations may have an even greater incentive to sway local politicians in their favour. Toronto's neighbourhood associations' perception of the relative merits and costs of a hearing could dictate whether they approach local politicians or appeal to the board, and whether they behave in a similar manner to their counterparts in the LPE approach, or in a different manner altogether. These contrasting possibilities relate to my third question: *Does the existence of the OMB affect the behaviour of neighbourhood associations in Toronto?*

LPE Literature and Neighbourhood Associations in Toronto

Although some early proponents of the LPE approach did not emphasize, at least initially, the role that neighbourhood associations play in the politics of urban development, some of their contemporaries already had begun investigating their behaviour and involvement in urban politics (see Thomas 1986), and the ramification of their emergence on policy making in cities (see Kantor 1987; and Kantor with David 1988). By the early 1990s, neighbourhood associations had grown in importance in local political economy literature, and are now, along with local businesses and developers, and local politicians, considered one of the central actors in the politics of urban development in many North American cities. Authors such as Vogel and Swanson (1989), DeLeon (1992a, 1992b; DeLeon and Powell 1989), and Purcell (1997, 2000) focus on such associations' involvement in anti-growth coalitions in Florida and California. In these cities, neighbourhood associations engaged in bitter battles with developers and their pro-growth allies. The two dominant characteristics of neighbourhood associations are their opposition to development (Logan and Rabrenovic 1990) and the fact that the most active associations comprise predominantly middle-income and upper-middle- income residents (Mesch and Schwirian 1996; Thomas 1986; Ley and Mercer 1980).

As with developers, neighbourhood associations seek to influence local politicians because of the latter's power over planning decisions. Downs (1981) and Logan and Rabrenovic (1990) suggest that most associations form, initially, to oppose development in their neighbourhoods. Neighbourhood associations lack the same monetary resources as developers, but are often successful in mobilizing the electorate for or against local politicians. They can be useful allies for local politicians, or formidable adversaries. Purcell (1997, 2000) and DeLeon and Powell (1989) demonstrate the power of middle- and upper-middle-class neighbourhood associations in curbing unwanted development in Los Angeles and San Francisco, respectively. The LPE literature on neighbourhood associations suggests that they will oppose development and will focus their efforts and resources on mobilizing the electorate and influencing local politicians.

In Ontario, the Ontario Municipal Board effectively removes final decision-making power on development and planning issues from the City, the main resource that attracts the attention of neighbourhood associations elsewhere. The board offers an alternative venue to oppose development. If one or more neighbourhood associations can raise the money to hire planning experts to oppose a proposal, they could succeed in scuttling a development at the board. A board decision in favour of a neighbourhood association would offer no avenue of appeal for a developer. Rose (1972) suggests this happened in the 1960s in Toronto: as opposition to development rose in the city, neighbourhood associations did turn to the OMB to oppose developers and a city council favourable to their interests. Thus, neighbourhood associations in Toronto could be inclined to bypass council and appeal directly to OMB as an alternative means to oppose development proposals.

However, since at least 2000, neighbourhood associations in Toronto have had little success at the board. The expense of a hearing favours developers, whose main resource is money, allowing them easy access to planning experts and lawyers. Neighbourhood associations' main resource, their ability to mobilize the electorate, is of little use before such an unelected body. Neighbourhood associations may have an even greater incentive to focus on influencing local politicians as a result, but may still view the board as a' means to object to unfavourable city council decisions. Just as developers adopt multiple strategies to ensure the success of their enterprises, so too may neighbourhood associations approach the board when lobbying local politicians has failed. How great an emphasis they place on either means of opposing development may be indicative of the strength and influence of the board. If they do not perceive the board as a viable option, then they should behave just like their compatriots in cities like Los Angeles and San Francisco. If the OMB is influencing neighbourhood associations' behaviour, however, then they should use the OMB as an alternative and possible replacement to lobbying local politicians, just as developers do.

The following two case studies examine the behaviour of neighbourhood associations and their perception of the board. The first case, 100 Yorkville, examines a well-publicised conflict over a condominium development in the city's posh Yorkville neighbourhood, from the initial proposal through the application process and OMB hearing. The second case, Bloor & Mill, focuses on a neighbourhood association's reaction and response to a townhouse development proposed by a small-time developer in the city's west end. Both cases examine neighbourhood associations' relationship with and behaviour towards City Planning, developers, and local politicians. The former case also examines neighbourhood associations' approach to the OMB.

100 Yorkville at Bellair

On 8 April 2002, Barclay-Grayson,[9] a medium-sized Toronto-based residential developer, submitted an application to the City of Toronto for a multi-phase, condominium high-rise and town home development for the city's Village of Yorkville (not far from Menkes's and Four Seasons' proposal from chapter 5) (Diamond 2002). The OMB had approved another contentious proposal for the site in 1994, but it was never built (Deverell 2003). Part of the site contained a City-run parking lot, which also doubled as a site for an open-air market during the Sierra Summer Festival (Urban Development Services 2000). The site also included the remains of the first Mount Sinai Hospital, built in 1932–4, which the City had designated a heritage building in 1983 (City Clerk 2003c).[10]

Well before submitting its application to City Planning, Barclay-Grayson began discussions with area residents, businesses, and the City (Diamond 2002). The developer had already won the support of the Bloor-Yorkville Business Improvement Area's board of management late in 2001 (Saunderson 2001). In addition, the City and the Toronto Parking Authority (TPA) had agreed to acquire part of the land from the developer to build and operate a parking garage. The agreement between developer, the City, and the TPA appeared to include an element of cost sharing for the construction of the garage (City Clerk 2001).

Barclay-Grayson's proposal included two towers, eighteen and eight storeys tall, a number of three-storey town homes, and two-storey retail at the base of the two towers. The proposal incorporated the façade of the Mount Sinai Hospital in the new development, but required its relocation on the site. It also incorporated the 150-space parking garage that the TPA would operate (Diamond 2002). In its preliminary report, City Planning noted that the developer would have to justify the proposal to demolish and reconstruct the façade of Mount Sinai by demonstrating that the structure could not remain in its current location. While Toronto's planning department acknowledged the larger proposed tower was adjacent to another, recently approved, eighteen-storey building, it noted that the floor plates[11] of the 100 Yorkville proposal were significantly larger. City Planning suggested the need for further study of any shadow or wind impact on the surrounding buildings and streets, and the proposal's contribution to traffic in the area. It also advised of potential section 37 contributions from the development. These included contributions to the City's plan to transform the streetscape of nearby Bloor Street, the provision of public art, and an investment in the redevelopment of the Toronto Reference Library (Community Planning 2002b). In its 4 June 2002 meeting, the Toronto East York Community Council (TYECC) adopted City Planning's report, which city council then adopted, beginning formal negotiations for the development (Clerk's Department 2002).

City Planning convened a community meeting on 27 June 2002. Roughly one hundred people attended. Most attendees expressed concerns over the height of the towers, the development's effect on traffic in the neighbourhood, and the proper preservation of the façade of Mount Sinai Hospital. Following its 9 January 2003 meeting, the

Toronto Preservation Board consented to the temporary relocation of
the Mount Sinai façade to allow for construction (Community Planning
2003b). City Planning submitted its final report on 5 February 2003, recommending the approval of the proposal. Planning noted in its report
that the tower portion of the development exceeded the size permitted
by by-law and the official plan. However, it concluded that the site's
proximity to a subway line and the downtown core rendered intensification appropriate, and that the developer had mitigated potential
negative effects emanating from the proposal (ibid.).

Before the 20 February 2003 meeting of the TEYCC, which included
City Planning's report on its agenda, local neighbourhood associations
and other concerned citizens offered their thoughts on the proposal.
The Save Yorkville Now (SYN) committee, the predecessor to the Save
Yorkville Heritage Association from the Four Seasons case, advised the
community council of its opposition to the proposal. SYN suggested
the proposal was "incongruous with [the] ... architectural integrity and
human scale" of the surrounding area (Stoffman 2003, 1). The committee also feared for the façade of the old Mount Sinai Hospital. SYN also
noted that in 1969, when it was first formed, it had succeeded in opposing another equally inappropriate development proposal for the
area, suggesting the "1969 'Save Yorkville' steering committee members have left [the City] ... a legacy to preserve" (ibid.). Famed planning
guru Jane Jacobs, a resident of the area, also noted her opposition to
both the 1969 proposal and to the Barclay-Grayson proposal. Jacobs expressed fears that the development would undermine the human scale
of the village, which she believed contributed to the area's attractiveness to tourists and residents, and that the proposal would set precedents for future development in the area (Jacobs 2003).

The tone of the submissions from the two main neighbourhood associations involved in the application process, the Greater Yorkville
Residents Association (GYRA) and ABC Residents' Association (ABC),
was more moderate than that of the SYN or Ms Jacobs. Although the
GYRA opposed the development, noting that the height and density of
the development troubled most area residents, it also made a number
of positive comments regarding the association's involvement in the
application process. The GYRA supported Barclay-Grayson's intent to
preserve the Mount Sinai façade, and commended the developer for
holding an open dialogue with the association, and for the inclusion of
some of the association's recommendations in the design of the building. It also noted the benefits the development would bring to the area

(Chung 2003). In a letter addressed directly to local ward councillor Kyle Rae, ABC thanked the councillor for his efforts to work with residents to improve the design of the building. The association suggested that while concessions made by the developer did not end all the concern over the height of the building, they did mitigate this concern. Lastly, in its parting remark, ABC noted that, while the final design was not perfect, it was satisfactory (Caliendo 2003b).

The contrast between the communications of SYN and Jane Jacobs and the two neighbourhood associations suggest the latter adopted a more conciliatory tone in addressing local politicians. Clearly, ABC felt Councillor Rae played an important role in facilitating the discussion between developer and local residents. The letters of SYN, Jane Jacobs, and the GYRA demonstrate a focus on local politicians as a means to oppose the development proposal. However, both the GYRA and ABC were heavily involved in discussions with City Planning and the developer before submitting their comments to the TEYCC and Councillor Rae, respectively.

Following a public meeting, and despite the continued opposition of some area residents and other concerned citizens (City Clerk's Office 2003), the TEYCC adopted the recommendations of City Planning, approving the development in principle, but requiring certain changes. City council adopted, in principle, draft by-laws amending the official plan and zoning by-laws, and entered into a heritage easement agreement for the site in a special meeting at the end of February. Among many provisions of the draft by-laws, the City precluded any dismantling of the Mount Sinai Hospital façade. Before passing the new by-law, the City required that the developer present another option for dealing with the heritage structure (City Clerk 2003c).[12]

A month after this decision, SYN submitted a list of "prominent leaders of Toronto" who were in opposition to the development.[13] These "prominent leaders," like SYN members, were not necessarily residents of the Village of Yorkville, and as such they did not constitute a neighbourhood association. However, SYN would play a major role in waging opposition to the development along with the support of such individuals (Milbrandt 2003b). Neighbourhood associations soon joined the SYN in voicing their opposition to the development. For instance, FoNTRA, the main opponent to Minto Midtown, voiced its concern over the proposal, even though it was beyond its jurisdiction (Milbrandt 2003a).

SYN sent another letter to council, noting that residents and local businesses intended to appeal the decision to the OMB should council confirm its earlier decision regarding the draft by-laws. The group also noted that the content of the 1994 OMB decision, which stipulated what developers could build on the site, might have misled a number of city councillors. Some councillors may have felt they were not in a position to oppose the development, though the new development actually exceeded the OMB's guidelines (Chu 2003b).[14] That SYN continued to oppose the development is not surprising. However, the ABC Residents' Association also forwarded a letter opposing the development, contradicting earlier statements suggesting it was satisfied with the final proposal. The beginning of ABC's letter states that it "would like to clarify its position" on the development (ABC 2003). The association stated that it, in fact, shared the same concerns that the GYRA had voiced in its earlier letter, and was in opposition to the development, largely because of its height. The association also echoed Jane Jacobs's fear that the development would set a precedent for future high-rise development in the area (ABC 2003).

Peter Milczyn, a councillor from Etobicoke, proposed to defer the decision at the upcoming council meeting, and to re-examine the development guidelines in place to protect the integrity of Yorkville (Deverell 2003). Perhaps in a bid to stem neighbourhood opposition, Councillor Rae seconded Councillor Milczyn's motion to re-examine the development framework for the area. Council passed the motion (Council Minutes 2003a). However, two days later, council enacted the draft by-laws it had adopted in February (By-laws 191-2003 and 192-2003).

SYN upheld its threat, and appealed the decision on 16 May 2003 (Chu 2003a). The ABC Residents' Association also appealed the decision. The association stated that the "development is not in the best economic interest of the taxpayers of Toronto and that it contravenes City Planning Policies" (Caliendo 2003a). In addition to SYN and ABC, the head of a law firm with an office adjacent to the development, Ball & Alexander, also appealed. Stacey Ball noted that her firm had purchased the location in Yorkville because it "chose to have a premise in a location in a high end European type of atmosphere, as opposed to being in the financial district" and that "the ambiance is important to [the firm's] ... client base, and ... staff" (Ball 2003b). Another lawyer operating in the area also appealed, based on similar reasoning as Ms Ball's (Howe 2003). Both lawyers later withdrew their appeals before the hearing (Ball 2003a; *1191777 Ontario Ltd. v. Toronto (City)*), leaving SYN, now incorporated as the Save Yorkville Heritage Association (SYHA) (Latham 2003) and ABC as the opponents to the development. In an interview following the SYHA's notice of appeal, Linda Chu, a realtor and resident of Yorkville, and member of the SYHA, stated that the neighbourhood felt as if it had "been sold out because the city went behind their [*sic*] back and approved the 18 storeys" (Hume 2003, B03). ABC and the SYHA joined forces and hired a planning lawyer to represent them at the OMB hearing (*1191777 Ontario Ltd. v. Toronto (City)*).

The Hearing

The board held the hearing on 30 April 2004, over two years after Barclay-Grayson's submission of the development application. Although it was not a party to the hearing, the GYRA participated in opposition to the development alongside ABC and the SYHA. The neighbourhood associations' two main reasons for opposing the development remained the height of the towers and the danger that the development would set precedents for future development in the area. Barclay-Grayson had already agreed to move the Mount Sinai façade as opposed to demolition, and agreed to build the development all at once, rather than in phases, ameliorating two additional concerns the associations had with the development. The associations did express an additional concern, however, with regards to the deal between the City, the Toronto Parking Authority, and the developer for the construction of the parking garage. They felt the agreement might have tainted the City's position towards the proposal.

Despite being the appellant, the neighbourhood associations did not call any expert witnesses to provide evidence against the proposal, or against the City and developer's expert witnesses. Given the lack of evidence demonstrating any significant negative impact emanating from the development, or evidence suggesting the City was biased in its decision to support the development, the OMB decided in favour of the City and Barclay-Grayson (*Toronto (City) Official Plan Amendment no. 252 (Re)*).

ABC's appeal and its willingness to raise money to hire representation for the board hearing suggest it viewed the appeal as a viable option to prevent the construction of 100 Yorkville at Bellair. However, ABC made the decision to appeal after exhausting all other means of scuttling the development. In addition, though neither SYN nor Ms

Jacobs were neighbourhood associations, that the GYRA also focused on swaying local councillors suggests neighbourhood associations in Toronto continue to focus some of their effort on local politicians.

Only when the SYHA and elements of the neighbourhood associations opposed to the development realized City Planning supported the proposal without altering the size of the development, and council appeared to support it as well, did they adopt more conflictual tactics. The associations and their allies mobilized significant opposition to the development at council hearings. Councillor Rae suggested that such meetings "too often ... have turned into 'ugly' shouting matches. Residents speaking in favour of more density have sometimes themselves become targets of those who don't, so they stay away and their views go unheard" (Cordileone 2004, P01). The neighbourhood associations used their main resource, the ability to organize and mobilize, to influence the final decision of city council, similar behaviour to neighbourhood associations' behaviour in cities like Los Angeles.

The two neighbourhood associations only resorted to an OMB appeal when appeals to local politicians and city council had failed, suggesting they appealed council's decision only because no other viable alternative was left. This fact suggests the neighbourhood associations did not perceive the OMB as an ideal means to oppose the development. In fact, comments about the "BAD" decision the OMB had made in 1993 (Chu 2003b, emphasis in original) suggest the associations were cognizant of the board's potential to render a decision against them. However, despite this perception of the board, the associations resorted to threats of appeal before city council rendered its decision.

Although the SYHA appeared to be the main protagonist in this case, the two neighbourhood associations (the GYRA and ABC) played an integral role throughout the application and appeal process. The GYRA and ABC heavily involved themselves in discussions with City Planning and the developer before submitting their comments to the TEYCC and Councillor Rae, and well before appealing to the OMB. Although the findings of chapter 4 suggest City Planning has little sway over neighbourhood associations, this case suggests that the latter are cognizant of the central role planning experts play in OMB hearings and perhaps in affecting council's position.

The changing tone and tactics of the associations demonstrate a more nuanced approach to dealing with unwanted development than is otherwise depicted in the LPE literature. At the onset, the two associations appeared willing to work directly with the developer towards a resolution of their differences. This consultation began before Barclay-Grayson even submitted its application for development to the City. Councillor Rae appears to have played an integral role in bringing developer and neighbourhood residents together. The neighbourhood associations' willingness to work with the developer and City Planning contradicts the standard depiction of their behaviour in LPE literature. Depictions of neighbourhood associations in cities such as Los Angeles (Purcell 2000, 1997), San Francisco (DeLeon and Powell 1989), and Gainesville (Vogel and Swanson 1989) suggest a highly conflictual relationship between the associations and developers, one that assumes conflict between pro-growth and anti-growth camps from the onset of any development proposal. This conflict, according to Kantor (1987; with David 1988), creates the situation where policy making turns to policy prevention. Although this case eventually led to conflict, initially the relationship between the opposing factions was cordial.

Bloor & Mill

Markland Wood is a community in the very west end of Toronto, in the former City of Etobicoke. Unlike Yorkville, which is part of downtown, Markland Wood is a suburban neighbourhood, though the neighbourhood shares a high level of affluence with Yorkville. On 14 May 2004, Manfred and Eleanore Jaenisch, small-time developers based in Bobcaygeon, Ontario, proposed to redevelop the site of a former Petro-Canada station. They proposed a townhouse complex consisting of thirteen four-storey town homes (Jaenisch 2004). The Jaenisches were apparently the owners of the site and had been leasing it to Petro-Canada.[15]

The loss of the Petro-Canada station upset some neighbourhood residents. As a result, well before any proposal to redevelop the site emerged, the president of the Markland Homes Association (MHA) contacted the Jaenisches to make them aware of area residents' concerns and to begin a dialogue concerning the future development of the site (Clifford 2004b). Among the MHA's concerns was that the corner "not decay like some other former commercial lots in the city" (Clifford 2004b, 2–4). Formed in 1962, the MHA comprises over 1250 homeowners in the Markland Wood area and is one of the most active neighbourhood associations in the city (Clifford 2004b). According to the board of the MHA, the community has the largest senior demographic in Canada (MHA interview 2009).

Before submitting its initial application, the developer held meetings with MHA board members, and additional meetings with the entire community (MHA interview 2009). Residents expressed concern over the built form, height and density, traffic and pollution, safety, and the development's effect on property values (City Clerk 2005b). Members of the MHA's board of directors that met with the developer's consultant (a former city employee) asked the developer to reduce the number of homes from thirteen and to lower their height. They were also concerned with the aesthetics of the development (MHA interview 2009). Regardless of the diminutive size of the project relative to the likes of the Four Seasons and Minto Midtown, many of the concerns residents raised were the same, notably the excessive size of the development and its effect on traffic in the area. Less than two months following the submission of its initial application, the developer submitted a revised proposal. The revisions explicitly addressed a number of residents' concerns. The most significant changes involved the reorientation of most of the town homes, in a bid to reduce traffic, so they faced the main road instead of another smaller road adjacent to the site, and reduction of the houses' heights from four storeys to three-and-a-half and three (Dickie 2004b).

A little over a month later, City Planning released its preliminary report. Both the height of the proposed houses and the number of houses exceeded zoning by-laws for the area. In addition, the site remained zoned for limited commercial use (Community Planning 2004c). The Etobicoke York Community Council (EYCC), on the motion of the local councillor, Doug Holyday, adopted City Planning's recommendations, and directed staff to begin consultation with the community (City Clerk's Office 2004b). Before the meeting took place, the Jaenisches once again revised their proposal for the site, in line with City Planning's preliminary report (Dickie 2004b).

Despite its already having undergone two revisions, most of the residents in attendance at a 4 October 2004 community meeting opposed the development. Residents' complaints did not differ significantly from those made during the initial consultation between the developer and the MHA. Due to the continued opposition, the developer again approached the MHA in order to address the continued concerns of residents in the area (City Clerk 2005b).[16] In a status update on the negotiations, the MHA noted that it had received short notice of the community meeting, and felt the high turnout was a direct result of its distribution of flyers to the community. The MHA also directed residents to express any concerns they had to Councillor Holyday (Clifford 2004a).

Despite the apprehension of some residents living near the proposed development, the board of the MHA expressed satisfaction with both the dialogue that had occurred between the developer and the association, and with the development proposal itself (MHA interview 2009). However, in another edition of its own paper, the *Marklander*, the association suggested it did not have an opinion, and wished to leave the final decision to residents in the immediate vicinity of the proposed development (Clifford 2005a). Supporting Logan and Rabrenovic's (1990) definition of neighbourhood association, members of the MHA's board of directors, in the interview I conducted in February 2009, suggested that the association in such situations focuses on the dissemination of information to neighbourhood residents (MHA interview 2009). During a meeting of the association's board of directors I attended, it became apparent the association is concerned about the public's perception. For instance, the board did not want people to perceive the MHA as purely a NIMBY organization.[17] Board members are likely cautious of supporting such a development for fear of residents perceiving them as pro-developer as well. The MHA seeks to foster a sense of community in Markland Wood, but among its most important roles is to act as an advocate for the neighbourhood, serve as a means to ensure the dissemination of information, and encourage community involvement in planning and other issues.

The association played a significant role in the application process. The developer appears to have recognized the importance of working with the association towards a proposal satisfactory to both, as it continued to consult with the MHA throughout the process. According to the MHA (2009), local ward councillor Holyday often leaves negotiations to area residents and the developer, but does oppose the MHA on occasion in support of certain developments. In this instance, aside from City Planning, the developer spent most of its time in consultation with the association. Councillor Holyday did not act as an arbiter between the developer and neighbourhood association as Councillor Rae did in the 100 Yorkville case, though he did attend the larger public consultations.

After months of consulting with the MHA and residents in the community, and revising its proposal twice, the Jaenisches appealed to the OMB, due to the City's failure to render a decision. In its notice of appeal to the City, the developer noted that seven months had elapsed since it submitted its first application. It felt that it had, since then, addressed all the concerns expressed by the City and residents, and suggested the development represented good planning (Dickie 2004a). The MHA noted the developer's change of tactic in a February 2005 update to neighbourhood residents, but again did not express support for or opposition to the development. The MHA did note when the OMB hearing would likely take place, and also noted the City's support for the proposal (Clifford 2005b). City Planning had endorsed the proposal following a third revision in January. Councillor Holyday and the EYCC recommended city council adopt City Planning's recommendations (City Clerk's Office 2005b). Council adopted City Planning recommendations to support the proposal at the OMB on 16 February 2005 (City Clerk 2005b).

The MHA again informed residents of the OMB hearing's time and location, but otherwise did not express an opinion regarding the development. The association continued to meet with the developer both before and after the hearing (Clifford 2005a). One area resident attended the hearing in opposition to the development. The OMB endorsed the City and developer's settlement without modification (*Toronto (City) Official Plan Redesignate Lands Amendment (Re)* [2005] O.M.B.D. no. 406). City council passed two by-law amendments pertaining to the development in 2007 (By-laws no. 643-2007 and 1126-2007 (OMB)).[18]

The Bloor & Mill case is unusual compared to other cases that involved neighbourhood associations (Four Seasons, Minto Midtown, 100 Yorkville, One Sherway). The main catalyst for involvement of neighbourhood associations in the other cases appeared to be opposition to the development. The MHA never expressed open support for or opposition to the development. However, members of the association's board of directors directly involved in negotiations with the developer were satisfied with the proposal (MHA interview 2009). Although the association was heavily involved in the application process, it appears to have adopted a neutral stance intentionally in its communications with area residents. According to LPE literature on neighbourhood associations, their primary reason for existing, and for mobilizing, is to oppose development. That such an organization would mobilize without such intentions driving it deviates significantly from the behaviour of neighbourhood associations in cities like Gainesville (Vogel and Swanson 1989), Los Angeles (Purcell 2000), or even Columbus (Mesch and Schwirian 1996).

Initially the MHA's basic behaviour did not deviate substantially from that of the GYRA or ABC in the 100 Yorkville or the Four Seasons cases. The MHA actively participated in a dialogue with the developer. However, the association appears to have done so without the intervention of Councillor Holyday. That a neighbourhood association would enter negotiations with a developer without the involvement of local politicians contradicts the general premise of most LPE theories. The addition of neighbourhood associations to urban-regime (Stone 1993) and growth-machine theory (Logan and Rabrenovic 1990) emphasized their opposition to development and their anti-growth leanings. However, the MHA approached the developer, not the local councillor, when the prospect of redeveloping the Petro-Canada site emerged. The MHA's public stance towards the development of the site, neither for nor against, suggests the organization, though initially concerned with the development, did not adopt an explicitly anti-growth attitude at the onset. Its primary goal, aside from keeping local residents informed, was to ensure its place in the dialogue on the development. Since the MHA prides itself on its activity and membership, it needs to ensure it maintains a sense of legitimacy in the community and among local businesses. Securing a primary role in discussions with the developer supports this perception.

Once formal discussions began between the developer and the City, the MHA, though maintaining its dialogue with the developer, also began to encourage residents to contact their local councillor and City Planning, and advised them of the times and locations of meetings on the planned development. The intent of the MHA was not to mobilize residents to influence the position of Councillor Holyday or the city council, however. Although the MHA's behaviour deviates significantly from what authors such as DeLeon and Powell (1989) or Purcell (2000) portray, there exists little evidence that the OMB influenced this change in behaviour. The MHA was ambivalent or even supportive of the development. Both LPE literature and this analysis focus on neighbourhood associations' opposition to development. This case suggests that conceiving of neighbourhood associations exclusively as organizations in opposition to development, or anti-growth in disposition, may be in error. The MHA played a role in the politics of urban development, even though it was not in opposition to development.

However, in advising residents to contact Councillor Holyday if opposed to the development, the MHA suggests the type of tactics it would adopt when openly opposed to a development proposal. Its emphasis on lobbying the local councillor suggests the association did not perceive the OMB as a viable alternative, but only as a last resort, as it did advise residents of the appeal. The board of directors of the MHA expressed apprehension and dislike of the OMB, and did not conceive of the board as a possible ally or alternative to local politician support (MHA interview 2009). The MHA did not attend the actual board hearing, nor did many area residents. In this case, the MHA's main motivation for involvement appeared to be its interest in maintaining its position as representative of the community.

Summary of Findings

In examining the behaviour of neighbourhood associations in Toronto, this chapter addresses my third question: *Does the existence of the OMB affect the behaviour of neighbourhood associations in Toronto?* Neighbourhood associations in Toronto adopt and use many of the same tactics to oppose development as their American counterparts. The OMB's existence does not remove their incentive to lobby local politicians. In fact, lobbying and cajoling local politicians appears to be their main tactic when opposing development. However, that neighbourhood associations continue to lobby local politicians does not entirely rule out the OMB's influence on their behaviour. After all, as the previous chapter suggests, developers continue to lobby local politicians, but use the OMB and planning experts as a foil to local politicians in opposition to development.

The MHA did not participate in the OMB hearing regarding Bloor & Mill. Its neutrality precluded such involvement. In contrast, the GYRA and ABC utilized both the threat of an appeal and the appeal itself in their opposition to 100 Yorkville, just as ABC did in the Four Seasons case. Unlike developers, neighbourhood associations can only appeal once council has rendered a decision. Thus, that the appeal was a final effort to oppose the development does not mean that the associations did not conceive of an appeal early on as a means to oppose the development. The associations used the threat of an appeal in an attempt to influence local politicians, an indication that the board influenced their behaviour.

The potential of an appeal is no idle threat either. Neighbourhood associations do not fare well at the board when they lack the support of council. However, if they can raise enough money to appeal a decision, they can increase the costs for the City and developer resulting from the proceedings themselves, and thereby postpone development. Eleven months passed after the SYHA and ABC initially appealed council's decision until the OMB rendered its final decision, adding almost another year before the developer could break ground. The threat of an appeal is a resource available to neighbourhood associations in Ontario that is absent in most other jurisdictions.

However, the fact that they use such threats as a means to influence local politicians suggests the focus of neighbourhood associations has not changed, even if their tactics have. Thus, the threat of appeal is another resource neighbourhood associations can use in pursuit of the same goal as their American counterparts, influencing the decision making of local politicians. To neighbourhood associations, the board does not provide the same alternative to lobbying local politicians as it does to developers, likely because of the cost involved, and because of their poor record at the OMB. However, the board provides neighbourhood associations with an additional resource beyond their ability to mobilize the electorate.

The behaviour of the neighbourhood associations in the 100 Yorkville, Four Seasons, One Sherway (which I discuss in the following chapter), and Minto Midtown cases suggests strong similarities exist between them and their American counterparts in cities like Los Angeles (Purcell 2000, 1997) and San Francisco (DeLeon and Powell 1989), as they adopted many common tactics. The GYRA and ABC, along with their ally, the SYHA, managed to garner significant media coverage, if not always favourable to them, and mobilized large groups of residents and other concerned citizens (Toronto "notables") to petition city council and to attend the public meetings in opposition to the development, something ABC and the SYHA duplicated in their battle over the Four Seasons Hotel. FoNTRA and Alderwood Community Involvement (ACII) achieved similar feats in the Minto Midtown and One Sherway cases, respectively.

In contrast, the MHA's behaviour in the Bloor & Mill case deviated significantly from the behaviour expected in the LPE approach. The MHA adopted a neutral stance towards the development proposal, though ostensibly supporting it. Despite its neutrality, the association participated in an active dialogue with the developer. This dialogue did not involve the ward's councillor. Such behaviour challenges the LPE literature's depiction of neighbourhood associations as predominantly anti-growth organizations. However, the case does not provide evidence of the OMB's influence. In fact, the MHA advised residents opposed to the development to adopt many of the same tactics as the associations involved in the 100 Yorkville case.

That Councillor Holyday did not involve himself in the dialogue with the developer in the Bloor & Mill case is another important finding, and may indicate some of the influence of the OMB on local politicians, which the following chapter addresses, even if it does not pertain to whether the OMB influences the behaviour and role of neighbourhood associations. More important, Councillor Holyday's lack of involvement in the Bloor & Mill case offers insight into the role of neighbourhood associations in Toronto that contradicts the standard depiction in the LPE literature.

The MHA's board of directors suggests that Councillor Holyday will oppose the association's stance on some development proposals (MHA interview 2009). Thus, like Councillor Rae in the 100 Yorkville case, Holyday may not fear the wrath of the electorate in such instances. However, the work of authors such as Purcell (1997, 2000), Vogel and Swanson (1989), and DeLeon and Powell (1989) suggest the conflict between developer and anti-growth advocates often places local politicians in uncomfortable positions. Cullingworth (1987) argues that the OMB allows local politicians to avoid involvement. Given such an aversion to involvement in development politics, local politicians in Toronto may be abandoning their role as the residents' representative in dialogues with developers. Neighbourhood associations, which often have an immediate interest in development issues, seem to have taken over the position of the residents' advocate in response. For neighbourhood associations to achieve this role, they need to establish their legitimacy with both residents and developers. The MHA engaged with the developer to demonstrate its leadership in Markland Wood, and from the onset of the dialogue made sure the developer was aware of the association's importance to the neighbourhood (for instance, by outlining the number of residents that were members). The EYCA pursued a similar course in the Pulse Condominium case, where the local councillor, John Filion, was also conspicuously absent from much of the proceedings.

ABC's apparent reversal of opinion also indicates that associations have a need for legitimacy, which they achieve by inserting themselves into any relevant policy processes as the de facto representative of residents. Kyle Rae's direct involvement in the dialogue concerning 100 Yorkville diminished the standing of the associations, but by working closely with Councillor Rae, ABC could manage an element of legitimacy as the representative of area residents' interests, especially when faced with opposition from City Planning and a city council in favour of the development. The SYHA's vehement opposition to the development, along with the GYRA's opposition, undermined ABC's ability to represent itself as the voice of area residents, as a vocal and highly visible minority of residents clearly were opposed to the development. ABC risked losing its appeal to area residents opposed to the development to the GYRA and the SYHA if it maintained that the development was acceptable.

The behaviour of the MHA, EYCA, and ABC suggest that opposition to development does not entirely drive neighbourhood associations' involvement in the politics of urban development, contradicting Logan and Rabrenovic (1990) and other LPE scholars. Organizations like the SYHA, which include elements well outside of the neighbourhood, are more indicative of the anti-growth advocates the LPE literature depicts. The driving force behind the MHA, EYCA, and ABC is to be the main advocates and representatives of their respective communities. Involvement in the politics of urban development is a means towards establishing and maintaining legitimacy. If the OMB allows local politicians to avoid making planning decisions, as Cullingworth (1987) suggests, then it may also provide space for neighbourhood associations to replace local politicians in their role as representative of residents' interests.

Without understanding whether and how the OMB influences the behaviour of local politicians, determining the board's exact role in influencing the behaviour of neighbourhood associations is difficult. The evidence from the two cases, and from the Four Seasons case, suggests that neighbourhood associations perceive the OMB as a last resort if they fail to sway local politicians. However, the board also provides neighbourhood associations with an additional resource for swaying local politicians' decisions: the threat of an appeal. Most political actors (specifically developers or municipal politicians) want to avoid the OMB (Blazevski interview 2008). Thus, threatening to appeal council's decision to the OMB may convince local politicians to continue a dialogue with both developer and neighbourhood associations to work towards a compromise. In addition, some politicians may simply choose to support neighbourhood associations in their opposition, if either refusal or approval will result in an appeal.

In threatening to appeal council's decision, neighbourhood associations may be hoping that council will decide to refuse the proposal, thus gaining an important and resourceful ally during the OMB appeal. The neighbourhood associations, in such a scenario, would conceive of the board as the main battleground against the developer, which, given developers' penchant for appeals, may be an accurate assumption. It appears that the board does influence neighbourhood associations' behaviour if such is the case. The Four Seasons, Minto Midtown, and One Sherway cases provide additional evidence of their behaviour. In the Four Seasons and Minto Midtown cases, as in the 100 Yorkville, Pulse, and Bloor & Mill cases, neighbourhood associations participated in early discussions with both City Planning and the developers. Only in the One Sherway case did the neighbourhood association involved eschew any direct dealings with the developer while at the same time limiting their relationship with City Planning. These findings again suggest that neighbourhood associations are cognizant of the role of planning in OMB hearings. Given the early and vehement opposition to the proposals in both the Minto Midtown and Four Seasons cases, it is unlikely that the neighbourhood associations would have engaged at all with the developers and City Planning if they felt the City or the OMB would side with them; still, in the latter case, city council appeared onside with the proposal, limiting the neighbourhood associations' options.

Neighbourhood associations expended significant effort in lobbying council in most of these cases. Clearly, such groups still rely heavily on the support of local politicians. Neighbourhood associations in Toronto continue to pressure and lobby local politicians as elsewhere in Canada and the United States. However, as both the 100 Yorkville and Four Seasons cases attest, the OMB affords them an additional resource for influencing local politicians: the threat of appeal. The two case studies above and the additional cases where neighbourhood associations engaged in the planning process suggest that that the OMB does influence their behaviour, which answers *Question 3*. Although neighbourhood associations in Toronto do focus most of their efforts on swaying local politicians, that they willingly engage in discussions with developers and planners deviates from the behaviour expected in the LPE literature. Neighbourhood associations in Toronto, much like the city's developers, exhaust all avenues, including appealing to the OMB, in a bid to influence policy decision making in their favour.

Either the LPE literature's depiction of neighbourhood associations is too simplistic, or the existence of the OMB plays a substantive role in influencing and shaping the behaviour of neighbourhood associations in Toronto. What LPE theories do fail to account for are the interests of neighbourhood associations, offering far too simplistic an explanation

150 Planning Politics in Toronto

of these interests, at least if applied to Toronto. While Logan and Rabrenovic's (1990) definition of neighbourhood associations suggests they
are more than simply agents against change, much LPE literature depicts neighbourhood associations solely in this light. Some associations
may well focus only on opposing development; however, the Bloor &
Mill, Pulse Condominium, and 100 Yorkville cases suggest that an urge
to ensure the representation of residents' interests drives neighbourhood associations' participation in the politics of urban development,
echoing Logan and Rabrenovic's (1990) definition. More important,
both cases suggest that neighbourhood associations need to involve
themselves in the politics of urban development for local residents to
perceive them as legitimate representatives, a fact overlooked by the
LPE literature.

8 Politicians and Urban Development in Toronto

In a June 2005 *Toronto Star* article, Councillor Mark Grimes expressed his significant disappointed over an OMB decision that allowed a major condominium development project to go ahead despite his and members of his constituency's opposition. In reference to the board's decision the councillor remarked, "This is another case of the community getting screwed by the bogeyman at the OMB" (Porter and Moloney 2005). While local residents were "dumbfounded" by the turn of events, having thought the proposal dead after council voted to refuse it (ibid.), one could ask whether Councillor Grimes's reaction was disingenuous or born out of naivety. Given the limited time he had spent in office to that point, the latter might be the better explanation, as any long-time observer of planning politics in the city and of the OMB would have seen the result as a foregone conclusion once city planners gave their enthusiastic support for the revised proposal for the site. It is easy to pick on Councillor Grimes in this instance, but he was clearly responding to the significant opposition of his constituents to a development that would have limited positive benefits for his ward, as it lay beyond its border. Whether Councillor Grimes truly believed the OMB would uphold the decision of council or was aware the development was a forgone conclusion, given the overwhelming support for the project from city planners, is beside the point. Councillor Grimes was making a political decision when he took it upon himself to oppose a development that fell outside his own ward, a decision that would win him support among his own constituents regardless of the veracity of his position. Toronto's local politicians are no different than their counterparts in other Canadian and American cities in this regard.

Paul Kantor (with David 1988), in his book *The Dependent City*, provides one of the most succinct explanations of the interests and motivations of local politicians in American cities. That politicians seek
to be elected and re-elected is a fundamental element of the liberal-
democratic order in both the United States and Canada. In this respect, local politicians do not vary from their state, provincial, and
federal counterparts. At the local level, according to Kantor, local politicians' electoral success "is intimately tied to the capability of the
local economy to generate jobs, governmental revenues, and social
order" (ibid., 241). Because of this fact, local politicians typically support pro-growth policies, as these policies generate jobs, additional
revenue for local government, and stability in cities. However, Kantor
suggests that local politicians are facing increasing opposition to such
policies from the electorate. This scenario unfolded in Toronto and in
other cities such as Los Angeles and San Francisco, where neighbourhood associations mobilized to defeat pro-growth city councils. Still,
Kantor (with David 1988) does not perceive the emergence of anti-
growth forces as simply signalling a shift in local government policy
directions, but as an "explosive dilemma," because, while local government is becoming more responsive to citizens' demands, it has become increasingly dependent on economic forces beyond its control
(5). He argues that "this conundrum of democracy amid dependency
explains why we face some of the most intractable urban policy problems of our time" (10).

Although Kantor was writing in the late eighties, the "explosive dilemma" remains an issue in many North American cities today. Toronto
is no exception, as anti-growth and pro-growth forces continue to align
themselves for battle. The dilemma arises for local politicians because
they stand in the middle of the battlefield between the two forces, acting both as participants and, occasionally, as mediators. Two important
factors define the role they play in the politics of urban development:
their aforementioned interest in attaining and maintaining power (election and re-election), and their authority over issues of planning and
development.

The dilemma that local politicians face arises from their affinity for
two increasingly divergent groups. Most American LPE scholars today,
including Kantor (1987; with David 1988), Molotch (1993), Logan and
Rabrenovic (1990), and Stone (1993) consider developers and middle-
class neighbourhood associations to be the two groups most attractive

to local politicians, although Stone still includes developers within the rubric of business. Local politicians' affinity for these groups derives from their respective resources, the former's wealth and the latter's ability to mobilize the electorate, and also accounts for Kantor's explosive dilemma, as the two groups are often at odds with each other. As a result, local politicians often must choose between the respective groups and the resources they offer.

The second factor that determines the role of local politicians in the politics of urban development, their authority over planning and development (what Dahl [1961] terms legality), dictates the relationship between them, developers, and neighbourhood associations. It also accounts for the central role they play in the battle between pro-growth and anti-growth forces. While the resources developers and neighbourhood associations control attract local politicians, local politicians' authority attracts developers and neighbourhood associations to them. Local political economy literature in the United States usually assumes the existence of this factor when studying the politics of urban development. One of the main purposes of this analysis is to challenge this basic assumption. Not all local politicians in North America enjoy such authority over planning and development. Lacking this authority, therefore, changes the role of local politicians, the basic pattern of politics, and the relationships between actors involved in the politics of urban development.

This chapter examines the role local politicians play in the politics of urban development in Toronto and addresses my fourth question: *Does the existence of the OMB affect local politicians' decision making and behaviour towards other actors?* The chapter considers two contrasting case studies. In the first, One Sherway, local politicians were heavily involved in the development's application process, as was a neighbourhood association. In the second case study, Lowe's, local politicians seem to have played a secondary role to the developer and City Planning. The first case involved a proposal for a multi-tower condominium development in the city's west end, while the second involves a proposal for a retail development including a large hardware store. The case studies investigate the behaviour of local politicians in two disparate instances, which are, however, indicative of two common scenarios local politicians face in Toronto. Finally, the chapter also compares and contrasts the behaviour of local politicians in Toronto with local political economy literature's depiction of their behaviour.

Toronto's City Council and Local Politicians

The City of Toronto is divided into forty-four wards, each electing one councillor to city council. In addition, the city has a mayor, elected at large. Toronto, like most municipalities in Canada, does not have a party system at the municipal level. It is further divided into four "communities," each with its own community council, composed of ten to twelve councillors whose wards fall within the territorial confines of the respective communities.[1] As the City's website states, one of the main purposes of a community council is to make "recommendations to City Council on local planning and development matters" (Toronto n.d.a). Peter Smith (interview 2008) refers to the forty-four wards as "forty-four separate fiefdoms," offering little overall direction for development in the city. In support of this depiction, both Councillor Walker (interview 2008) and Councillor Rae (interview 2008) suggest that, in most instances, other city councillors would not oppose the position of a councillor in whose ward a development was proposed. The lack of a party system and the weakness of the mayor account for the power of individual councillors, much as they do in Los Angeles (Purcell 2000). As regards the role of local politicians and city council as a whole in the politics of urban development in Toronto, individual councillors typically have the greatest influence on the success or failure of a development proposal, followed by the respective community councils and, lastly, city council as a whole, though council makes the final decision (Paton interview 2008).

City councillors in Toronto vary in their response to development proposals. Some councillors are openly hostile to most development, while others tend to be favourable. The reception developers receive from local politicians can thus vary substantially from ward to ward (Blazevski interview 2008; Paton interview 2008; and Smith interview 2008). Councillors Rae and Walker represent the poles of sentiment towards development with other councillors falling somewhere between the extremes (Keefe interview 2008; Paton interview 2008). Councillors also have long tenures in city council. For instance, Councillor Walker served in office for almost thirty years before retiring. Councillor Milczyn, involved in the One Sherway case below, has served as a councillor for the former City of Etobicoke and the new City of Toronto for twenty years. Councillor Filion, from the Pulse Condominium case has served for twenty-five years, while Councillor Rae served for twenty years before his retirement (Toronto n.d.b). Not surprisingly, the city has a low turnover rate of councillors as well. Of the thirty-seven incumbents who ran in the 2006 municipal election, only one lost his seat and that to a former city councillor (Toronto 2003, 2006). Only two of the other contests involving incumbents resulted in a close race with opponents (Ward 18 and Ward 30). Donald Beggs, president of the Markland Homes Association, suggests that councillors' long stays in office and relative job security have made them less receptive to the interests of city residents (MHA interview 2009). Councillor Walker (interview 2008) suggests that the adoption of elections every four years (as opposed to two or three) will further distance local politicians from the citizens, as the former face less pressure from the electorate.

The findings from the previous chapter and chapter 4 suggest that city councillors continue to respond to citizens and neighbourhood associations on issues of development. However, that the OMB removes final decision making from city councillors may help them stay in office, if the board allows them to avoid responsibility in the contentious policy area of development. Otherwise, if neighbourhood associations can successfully mobilize the electorate, they should be able to topple unsympathetic councillors, regardless of their time in office or the years between elections. Many councillors suffered such a fate in the late 1960s and early 1970s at the hands of an organized and mobilized electorate.

While the behaviour of both developers and neighbourhood associations in Toronto diverges from that of their American counterparts, they still seek to win the support of city councillors and devote resources to that end. The existence of the Ontario Municipal Board may diminish the importance of local politicians to the politics of urban development in Toronto, but they remain key players nonetheless. For both developers and neighbourhood associations the support of both individual councillors and city council as a whole remains an important asset, whether a development application makes its way to the OMB or not.

Toronto's Local Politicians and LPE Literature

Toronto's city council and local politicians do not deviate significantly from their American counterparts.[2] Thus, local politicians in Toronto would behave in a similar manner to their counterparts in comparable American cities if the OMB did not exist, or did not influence their behaviour. Upper-middle-class neighbourhood associations have become increasingly effective at foiling developers' interests, emerging as an alternative partner for local politicians. As Kantor (1987) notes, local politicians in the United States "are constrained to reconcile their responsiveness to the citizenry (popular control) with the promotion of their economies (market control)" (495). They must choose between their electorate, which opposes development (and the neighbourhood associations that mobilize it), or the development corporations that fund their election campaigns and provide needed fiscal resources for development projects in the city. Having to choose between developer and neighbourhood association, when the two are at odds, places local politicians in an unenviable position, resulting in the "intractable urban policy problems" Kantor speaks of (Kantor with David 1988, 10). In cities like San Francisco, this intractability results from city council splitting between anti-growth and pro-growth camps, which undermines the proper functioning of council (DeLeon and Powell 1989; also DeLeon 1992b).

Regardless of the actual outcome, local politicians in many American cities must decide between the support of strong neighbourhood associations or the development industry and its allies. Concurrently, each group will seek to elect candidates favourable to their cause. In either event, local politicians will play an active role in the politics of urban development, whether they are for or against growth. They will choose the side of either anti-growth neighbourhood associations or pro-growth developers.

Given the attitude and behaviour of Councillor Rae and Councillor Walker, Toronto's local politicians would appear to mimic their American counterparts, as the two appear to reflect the pro-growth and anti-growth poles common in other North American cities. However, both councillors consider themselves outliers in city council (Rae interview 2008; Walker interview 2008).[3] In fact, the typical portrayal of local politicians' behaviour in Toronto diverges significantly from the portrayal of their behaviour in the LPE literature. Journalists and academics tend to attribute this divergence to the existence of the OMB.

Both councillors (Rae interview 2008; Walker interview 2008), as well as city staff (Keefe interview 2008; Paton interview 2008), a developer (Blazevski interview 2008), and an external planning expert (Smith interview 2008) suggest that when conflict between developer and neighbourhood association arises, many of Toronto's local politicians will use the OMB to avoid responsibility for any decision on development. Tom Keefe (2008) suggests that in many ways local politicians see themselves as only one step towards the board. Either local politicians will use the spectre of a board decision to convince neighbourhood associations to compromise on the proposal (Paton interview 2008; Smith interview 2008) or, given significant opposition, will support the wishes of the neighbourhood associations, despite either supporting the proposal or foreseeing the consequence of a board hearing (Walker interview 2008; Keefe interview 2008). Either way, when conflict between developer and neighbourhood association arises, the OMB, not city council, will inevitably bear responsibility for the final decision on development, allowing local politicians to avoid significant fallout from choosing sides in the conflict.

Academic literature on Toronto and the OMB does not address this point at any length. However, Cullingworth (1987) did note this behaviour in passing when discussing planning practices in Ontario. In his survey of planning institutions in Canada, he suggested that the OMB "nicely allows politicians to abrogate the responsibilities which properly fall on them" (440). In addition, journalists have remarked on Toronto politicians' tendency to avoid making substantive decisions on controversial planning issues (see Gillespie 2007; Barber 2005). This anecdotal, though informed, conception of local politicians' behaviour in Toronto suggests that most Toronto politicians will avoid taking responsibility for planning decisions. The following case studies focus on the behaviour of local politicians engaged in the politics of urban development in Toronto.

One Sherway

On 4 July 2003, Lifetime Homes Inc.[4] applied to the City of Toronto for amendments to the official plan and pertinent zoning by-laws (Council Minutes 2005a). The original application proposed the construction of two thirty-five-storey and two thirty-storey condominium towers on vacant land adjacent to the Sherway Gardens Shopping Centre, a large mall in the city's southwest corner (Diamond 2003). The City and developer held a meeting for the public a month following the submission of the application. City Planning noted that Lifetime's proposal substantially exceeded the density permitted under the Sherway Centre secondary plan. Lifetime proposed a development 5.2 times the size of the lot area, as opposed to the 1.5 times the secondary plan allowed (Community Planning 2004b).[5]

The piece of land subsequently changed hands from Lifetime Homes to Sherway Gate Development Corporation (SGDC), a partnership between Menkes and Great Gulf Homes (the latter a subsidiary of international developer Great Gulf Group).[6] On 4 March 2004, the new owners submitted a revised proposal for the site. The new proposal maintained four towers, but significantly reduced their heights to 32, 27, 26, and 19 storeys. In addition, although the proposal still exceeded the density limits of the secondary plan, SGDC reduced the density from 5.2 times the lot size to 3.75, and reduced the number of units below the maximum number permitted (1,350) for the site. The City and developer held another community meeting on 21 July 2004 (Community Planning 2004b).

The proposed development was located in Ward 5, Councillor Peter Milczyn's ward. Councillor Milczyn attended both public meetings. Because of the close proximity of the site to Ward 6, Councillor Mark Grimes also involved himself in the process. Most of the residents who attended the meetings were from Councillor Grimes's ward, from a community called Alderwood. Councillor Grimes held an additional meeting with these residents in October of the same year. The Alderwood residents were vehemently opposed to the development. As in several of the previous case studies, residents were concerned over the density and height of the development, increased traffic, loss of privacy due to the buildings' heights, and the effect of the development on the neighbourhood's schools. In addition, residents felt that the development would result in greater pollution and noise, and that the site lacked the proper infrastructure for such a large development (Community Planning 2004b).

Despite local residents' concerns, the City's planning experts, in their final report to the Etobicoke York Community Council (EYCC) of 17 October 2004, recommended that the City approve necessary amendments to the official plan and zoning by-laws so the developer could proceed with the development. In its report, City Planning noted that any shadow cast by the buildings would fall solely on the Toys"R"Us and Sherway Gardens, and would be limited. The report also noted that the Queen Elizabeth Way (QEW), a major expressway that separates the site from the Alderwood community to the south, produced far more noise than could possibly be generated by the new development. The city's school boards did not oppose the development. Finally, City Planning had accepted a traffic study from the developer, which concluded that the existing road network in the area could accommodate any increase in traffic resulting from the development. City staff noted that SGDC had already committed itself to a minimum of

$500,000 for provision of open space and public art under section 37 of the Planning Act (Community Planning 2004b).

In an EYCC meeting held on 16 November 2004, Councillor Grimes, at the behest of residents from his ward, requested that the City hire an outside consultant to conduct a peer review of the traffic study the developer had submitted to City Planning. His motion passed (City Clerk's Office 2004a). City staff submitted the findings of the external peer review to the EYCC on 13 January 2005. According to the staff report, the firm responsible for the peer review agreed with the original report on most points. The proposed development would have a modest impact on traffic. Most of the congestion in the neighbourhood was a product of traffic on the QEW and Highway 427, another major expressway in the area. The review also considered the site a suitable location thanks to easy access to transit (City Clerk 2005c).

Despite City Planning's support for the project, and the support of Councillor Milczyn, the EYCC voted eight to two against it (City Clerk 2005c; Barber 2005).[7] In an interview with John Barber of the *Globe and Mail*, Councillor Milczyn vented his frustration with the decision, noting that the proposal was "precisely the type of development we want in precisely the place we want it" (Barber 2005). At the city council meeting of 1 February 2005, Councillor Grimes submitted a petition with 814 signatures in opposition to the development. During this session of city council, Councillor Milczyn proposed to amend the EYCC clause, and adopt city staff's recommendations instead. Despite the support of the mayor, Milczyn's motion lost by one vote, twenty votes against to nineteen in favour. Council subsequently adopted the EYCC's rejection of the proposal, twenty-two to seventeen (Council Minutes 2005b).

The Appeal

On 4 February 2005, solicitors representing SGDC served notice to the City of the developer's intent to appeal council's decision to the OMB (Diamond 2005c). In response to the appeal, residents of Alderwood, the main opponents of the proposal, incorporated a neighbourhood association called Alderwood Community Involvement Inc. (ACII). ACII retained its own lawyers to oppose the development at the OMB. The lawyers' first act was to ask the board to push back the proposed hearing date, scheduled for 16 May 2005, and convene a pre-hearing beforehand (Kusser 2005). City lawyers supported ACII's request (Whicher 2005), while the developer suggested seventy days (following the notice of appeal) was substantial time for ACII to prepare its case and retain experts (Diamond 2005b). At this juncture, Councillor Grimes re-entered the fray. He wrote to the OMB, requesting a postponement of the hearing, due to the City's delay in hiring external planning experts of its own (Grimes 2005). Councillor Grimes did not, however, involve himself directly in the appeal process. Councillor Milczyn also attempted to intervene. Citing a confidential report from the city solicitor, Milczyn asked council to reconsider its decision to refuse the development. Mayor Miller ruled the motion out of order, however (Council Minutes 2005a).

On 1 June 2005, the OMB allowed the appeal. As in other cases where city council has opposed City Planning, the board relied heavily on the testimony of city planners in favour of the development. The City's external planning expert suggested the City needed to revisit the secondary plan for Sherway Gardens to determine what was appropriate for the area. His testimony did not suggest the proposal involved poor planning, however. The board did not give significant weight to Alderwood residents' fears, noting, as did City Planning, that the QEW was responsible for most of the noise and traffic in the area (*Toronto (City) Official Plan Redesignate Land Amendment (Re)* [2005] O.M.B.D. no. 595). Following the decision, certain residents from Alderwood contacted the board member responsible for the decision, as well as the premier of Ontario, but to no avail (Affleck 2005).[8]

Both Councillor Grimes and Councillor Milczyn played important roles in the application process, though on opposing sides. They also continued opposing and supporting the proposal, respectively, during the appeals process. The close vote in favour of refusing the development application suggests a city council heavily divided, similar to De-Leon and Powell's (1989) depiction of the San Francisco City Council. The two councillors' actions, and the actions of city council as a whole, in this case suggest that the behaviour of local politicians in Toronto deviates little from what the LPE literature predicts. Councillors Grimes and Milczyn participated actively in the politics of urban development, and they and the rest of council openly took sides on the issue, much as their American counterparts do. However, the One Sherway case is unusual.

In Toronto, neighbourhood residents' opposition to a development typically emerges in the same ward as the proposed development. In this instance, there was limited opposition to the development in Councillor Milczyn's ward, so he was free to support the development without repercussion to his standing with residents in Ward 5. The opposition arose from a community to the south of the proposal in Councillor Grimes's ward (Ward 6). Councillor Grimes clearly felt pressured to oppose the development. Had no opposition arisen in Ward 6, or had the proposal arisen in that ward, council may not have split in the fashion it did. The unusual features of the case may not represent the typical behaviour of local politicians in Toronto, but does suggest that strongly opposed neighbourhood associations may turn a specific development proposal into something salient for local politicians.

Such a finding is important, because it suggests that local politicians in Toronto will enter into the morass experienced by their American counterparts, resulting in a council split along pro-growth and anti-growth lines. However, they will only do so when a development proposal in some way encroaches on more than one ward, or "fiefdom." Minto Midtown parallels the One Sherway case in this respect, as the former development sits at a juncture of three wards. The division in council in such instances may not even relate directly to an anti-development/pro-development divide. Councillors could simply be voting based on other traditional cleavages, or as a favour to one councillor or another.[9] There is little indication in this case that other councillors took an active interest in the development beyond voting their mind.

Lowe's

On 21 May 2003, Toronto City Council approved the demolition of a building used for paint manufacturing on a site straddling the former cities of North York and York (City Clerk 2003b). Over two years later, on 26 September 2005,[10] the owner of the site, North American Development Group,[11] a developer of shopping centres in the United States and Canada,[12] applied for a site plan control[13] to permit the construction of a large retail hardware and home improvement store, and seven smaller satellite buildings with additional retail (Macaulay 2006).

Unlike the previous seven cases, the developer's proposal did not require an amendment to either the official plan or existing zoning by-laws. According to North American's solicitor, the developer had been in talks with City Planning for almost two years before the application's submission (Makuch 2005a). Lowe's Companies Canada, UCL (Lowe's), a new subsidiary of the giant American home hardware retailer, also joined in discussion with City Planning after signing a lease for the site with North American (Harbell 2005a). Despite the consultation, City Planning staff approached city council in late October of 2005, recommending that the City pass an interim control by-law (ICBL) preventing most types of development in the Castlefield Caledonia Design and Décor District, which included the North American development site. Because the district straddled two former cities, the existing by-laws and official plans provided for conflicting planning principles, and neither conformed to the proposed use of the area as envisioned in the new official plan (Tyndorf 2005).

In its report to city council, City Planning suggested the new ICBL exclude two sites proposed for development, as City Planning had been reviewing these applications for some time. However, City Planning did not suggest North American and Lowe's site should be exempt, though it acknowledged in its report that it had recently received an application for the site. City Planning suggested the proposal could affect the review and alter the character of the area. Councillor Howard Moscoe, whose ward encompassed the district, moved that council adopt City Planning's recommendation (Tyndorf 2005). City council subsequently passed two interim control by-laws, By-laws no. 862-2005 and 863-2005, one each for the former City of North York and the former City of York, on 26 October 2005. The latter of the two ICBLs effectively ended City Planning's consideration of Lowe's and North American's development proposal for at least one year (the duration of the initial by-law).

On 21 December 2005, North American appealed By-law no. 863-2005 to the OMB. The developer stated that it had engaged with City Planning in discussions concerning the development of the site for almost two years, and at no time did City Planning mention the possibility of a development freeze on the site. The developer also argued that the new official plan already addressed the issues of large-scale retail development, and was now under appeal to the OMB. As a result, the ICBL was premature, since the board had yet to rule on the new official plan in regard to such retail development (Makuch 2005a). Lowe's appealed both ICBLs the following day. In its notice to the city clerk, Lowe's noted that it had approached City Planning months before submission of the application concerning the development, and reiterated North American's claim that it had no prior warning of the ICBLs. Lowe's argued that its proposal for the site was completely in keeping with the existing official plan, and the City was wrong to pass the ICBLs based on the new official plan, as it had yet to come into force.[14] Finally, Lowe's claimed that the ICBL was "unnecessary, unreasonable, was passed for an improper purpose and does not represent good planning" (Harbell 2005a).[15]

Presumably, North American or Lowe's approached the ward's councillor, Howard Moscoe, with their proposal at some point during the proceedings. They or their counsel also may have made assumptions regarding Councillor Moscoe's support for the proposal. However, there is little evidence of continued dialogue between Councillor Moscoe and the developers. In their appeals to the OMB, both Lowe's and North American spoke of their dialogue with City Planning, and of their feeling that the City's planning experts had not dealt with them in good faith, but made little mention of local politicians. While Councillor Moscoe may have been apprised of the development and the effect of the ICBL on it, City Planning's limited mention of the development in its report to the NYCC may have left much of the community council and city council unaware of these facts.

Following notification of the appeal, City Planning sought city council's direction on the specific development. In a report to council regarding the impending OMB hearing, City Planning recommended council oppose the site plan application of the developers, as the site plan did not conform to the newly passed ICBL. Councillor Moscoe moved that the NYCC adopt City Planning's recommendations and pass them on to city council (City Clerk's Office 2006). Council adopted City Planning's recommendations a week later. In its justification for opposing the site plan application, City Planning noted that while the developer had submitted the initial application on 26 September 2005, the application was not completed until the middle of October, and did not begin circulating among staff until 26 October (the day council passed the two ICBLs) (City Clerk 2006b).

The Settlement

On 21 June 2006, solicitors for Lowe's and North American submitted a proposal for settlement to the City for the ICBL appeal, and preliminary terms for a settlement on the site plan application. The proposed settlement involved Lowe's and North American withdrawing their appeals of the ICBLs, effectively postponing construction until October 2006 (roughly the time when the initial ICBLs would run out). The City would agree to exempt the developer's application from the ICBL, allowing City Planning to process the site plan application. The City would also commit to processing the application before the end of October (Rovazzi and Shelton 2006). The city solicitor approached council directly with the proposal, and recommended its adoption in a confidential report. In addition, city council considered a confidential fiscal impact statement from the City's CFO and deputy city manager. Lowe's and North American gave the City until 30 June to accept the proposal. The OMB hearing was scheduled for 12 July. Councillor Moscoe moved that council adopt city staff's recommendations. City council approved the settlement on 27 June (Council Minutes 2006).

The City advised the board of the settlement on 30 June 2006 (Haley 2006). The board's decision of 12 July 2006 suggests the final settlement did not deviate significantly from the developers' proposal. City Planning and the developers began discussion on the site plan application (*Toronto (City) Interim Control By-law 862-2005 (Re)*). In late August 2006, City Planning recommended to city council that the City extend the ICBLs for another year. However, the new ICBLs would exempt the North American and Lowe's site (Tyndorf 2006).[16] While the city solicitor's report and the fiscal impact statement are inaccessible, one can infer that the City faced potential legal action had it continued to disregard North American and Lowe's application. Alternatively, the City's solicitor may have advised council that the City likely would lose the appeal of the ICBL, which would render the by-laws void (allowing for additional applications for development in the area).

City council in this instance relied heavily on the advice of the City's planning experts and later on the advice of the city solicitor and top bureaucrats. In contrast with the One Sherway case, council did not split when voting in support of the ICBL, nor in support of the settlement. Planning and development issues in this case did not have the same salience for local politicians in Toronto as they did in the previous case. The behaviour of city councillors in this case contrasts sharply with the LPE literature's portrayal of local politicians' behaviour. Given the absence of neighbourhood association involvement in this case, local politicians should have supported the development, at least according to Kantor's (with David 1988) portrayal of their behaviour. Without citizen involvement, there is no dilemma for local politicians. Conversely, Purcell (2000) and DeLeon's (1992b; and DeLeon and Powell 1989) respective accounts of local politicians' behaviour in Los Angeles and San Francisco suggest the divide between pro-growth and anti-growth forces should permeate policy decisions on planning. That divide clearly was not in evidence in this latter case.

City council's heavy reliance on the advice and expertise of members of the planning community and the City's top bureaucrats suggests it relinquished the decision making to its bureaucracy, not the OMB. After all, council opted to settle with the developers to avoid a hearing (on the advice of the city solicitor, CFO, and deputy city manager). However, effectively delegating the decision making in this matter suggests city council, if not avoiding responsibility for the decision, did not perceive the issue as salient enough to become actively involved in the process.

Summary of Findings

This chapter, along with considering the behaviour of local politicians involved in the politics of urban development in Toronto, addresses my fourth question: *Does the existence of the OMB affect local politicians' decision making and behaviour towards other actors?* In comparable American cities like San Francisco and Los Angeles, as the local political economy literature depicts them, local politicians play an active role in the politics of urban development, and often adopt explicit pro-growth or anti-growth platforms when running for office, and when voting in council. If local politicians in Toronto behaved in a similar manner, it would indicate that the OMB has limited influence on their behaviour. However, many depictions in the media and limited academic accounts of local politicians' behaviour in Toronto suggest they will try to avoid responsibility for development decisions. These accounts of local politicians' behaviour all suggest the OMB's presence allows local politicians to avoid decision making. Therefore, if these accounts are representative of common occurrences, they provide evidence of the OMB's influence on local politicians' behaviour.

The contrast between the One Sherway and Lowe's cases is pivotal for understanding local politicians' behaviour in Toronto. The former case suggests local politicians in the city behave similarly to their counterparts in comparable American cities, where strong neighbourhood associations compete with developers for the support of city council. Councillor Grimes and Councillor Milczyn were heavily involved in the application and appeals process, and council appears to have split along pro-growth and anti-growth lines. The dispute over Minto Midtown led to a similar stand-off, but with the pro-growth forces victorious. In sharp contrast, Councillor Moscoe was significantly less involved in the discussion with Lowe's and North American. In addition, city council relied heavily on the advice of the City's planning experts and other bureaucrats. Council voted en masse in favour of the two ICBLs that effectively prevented the development, and then voted to accept a settlement allowing the development proposal. Council did not relinquish its decision-making role to the OMB in the Lowe's case; in fact, it voted in favour of the settlement to avoid a hearing. However, city council, equally, did not engage actively in the application process, effectively delegating decision making to City Planning and other city staff.

The two cases provide contradictory evidence of local politicians' behaviour. However, two important contextual differences exist between the two cases. First, in the One Sherway case, a well-organized neighbourhood association actually opposed the developer, whereas the public was largely absent from the dialogue surrounding the Lowe's proposal. Second, the opposition in the One Sherway case arose predominantly from residents in an adjoining ward, as opposed to the ward in which the site lay. According to Keefe (2008) and Walker (2008), the politics of urban development usually plays out within a specific ward. Councillors from other wards usually accept the will of the specific ward's councillor. Aside from the Minto Midtown case, the other cases examined in this book support this conclusion. Even among the more contentious developments, the Four Seasons and 100 Yorkville, there was little opposition to Councillor Rae's stance on the development (though Councillor Walker did vote against the former [Walker interview 2008]). In the Aldergreen Estates, Pulse, and Bloor & Mill cases, there is little evidence of any dissension among council.

This second difference accounts for the split among council members. Councillor Milczyn supported a proposal he felt would benefit his ward and represented good planning. Residents of his ward appear to have accepted the proposal. Councillor Grimes, in contrast, responded to significant opposition to the development among residents from his ward, and opposed the development. The opposition of residents in a neighbouring ward made the development proposal salient beyond Councillor Milczyn's ward. Council divided in response to the increased salience of the specific proposal, possibly demonstrating ideological leanings or an affinity for one of the two councillors over the other. For Councillor Grimes, neighbourhood associations' opposition made the issue of development particularly salient. That Grimes was not in the ward where the developer proposed to build, and Councillor

Milczyn was supportive of the development, made the issue salient for the entire city council, as it forced councillors to choose between the neighbourhood associations or the developers. Similarly, in the Minto Midtown case, the proximity of the proposed development to Anne Johnston's ward made the issue more salient for her, resulting in her support for the proposal and opposition to Councillor Walker, although members of her own constituency opposed the development.

The Lowe's case, in contrast, suggests development is less salient to city council when opposing neighbourhood associations are absent. Local politicians in the city may favour anti-growth or pro-growth policy or sentiment. However, the Lowe's case suggests that Toronto politicians do not perceive the issue of development in the same light as their American counterparts. Both the Bloor & Mill and Pulse cases support this finding, even though neighbourhood associations were involved in both cases (though to a much lesser extent in the latter). In both cases, Councillor Holyday and Councillor Filion left negotiations to the neighbourhood associations, developers, and City Planning. Neither councillor demonstrated significant interest in the proposed developments.

In the LPE approach, resources structure the relationship between different actors. Local politicians enjoy the resource of authority – the ability to decide on issues of planning and development. However, boasting such a resource makes local politicians the main target of developers and neighbourhood associations who wish to influence urban development. Influencing local politicians is not the main focus of developers in Toronto (though they have not left local politicians to their own devices), but neighbourhood associations still rely heavily on local politicians' support. Local politicians in Toronto face less pressure from developers due to the latter's reduced interest in them. That local politicians become heavily involved when neighbourhood associations oppose a development proposal demonstrates both the latter's continued focus on and mobilization of local politicians and the reduced pressure on local politicians from developers.

In addition, city council is aware that planning experts play a vital role in OMB hearings (Keefe interview 2008; Walker interview 2008). Thus, when neighbourhood associations are not involved or interested in a specific development proposal, as in the Lowe's case, council effectively delegates decision making to City Planning. In a sense, both Councillor Holyday and Filion did the same in the Bloor & Mill and Pulse cases, respectively. Both councillors supported the final recommendation of City Planning, and in the latter case, City Planning clearly had the most significant effect on the outcome of the negotiations, as the developer did all it could to address the concerns of the City's planning experts. Following the advice of City Planning usually ensures the City will be in a position of strength if an OMB appeal makes it to a hearing. Thus, that local politicians leave the decision making to planning experts may be more than simply an effort to avoid responsibility. They could be making a strategic attempt to ensure the interests of the City are protected. However, the Lowe's case suggests councillors rely on City Planning without much reflection. They accepted the advice of City Planning when passing the ICBLs, but quickly had to shift course once the City's top bureaucrats revealed the possible negative consequences of supporting City Planning's stance. The case undermines the notion of strategic decision making in council. Regardless, the findings from these two cases provide an answer to *Question 4.*

The OMB does allow local politicians to avoid making difficult planning decisions. Local politicians in Toronto can and do abdicate responsibility to City Planning. Should an appeal of council's decision result in a board hearing, the expert testimony of the City's planning experts, not the opinion of city council, plays the pivotal role in determining the board's decision. Developers' reduced interest in local politicians allows the latter to delegate responsibility because the pressure to support development is less than the local political economy literature suggests, especially when compared with Logan and Molotch (1987) and Kantor's (with David 1988) accounts.

In Toronto, local politicians must make controversial decisions on planning and development issues when neighbourhood associations mobilize against a proposal, at least when these groups can threaten local politicians' electoral base. The issue of development becomes far more salient for local politicians when residents are opposed to development. However, local politicians need not live with the consequences of their decisions, as the OMB often will make the final decision, regardless of councillors' respective stances on the issue. In many respects, the existence of the OMB allows local politicians greater freedom by reducing their role. While some politicians will develop a specific anti-growth or pro-growth attitude, they need not do so. Developers focus less on opposing local politicians who express anti-growth sentiment, reducing the consequences of opposing development. In contrast, local politicians can adopt a pro-growth stance without sustaining significant damage to their standing with residents, as they can focus on the opinion of City Planning and the likelihood of winning an OMB appeal to justify their stance.

Finally, evidence from chapter 4 (see especially chart 4.4) suggests that local politicians will often support measures to avoid a hearing. Council may support settlements because an OMB decision against the City erodes the standing of local politicians among the public. Alternatively, settlements among the various parties to a dispute over development may be a means to prevent development issues from becoming too salient in the general politics of the city. The OMB may help local politicians in Toronto confine controversies over planning to the initial application process and OMB appeals, preventing them from becoming salient issues during elections. Keeping the politics of urban development out of election campaigns could also explain why developers do not actively oppose anti-growth councillors. In the past, when conflicts over development spilt into elections campaigns, as they did in the late 1960s and early 1970s, the city's developers lost the support of council. Thus, preventing development from becoming a salient issue in elections could benefit them as well.

9 The OMB and Local Political Economy

In chapter 1 I outlined three central objectives I had for this book: first, to address the failure of local government literature in Canada to account for the Ontario Municipal Board's role in the politics of urban development in Toronto; second, to provide an updated account of the politics of urban development in the city; and third, to examine whether the local political economy approach to studying urban politics can address and accommodate the divergent planning institutions that shape and direct planning policy and decision making in North American cities. The findings of my analysis demonstrate that the OMB significantly influences the behaviour of actors and the politics of urban development in the city such that these actors' behaviour deviates, to varying degrees, from that of their counterparts in other North American cities.

However, the manner in which actors behave, and the roles they play, are not necessarily what one would expect given the board's existence. The OMB significantly contributes to a politics in the city that simultaneously pushes actors towards compromise while fanning conflict. The American theories of urban politics that draw on the local political economy approach cannot account for the politics of urban development in Toronto. While the interests of actors and socio-economic structure assumed to exist in the LPE literature both hold in Toronto, the OMB alters the distribution of resources among actors in the city. The current local political economy literature cannot address this change in resource distribution, because it assumes a specific distribution of resources. It fails to account for differences in planning institutions, and the role they play distributing resources among actors and shaping and constraining their behaviour. However, the underlying elements of the LPE approach to studying urban politics provide the foundations for a model that can accommodate much wider variation. Such a model explicitly recognizes how the confluence and interaction of actors' interests, resources, institutions, and structures affects their behaviour and the politics of urban development.

The OMB and Political Actors in Toronto

Local political economy literature depicts the politics of urban development in American cities as a product of the interaction of developers (and other businesses), neighbourhood associations, and local politicians. Such interaction can result in a strong and enduring coalition between two of the three actors, as in Atlanta, or lead to conflict between developers and neighbourhood associations, resulting in policy deadlock, as in Los Angeles. Early literature on the politics of urban development in Toronto suggests that before the late 1960s, the former situation existed (though not necessarily in the form of a regime), as pro-growth forces clearly dominated city council. Urban development politics in the city then shifted, becoming more conflictual in nature. However, neither conception of actors' relationships and behaviour captures that of the political actors in Toronto during the seven years this analysis focuses on.

The most important factor altering the politics of urban development in Toronto is the existence of the Ontario Municipal Board. The board's role as final decision-maker on planning issues is pivotal to understanding urban development politics in the city. However, it is not sufficient in accounting for actors' behaviour. The conflictual nature of board hearings and the board's focus on expert testimony substantially shape the behaviour of developers, neighbourhood associations, and local politicians. In addition, these two factors highlight the integral role planning experts and expert testimony plays in shaping not only the built form of the city but the behaviour and relationships of political actors. The board's main role in the politics of urban development is to shift resources among actors.

The Role of Planning Experts in Toronto

The first of four questions I posed asks whether *the existence of the OMB affects the role of Toronto's planning community in the politics of urban development*. Given that most LPE literature does not address the role that planning experts or the entire planning community play in the politics of urban development, a conclusive answer to this question is impossible. However, planning experts clearly are important actors in urban development politics in Toronto. The court-like, conflictual atmosphere of OMB hearings results in the "contest among duelling experts" of which Bowman (2001, 3) speaks. The OMB bases its decisions on which expert's testimony it prefers, and will even chastise planning experts when it feels their work is substandard. Thus, the strength and quality of expert testimony and research plays a substantial role in determining the outcome of OMB hearings. This fact places significant pressure on planning experts, but also plays an important role in shaping their influence on policy decision making in the city.

The board's focus on planning experts and the strength of their evidence affects parties to OMB hearings in two ways. First, it requires all parties to hire their own planning experts if they are to have any chance of winning. This fact hurts neighbourhood associations and lone citizens who cannot afford the same expertise available to the City and developers. Second, it provides the City's planning experts with an advantage over private-sector planners. Because the City's planning experts act in an advisory role to city council, the sentiments of non-experts, including local politicians and the public, influence them to a lesser degree than private-sector planning experts. Private-sector experts are retained, in theory, to defend the position of their clients. Thus, they must try to limit their judgment of a specific proposal to a position supportive of or at least neutral to those who hire them. In theory, City Planning's advice to city council precedes council's involvement in the process. While some councillors, like former councillor Michael Walker, clearly establish their opinion before planning advises council, just as often the developers approach planning before apprising local politicians or residents of their intent. As a result, local politicians and residents have fewer opportunities to influence the City's planning experts, in contrast to the private-sector planners developers may retain. It is the latter planning experts who have the most direct influence on city planners, and it is through planning rationale that they try to influence City Planning's position. The City's planning experts have more autonomy than their private-sector counterparts. They are better able to base their position and advice to city council on their own assessment of the planning rationale for a project, in contrast to private-sector planning experts, whose position is largely influenced by that of their employers. As a result, private-sector experts often provide weaker evidence than City Planning, or eventually yield to the opinion of City Planning, as in the One Sherway case.

As Smith (interview 2008) and Rae (interview 2008) note, despite the advantage the City's planning experts enjoy at the OMB, their limited experience in comparison to private-sector planning experts and excessive workloads often undermine their influence on the board. The board has chastised the City's planning experts on some occasions as a result. However, the advantage City Planning has at the board is not insignificant, and is largely responsible for the influence of planning experts on actors' behaviour during the application process. The OMB provides City Planning with the resource of legitimacy and, at least, the appearance of increased autonomy. The former, in some respects, follows from the latter. The opinion of the City's planning experts is somewhat more legitimate than that of the private sector's because of their increased autonomy. It is this sense of greater legitimacy that developers especially covet. The modicum of autonomy that City Planning has, or at least the perception of such autonomy, influences the behaviour of actors involved in the politics of urban development in Toronto, as evidenced by the attention developers and local politicians pay to City Planning's opinion.

This focus on expert testimony also changes the language of development disputes. The disputes that arise between developers and neighbourhood associations relate directly to the traditional exchange value versus use value debate that informs most of the politics of urban development in the LPE literature. However, both parties to the debate must couch their position exclusively in the language of land use planning when arguing before the Ontario Municipal Board. The mastery of the language of land use planning becomes a must for any party to a hearing. As a result, even when a party to a hearing lacks its own planning expert, it will try to co-opt planning documents and the testimony of other experts to support its position before the board. Both the Minto Midtown and Four Seasons cases are good examples of this tactic, as in both instances neighbourhood associations tried to use the testimony and research of others to support their position. That they failed is largely indicative of their lack of mastery of the language of land use planning, and only serves to reinforce the importance of planning experts, who speak the language fluently.

That the LPE literature omits planning experts from its discussion of urban development politics is an unfortunate error. Although such experts in other jurisdictions may not enjoy the same influence that the planning experts in Toronto enjoy, there is enough variation among planning institutions in North America to suggest that planning experts and the greater planning community may play a significant role in the politics of urban development in jurisdictions beyond Ontario. Leo's (1998) case study of growth management in Portland, Oregon, demonstrates one such instance, where a variety of institutions (Metro Portland, the LCDC, the LUBA) serve to direct urban planning in a very different direction than in other American cities. Both the LCDC and LUBA, in particular, draw heavily on the type of planning expertise the OMB demands when rendering a decision. Such variations could result in significant differences in the unfolding of urban development politics in other North American cities that could challenge some of the LPE theories.

Clearly, when assessing cases like Toronto and Portland, it is necessary for analysts to be cognizant of the place of planning experts in the politics of urban development and to understand the language of land use planning. Even where institutions like the OMB or LUBA are absent, an understanding of both the role of experts and of land use planning can only add depth to the analysis of urban development politics. The LPE approach to studying urban politics can adjust to accommodate variation in planning institutions and the role of planning experts, as well as variations among the other factors that shape actors' behaviour, so long as scholars broaden their scope of analysis.

Developers and the City

My second question asks whether *the existence of the OMB affects the behaviour of developers in Toronto*, as the OMB erodes the right of local politicians to make authoritative decisions on planning issues. Developers in Toronto continue to engage with and attempt to influence the city's local politicians, much as they do in LPE literature. Their contributions to election campaigns testify to this fact. In addition, developers actively lobbied city councillors in at least two of the cases I examined: Minto Midtown and 100 Yorkville. In the latter instance, the developer's solicitor sent a lengthy letter to Mayor Lastman and council providing details of the proposal and its purported benefits to the neighbourhood and city (Diamond 2003).

However, in many of the cases, the developers focused most of their effort on winning the support of City Planning. In the Aldergreen

Estates case, the developer engaged with both Councillor Rae and local residents, but expended most of its energy on ensuring that its development proposal adhered to most of City Planning's guidelines. The developer did the same in the Pulse case, where it engaged local residents, but focused most of its effort on assuaging the criticism of City Planning, and in the Lowe's case. Developers' behaviour in Toronto is distinct from the behaviour the LPE literature portrays. The existence of the OMB, and its processes, particularly its focus on expertise, explains this divergence from the LPE theories. However, the divergence is not as great as one might expect. Developers in Toronto are not merely by-passing council in favour of the board.

What authority council still has over planning remains an important resource, even if the presence of the board erodes its practical use in comparison to other jurisdictions beyond Ontario. After all, developers incur costs whenever they appeal a decision to the board: first, the cost of the hearing itself, and second, the cost in terms of lost time before the developer can break ground and begin construction. Given these costs, developers still benefit from having the support of city council, especially when other actors, such as neighbourhood associations, are not actively opposed to the development. Without opposition from residents, developers can begin development once council signs off on the proposal. That the majority of appeals from developers arise from council's neglect to render a decision is evidence of developers' attempts to expedite the process of decision making, not avoid city council altogether. That the majority of OMB appeals resulting from neglect result in settlements also attests to this fact.

From 2003 through 2005, developers applied for 320 official plan amendments or zoning by-law amendments (City Planning 2005, 2004). Of these, 131 resulted in appeals (41 per cent). However, developers and city council opposed one another only forty-two times in front of the board, or in 32 per cent of all appeals from 2003 through 2005.[1] Thus, of the 320 applications for OPAs and ZBLAs, developers and the City were able to negotiate a settlement among themselves 87 per cent of the time. Developers do not rely solely on the OMB to render decisions in their favour, or try to avoid council altogether. If the board's influence on developers was confined to its role as decision-maker, this evidence suggests such a role would have minimal effect on Toronto's development industry, as local politicians would retain much of their importance. However, the board's power of decision making alone does not account for its effect on developers in Toronto. The OMB's focus on expertise significantly alters the strategy and behaviour of developers in the city.

As evidenced in the Aldergreen Estates, Pulse, and One Sherway cases, developers will shape their development proposals to conform to City Planning's desires, even if city council, neighbourhood associations, or individuals oppose the development, because the support of City Planning almost assures a victory at the OMB. Although developers will still appeal council decisions to the board when City Planning is opposed to development, settlements and decisions favouring developers are more likely with City Planning's approval. The OMB provides City Planning with an important resource, legitimacy, which developers covet whether they appeal to the board or not. When neighbourhood associations or residents are not opposed to a development, winning the support of City Planning almost assures the support of city council as well, as the latter will devolve decision making to its planning experts. Thus, the OMB shifts much of developers' focus away from local politicians and towards City Planning.

As Paton (2008) suggests, developers in Toronto adopt a "multi-front operation" when seeking approval for a development proposal. Unlike developers in the LPE literature, developers in Toronto place most of their focus on City Planning, not local politicians. However, the OMB does not remove all the benefits of lobbying city council. For instance, if developers fail to persuade City Planning of the merits of a proposal, they can still seek city council approval. After all, City Planning cannot appeal the decision of council. In addition, if council approves the development despite opposition from neighbourhood associations and City Planning, the City will not send either planning experts or counsel in opposition to the development (and may even send individuals in support, as in the Minto Midtown case). If no opposition exists or if neighbourhood associations align with the developer and city council, a developer can avoid an appeal regardless of City Planning's position on a development. The motives and interests of developers in Toronto are, thus, the same as the LPE literature depicts. However, by redistributing resources among planning experts and local politicians, the OMB alters the behaviour of developers, and provides them with other avenues to pursue development in the city.

Toronto's Middle-Class Neighbourhood Associations

The OMB affords developers multiple avenues to pursue their goal of development beyond lobbying local politicians. Many of these

avenues, including appealing to the board, are available to neighbourhood associations as well in their attempt to protect the integrity of
their communities. As Rose (1972) suggests, in the late 1960s and early
1970s, neighbourhood associations in Toronto used the OMB successfully to counter the city's developers and a council supportive of them.
Thus, the OMB may influence the behaviour of neighbourhood associations much as it does that of developers. However, developers' main
resource, wealth, is integral to their use of the board, as OMB hearings
can be expensive. If the cost and length of an OMB hearing is a hin-
drance to many developers, then they are prohibitive in many ways
for Toronto's neighbourhood associations. Despite their affluence, the
cost of hiring planning experts and lawyers, a necessity for success at
the OMB, can make participating in a hearing difficult. That neighbourhood associations have an additional means to challenge developers,
but may lack the resources necessary to use it successfully, complicates
matters when considering their behaviour. My third question considers
this ambiguity and asks whether *the existence of the OMB affects the behaviour of neighbourhood associations in Toronto.*

In many respects, the behaviour of neighbourhood associations in
Toronto is prototypical of the behaviour expected in the LPE literature, particularly as expressed by the likes of Purcell (1997, 2000) and
DeLeon and Powell (1989). Opponents of Minto Midtown, the Four
Seasons, 100 Yorkville, and One Sherway all lobbied local politicians
heavily, with varying success, to prevent the realization of these proposals. Their main tactic was to mobilize as many residents as possible
to attend community and city council meetings in opposition. Based on
such accounts of neighbourhood associations' behaviour, the OMB has
little effect on them. Where it does affect them, it only strengthens their
dependence on local politicians, as these groups require city council's
support and resources to oppose developers at the OMB. However, in
two of these cases, 100 Yorkville and Four Seasons, the neighbourhood
associations (largely the same in each case) turned to the OMB when
their bid to influence city council failed. Opponents of Minto Midtown
also continued to oppose the development at the OMB hearing despite
the City and developer having reached a settlement. That they failed in
each case is indicative of their inability to wield sufficient expertise at
the hearing or a lack of mastery of the language of land use planning.
However, they maintained their opposition despite the odds against
them. In addition, particularly in the 100 Yorkville case, the neighbourhood associations attempted to use the threat of a hearing to win concessions from the developer and City. That neighbourhood associations

can threaten to prolong the length and cost of an appeal before a developer can begin construction on a development is an important resource that would otherwise be unavailable to such groups without the existence of the OMB. Thus, the board does influence the behaviour and resources of neighbourhood associations to a limited extent.

The board also has some influence on neighbourhood associations' perception of and behaviour towards City Planning. However, their focus on City Planning is not as great as the developers'. This fact suggests that the board's focus on planning expertise has less of an influence on neighbourhood associations' behaviour than it has on developers'. Only in the Minto Midtown case did neighbourhood associations appear explicitly to be seeking the support of the City's planning experts. However, that neighbourhood associations in the Four Seasons, 100 Yorkville, Pulse, and Bloor & Mill cases all worked with both the developer and City Planning, at least initially, suggests their awareness of the importance of planning expertise. That the neighbourhood associations often ended at odds with City Planning suggests intractability on their part, as opposed to developers' willingness to compromise with city planners. Because of this intractability, and neighbourhood associations' relative lack of resources, the OMB's presence does not provide them with as many opportunities to affect policy decisions as it does developers. However, they still enjoy more than their counterparts in other jurisdictions do.

In addition, the case studies in the previous four chapters suggest that the LPE literature's portrayal of neighbourhood associations may be overly simplistic regardless of the OMB's existence. Early in the 100 Yorkville case, one of the neighbourhood associations, though attempting to protect the interests of its residents, had agreed to a proposal for the site after extensive dialogue with the developers, ward councillor, and City Planning. Only after other associations began voicing their dissent did the neighbourhood association in question begin to oppose the development. In the Bloor & Mill case, the neighbourhood association never opposed the development, seeking solely to have input on its design and construction. Likewise, the neighbourhood association in the Pulse case conceded to the developer once the latter had addressed a number of the residents' concerns. In these instances, the neighbourhood associations were not solely interested in opposing development, as authors such as Downs (1981) and Mesch and Schwirian (1996) portray them. Rather, the associations in each case sought to maintain involvement in the process and in the dialogue with the developer, both to ensure that the developer and City Planning were aware of residents' opinions and concerns and to establish the associations' legitimacy with the broader public. These findings suggest that the LPE literature defines the interests of neighbourhood associations too narrowly.

City Councillors' Role in the Politics of Urban Development

Local politicians still play an important role in the politics of urban development in Toronto. Although the OMB erodes their power, it does not completely remove councillors' authority over planning, their main resource. Local politicians' support can be an asset to both developers and neighbourhood associations. For the former, the support of city council can expedite the application process, and in instances where other actors appeal council's decision, its support ensures the City will be absent at OMB hearings or present in a supporting role to the developer. For neighbourhood associations, winning the support of local politicians is pivotal if they wish to oppose developers at the OMB. Without the support of council, neighbourhood associations must fight with limited resources against the City (and often City Planning) and wealthy developers.

Despite their continued relevance to the politics of urban development, however, many participants in the politics of urban development in Toronto, and scholars familiar with the city, suggest the city's politicians use the existence of the OMB to avoid making difficult decision on planning issues. Based on this belief, my fourth question asks whether *the existence of the OMB affects local politicians' decision making and behaviour towards other actors.* After all, the OMB, not local politicians, will invariably bear the responsibility for a planning decision, if an actor appeals city council's decision (or its failure to make one). Kantor's (with David 1988) discussion of the "explosive dilemma" facing American cities, and the depiction of urban development politics in cities such as Los Angeles and San Francisco, suggest local politicians must adhere to the demands of either developers or neighbourhood associations, which effectively forces them to make a choice between funding for their campaigns and economic growth, and the support of the electorate. The OMB's role and influence in the politics of urban development in Toronto may allow the city's politicians to avoid such decisions altogether.

The One Sherway case, and to a lesser extent the Minto Midtown case, suggest that the behaviour of local politicians in Toronto deviates little from that of local politicians in other jurisdictions. Council divided almost evenly between pro-growth and anti-growth forces in One Sherway, and while the division among councillors in the Minto case was not so great, significant dissention still manifested itself. The other six cases suggest varying levels of involvement of city councillors in the development process. In the 100 Yorkville, Four Seasons, and Aldergreen Estate cases, Councillor Rae played an active role in application process, supporting the first two proposals and opposing the last. These cases suggest that some councillors do not abandon their role in urban development policy making, and will take sides on a case-by-case basis. Councillors in the remaining three cases played a far more muted role, however. In the Pulse and Bloor & Mill cases, Councillors Filion and Holyday, respectively, left neighbourhood associations and developers to negotiate among themselves. In the Lowe's case, council as a whole appears to have relied entirely on the opinion of City Planning, and then the City's top bureaucrats, when rendering its decisions.

These cases portray actively engaged local politicians in certain instances, and in others, councillors removed from the process entirely. The main distinguishing feature between the cases where local politicians engage in the planning process and those where they do not appears to be whether significant opposition to a development exists among residents. Thus, for most local politicians, development issues only become salient when neighbourhood associations actively oppose a development. This behaviour differs significantly from that which the LPE literature portrays. Kantor (1987; with David 1988), Stone (1989), Elkin (1985), and Logan and Molotch's (1987) respective theories suggest development is always a salient issue for local politicians. LPE literature in Canada argues the same. As Sancton (1983) suggests, the cleavage over development defines politics in Canadian cities.

In Toronto, the presence of the OMB lessens developers' focus on local politicians, placing it instead on City Planning. As a result, the pressure that local politicians in other North American jurisdictions endure from developers is absent or lessened, because the politicians' attention is directed elsewhere. Councillors are also aware of the important role planning expertise plays at OMB hearings, and as a result are likely to adhere to the advice of City Planning. In contrast, the pressure that neighbourhood associations opposed to development apply to local politicians is far greater. If such associations legitimately threaten the electoral support of a local politician, he or she must respond. The OMB allows them to do so without suffering any significant consequences, however. If they choose to oppose a development that would otherwise bring benefits to the city or their ward, local politicians can rely on the OMB to support it, especially if City Planning is onside with the developer. If they choose to support a development, they can do so focusing on City Planning's position on the development and the possible consequence of an OMB decision against the city, namely, the possibility that the City and residents could end up worse off if the board is left to decide. Councillors in the Minto Midtown case purportedly used such justification for their support of the development, as did councillors in the 100 Yorkville case (Deverell 2003).

Local politicians in Toronto have not vacated their role as decision-makers entirely. In fact, they have a proclivity for settling disputes over development before they result in a hearing (or at the very least a proclivity for telling the City's solicitor and planning experts to come to some sort of a resolution). Settlement is a useful means for the City to procure benefits from a developer. An OMB hearing can leave the City with nothing but the development fees (if any). The City settled with the developer in the Minto Midtown case in part to procure such benefits. The OMB allows local politicians to avoid the consequences of their decisions. However, allowing the board to render decisions in too many appeals could substantially erode what standing local politicians have with developers and neighbourhood associations. Just as the threat of an appeal is more useful to neighbourhood associations than the appeal itself, so too is the possibility of an OMB decision more useful to local politicians than actually allowing the board to render a decision. Local politicians can use the spectre of the board to justify their decisions, but avoid having the board render a decision, so as not to lose the benefits of a brokered deal with developers. In addition, by settling before the board renders its decision, council may be able to limit the overall salience of development issues to the greater voting public. Determining an individual councillor's or the entire council's stance on development in the city is difficult when many of council's decisions are predicated on avoiding OMB hearings.

The previous point leads to one of the more interesting findings concerning local politicians' behaviour. Clearly, the presence of the OMB allows local politicians significant flexibility when making decisions or in delegating decision making to City Planning. The MHA Board of Directors (2008) account of Councillor Holyday is suggestive of this flexibility. In the Bloor & Mill case, Councillor Holyday left negotiations to the neighbourhood association, developer, and City Planning.

However, in other circumstances, where Holyday felt a specific development was beneficial for his ward, he opposed the association and residents. This flexibility allows local politicians to pick and choose their battles. When they need to, they can deflect criticism and anger away from themselves and onto the board. They can also support development when they feel a proposal warrants it, so long as opposition is not concerted enough, and can vehemently oppose a proposal when they feel it politically advisable to do so. Local politicians can affect the salience of development issues, and can use the flexibility the OMB affords them to prevent such issues from permeating electoral campaigns. That developers limit their involvement in such campaigns suggests they are implicitly acquiescing to this tactic. Both past experience in the City of Toronto and the history of many other North American cities offer telling accounts of what happens when development issues permeate municipal elections. The results are often catastrophic for both developers and local politicians. Thus, the OMB provides local politicians in Toronto with a resource their counterparts in many other jurisdictions may well covet, the ability to distance themselves from planning issues.

Conflict or Cooperation?

Since the emergence of strong middle-class neighbourhood associations opposed to development, the politics of urban development in the United States has become a politics of conflict. Kantor's (with David 1998) book *The Dependent City* captures best the ramifications of their emergence, as it details the intransigence that can develop in cities when local politicians are unable to mediate between business and citizen interests. This intransigence is evidenced in cities such as Los Angeles (Purcell 1997, 2000), San Francisco (DeLeon 1992a, 1992b), Gainesville (Vogel and Swanson 1989), and Columbus, Ohio (Mesch and Schwirian 1996), where anti-growth advocates confront pro-growth coalitions in continued battles over the built form of their cities. Media accounts of the politics of urban development in Toronto suggest the same occurs there. Often, the media, local politicians, and citizens portray or conceive of the OMB as sinister, supportive of developers in opposition to the will of the public and its elected officials (see Rochon 2005; Lorinc 2007). Four of the cases I examined typify this portrayal of the politics of urban development in the city, and of the OMB's role. However, these four cases (Four Seasons, Minto Midtown, One Sherway, and 100 Yorkville) are conducive to such media portrayals precisely because of the conflict between the developers and neighbourhood associations. Thus, both these cases and the media's portrayal of the politics of urban development may not reflect the norm for political behaviour in Toronto.

The City settles disputes over planning that result in appeals 43 per cent of the time. Furthermore, neighbourhood associations were involved in less than a third (32 per cent) of the appeals requiring a board decision, and their participation does not entail their opposition in every case. While conflict between neighbourhood associations and developers and their respective allies does occur in Toronto, such conflicts are not the norm. Roughly half of all applications for OPAs and ZBLAs result in an appeal; of those, only approximately 9 per cent result in the kind of conflict typified by the four cases mentioned above.[2] Despite portrayals to the contrary, cooperation, not conflict, is the norm for actors involved in the politics of urban development in Toronto. The findings from the preceding chapters suggest the OMB may play an important role in forcing actors to negotiate with one another.

As Blazevski (interview 2008) says, no one likes to go to the OMB. The process is costly for all actors involved. OMB appeals can take from many months to years. Developers are unable to begin construction during these intervals, which can cost them significant money depending on fluctuating market conditions. For neighbourhood associations, the cost of planning experts and lawyers is often exorbitant, while the City can lose any section 37 benefits from a proposed development if the OMB decides against it. The costs and consequences of a board hearing are sufficient reasons for all parties to work towards a compromise. Whom such compromises tend to favour is debatable, but the pressure to negotiate appears to be a strong force in the politics of urban development in Toronto, and the powers and procedures of the Ontario Municipal Board appear to be the source of such pressure. Despite the existence of an active development industry and organized neighbourhood associations, the politics of urban development in Toronto is far less conflictual than LPE theories portray.

The Ontario Municipal Board and Urban Planning in Ontario

Despite the fact that the OMB seems to relieve tension over development more often than it generates it, people's perception of the board's role in planning results in debates over its very existence. Thus, any discussion of the board's role in planning in Ontario is bound to raise questions regarding the purpose of and need for the board. The aim of this analysis was not to address whether the board should exist or not. Nevertheless, my findings shed significant light on why the board persists despite significant opposition from the public. While belief in the collusion between provincial governments and developers offers an explanation to many observers, a very important factor is often overlooked in both academia and in the media when considering the purpose and existence of the OMB: the broader institutions of planning in Ontario.

Municipal governments in Ontario can easily manipulate and amend their own planning laws. Unlike many other jurisdictions in North America, there is no limit to or direct oversight over either zoning by-laws or official plan amendments in the Province of Ontario. In addition to the ease with which municipalities can amend their planning laws, section 37 of the Planning Act allows them to procure benefits from developers in exchange for permission to build beyond existing height and density restrictions. Combined, the ease of amending planning laws and the benefits of doing so ensure that municipalities in Ontario will amend their zoning by-laws and official plans, and amend them often. In fact, John Barber (2008) suggests the City of Toronto intentionally places significant height and density restrictions on sites throughout the city with the purpose of amending them so as to receive additional benefits from developers.

Regardless of such possible intent, Toronto's constant amending of its own by-laws and official plan (or plans, prior to the coming into force of the new plan) ensures a steady stream of appeals to the OMB, as the City picks and chooses among the proposals it likes and dislikes. This process of constant amendment erodes any significance the City's planning laws may have. As a result, the OMB bases its decisions entirely on its own perception of good planning. The board persists because without it there would be little rhyme or reason to planning decisions in Ontario's municipalities beyond municipal councillors' political calculations. The board effectively removes actual planning decisions from the realm of the entirely political by exalting the role of planning experts. Although local politicians in Toronto use political calculations when deciding when to support or oppose a development in many cases, their calculations are often based on the planning rationale behind a specific proposal. The board, thus, is a means to curb the decision-making authority of local politicians in Ontario.

Implications for Local Political Economy Research

A specific understanding of the relationships among individuals' interests, their resources, and the institutions and structures that constrain them informs the local political economy approach, and permeates every theory that derives from it. Authors with very distinct theoretical perspectives adopt and utilize the same approach when studying local political economy. Thus, authors such as Stone (1989), Kantor (with David 1988), and Elkin (1985) work within the same approach as authors such as Logan and Molotch (1987), Fainstein and Fainstein (1983), and Harvey (1983). All of them reject pluralist and economic determinist models or theories of urban politics. The political economy model they and other local government scholars adopt explicitly recognizes the role of both socio-economic forces and human agency in determining actors' behaviour. In all these theories, institutions, economic structure, and actors' interests play a pivotal role in determining the behaviour of political actors. In addition, academics who adopt the LPE model recognize the importance of the uneven and differing resources distributed among the different actor groups in shaping their behaviour and relation to one another, although how they perceive the distribution of resources may vary. Figure 9.1 depicts a model of the local political economy approach to the study of urban politics.

In this model, the confluence of actors' interests, their resources, institutions, and structures determines their behaviour. Each actor group involved in the politics of urban development pursues its own interest. Developers pursue profit. Local politicians seek office, and neighbourhood associations seek to protect the integrity of their communities. Each group also controls, as Dahl (1961) argues, unevenly distributed resources. Developers control wealth, local politicians authority over planning, and neighbourhood associations the ability to mobilize the electorate. The global socio-economic structure and the institutions governments impose shape actors' agency. As the diagram shows, interests, resources, institutions, and structures are interdependent.[3] For instance, socio-economic structures shape actors' interests, while institutions can shape the distribution of resources. The interests of actors can also determine what resources are valuable to respective actors, while the availability of resources to different actors can shape both the economy and institutions. The interests of actors also subtly (and sometimes not so subtly) affect the economy and institutions.

Figure 9.1. The local political economy model

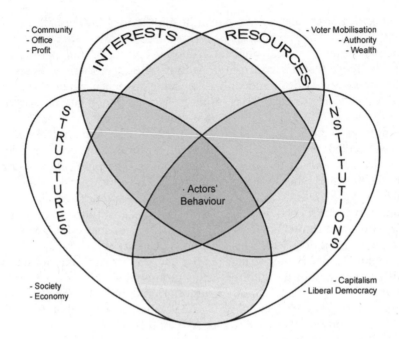

Causal relationships exist among these four factors, but at any one point in time they are set, and the confluence of these factors in time will determine the actors' behaviour. Changes in actors' behaviour represent a change in one of these factors. For instance, as both Elkin (1987) and Kantor (1987; with David 1988) note, middle-class residents in America's cities and suburbs used to be members of the growth co-alitions. However, when governments threatened their communities with new development and highways, residents' interests shifted from pro-growth to anti-growth. The shift in interests resulted in a shift in behaviour, which fundamentally altered the politics of urban develop-ment. This chain of events occurred in cities such as Los Angeles, San Francisco, and Toronto.

This approach to understanding political behaviour has significant explanatory power. This book adopts the same approach when analys-ing the role of the Ontario Municipal Board in Toronto's politics of urban

Figure 9.2. Revised local political economy model for Toronto

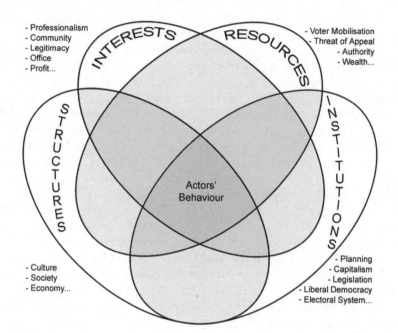

development. The findings from this analysis suggest the strength of the approach, but highlight the limits of the local political economy literature that utilizes it. Growth machine theory, urban regime theory, and their derivatives recognize the important role that all four factors play in urban politics and the politics of urban development. However, both theories adopt narrow conceptions of the content of each factor. While literature on neighbourhood associations recognizes a change in actors' interests, it assumes that resource distribution and institutions remain unchanged. It makes such assumptions despite the fact that, for example, the creation of urban growth boundaries in some American cities significantly influenced patterns of urban development, and presumably the politics of urban development (for example, in Portland, Oregon; see Liberty 1998). Thus, changes in institutions also play a role. The local political economy in North America is more dynamic than most theories suggests.

Kantor (1987; with David 1988) is one of the few authors to recognize the dynamic nature of local political economies. However, he fails, as do most scholars of local political economy, to account for the low-level institutional differences across jurisdictions that influence and shape urban politics, such that they can deviate from place to place. Frug and Barron (2008) recognize their importance, but do not address their influence in local political economy. The failure of growth machine theory, urban regime theory, and other theories drawing on the LPE approach to account for the politics of urban development in Toronto derives from their failure to consider additional constraints on actors and the availability of additional resources to some actors. Figure 9.2 broadens the content of these factors within the LPE model to include variables pertinent to this analysis of Toronto. In fact, the content of each factor may well be infinite. Scholars of urban politics, LPE, and the politics of urban development should expand their research to address the content of each factor, and search for additional variables within each that may account for further variation in actors' behaviour. In addition, scholars must examine all relevant actors. The findings of this analysis suggest that differences in planning institutions can have a significant effect on actors' behaviour. However, the existence of the OMB does not affect such behaviour solely by further constraining actors' agency. The board also alters the distribution of resources among actors.

The OMB erodes local politicians' authority over decision making, though it does not remove it entirely, and provides local politicians with flexibility in decision making. In addition, it provides both neighbourhood associations and developers with an additional resource, the threat of an appeal to the OMB. Most important, the board's focus on planning expertise provides City Planning with the resource of increased autonomy and, subsequently, increased legitimacy. Indeed, the role and influence of all planning experts in the city increases because of their mastery of the language of land use planning. Understanding the politics of urban development in Toronto requires understanding the content of the interests, resources, institutions, and structures that shape political behaviour in the city. Growth machine and urban regime theories have limited applications in comparative analysis; however, the LPE approach to urban politics that underlies them both provides a powerful means for cross-city and cross-jurisdiction comparison, so long as scholars can account for the variations in actors' interests, resources, institutions, and structures, and do not define each factor too narrowly.

Appendix A
Studying Local Political Economy

Tom Keefe, Toronto's current director of community planning, Etobicoke York District, discussed the ambiguous nature of OMB rulings during an interview I conducted for this analysis. This ambiguity arises when one tries to establish who won the hearing. To illustrate this ambiguity, Keefe recounted an anecdote from one of the City's lawyers concerning an appeal won by a developer. Despite the fact the developer had won its appeal of city council's refusal to amend the planning law, the City's lawyer felt the City had won a favourable decision from the board. Although the OMB allowed the appeal, it significantly curtailed the height of the proposed development. City Planning's central reason for recommending refusal of the developer's application was the development's excessive height. Thus, the board had actually supported the position of city staff (Keefe interview 2008). Despite technically favouring the developer in its appeal, the OMB actually sided with the City's planning experts.

The ambiguousness of OMB decisions makes studying the board and its role in the politics of urban development very difficult. However, this ambiguity in many cases is largely reflective of the board's powers and the relative ease with which municipalities in Ontario can manipulate their own planning laws. Thus, despite the difficulties this ambiguity presents for studying the OMB and the politics of urban development in Toronto, navigating and integrating the nuances and scope of the board's decisions is necessary for any analysis.

The methods of evidence gathering and analysis I adopted when conducting my research largely reflect an attempt to capture the richness of the board's decisions, the nature of the appeals process, and the politics of urban development in Toronto as a whole. To achieve this goal,

I utilize multiple methods of evidence gathering and analysis, what Dahl (1961) would call "an eclectic approach ... adopted deliberately, not only to avoid putting all our eggs in one methodological basket but also to take advantage of the existence of a very wide assortment of data" (330–1). This appendix outlines the quantitative and qualitative methods of analysis I used when conducting my research for this book, and provides an in-depth account of the methods I used to gather and handle evidence and data for the analysis. In selecting certain methods and approaches over others, I tried to avoid some of the pitfalls of the different methods common to the LPE literature, while drawing on their strengths.

Methods of Analysis in Local Political Economy Literature

The single-city study is probably the most common method of analysis in LPE literature. By focusing on a historical account of politics in one city, authors are able to provide a rich, in-depth, account of political behaviour. Such works often provide very compelling evidence for a specific theory. In addition, these city studies usually involve implicit or indirect comparisons to other cities, helping to place the specific city in context. Elkin's (1987) study of Dallas is a good example, as he often contrasts the city with other American cities like Chicago and Philadelphia. The main limitation of this approach is the level of context involved in such an analysis. While an accumulation of single-city studies can provide the strongest evidence for a given theory, theories rarely survive intact through each study as authors attempt to fit a theory to their specific case. Mossberger and Stoker (2001) suggest that such is the case with urban regime theory. Theories or concepts based largely on a single case may be limited by the context of that case.[1]

Authors using the second approach to local political economy analysis use multiple cases or examples to illustrate the strength of their theory. This approach is not strictly comparative, as the author does not directly compare and contrast his or her examples. Each case is evidence supporting the theory or concept the author proposes. Logan and Molotch (1987) built their growth machine theory through this process. Such an approach or method of analysis avoids the trap of context. Examples drawn from different cities help establish the explanatory power of a theory. Unfortunately, a single limited account from a city's history may not reflect political behaviour in the city as a whole. Sanders and Stone's (1987) critique of Peterson's (1981) *City Limits* reflects this limitation. The two authors, in reviewing Peterson's account of New Haven and Oakland, focus on the supposed consensus for redevelopment policies in the two cities. The two authors argue that Peterson's account fails as it focuses solely on the "preexecution promotion" of redevelopment, rather than the entire redevelopment process, which was far more conflictual (Sanders and Stone 1987, 524). A graver problem with this method is the lack of contrast with divergent cases. There is potential for significant selection bias when using such a method, as scholars look for specific examples to support their theory or concept.

Lastly, comparative urban political research, as Denters and Mossberger (2006, 551) refer to it, is developing increasing prominence in the study of local political economy. Unlike the other two methods of analysis, this method is explicitly comparative. Literature utilizing the comparative method compares and contrasts cities in different jurisdictions with different institutional constraints. Savitch and Kantor (2002) and Sellers (2002) both use the method to test whether cities are growing more powerful and whether city politics in North America and Europe are diverging or converging due to globalization. This approach can provide a stronger test of a theory, as the authors employ multiple divergent cases in their analysis. However, the resulting depiction of the cities can often be a caricature of reality. Limited space and resources can minimize the number of sources or observations an author can collect for each city, which can result in a misleading representation of a city. If the depiction of the city is misleading, then so are the author's findings.

Analysing the OMB and Political Behaviour in Toronto

As with Dahl's (1961) *Who Governs?*, I have used an eclectic mix of methods of analysis. For instance, I used demographic information for Toronto's neighbourhoods and created a map plotting OMB cases to investigate the make-up of the city's neighbourhood associations. To establish developers' attitudes towards local politicians, I examined the amount of campaign contributions emanating from developers in the city. The majority of my work relies on two methods of analysis, however. For my analysis of general trends in OMB appeals and decisions from 2000 through 2006, I utilized quantitative methods. While this quantitative analysis offered a strong account of trends in actors' behaviour during the OMB appeals process, it offered limited explanation accounting for this behaviour. Nevertheless, my findings from these data provided a useful background for the remainder of my analysis. For that, I adopted the multiple-case-study approach as my method. I conducted eight in-depth case studies of development proposals in the city. I then compared and contrasted my findings from these cases, the behaviour of Toronto's political actors, against the behaviour typified in American LPE literature.

This study is city-specific. However, it does not employ a historical account of political behaviour in the city. Because the role or perception of the OMB appears to have changed since the late 1960s, a historical account would not necessarily capture the politics of urban development in the city today. An analysis of why the board's role changed would be interesting in and of itself; however, why the board's role may have changed was not the focus of my research. I also focused on a specific period in time, 2000 through 2006, to avoid any complications for analysis arising from the amalgamation of Metro Toronto in 1998 and the coming into force of significant changes to the Planning Act in 2007. From 2000 through 2006, the board's role and people's perception of the board deviated little, and the board played a substantive and direct role in influencing the shape of development in Toronto and, possibly, the politics of urban development. Whether the board's role has changed over the decades is of less importance than whether the existence of such a planning institution in Ontario and Toronto affects how the politics of urban development unfolds in the city. Limiting the scope of analysis allows for a more in-depth analysis over a period of time (seven years) where other elements remain the same. Focusing too heavily on the past would limit the analysis of the present. As for the limits of a single-city study, I did not set forth to generate a new theory of political behaviour or political economy for application in other cities (though I do suggest a framework for such analysis). Rather, along with providing an updated account of the politics of urban development in Toronto, I attempted to address a potential problem in LPE literature: the failure to account for different planning institutions when studying urban development politics.

Focusing on multiple case studies within the same city avoids some of the pitfalls of cross-city comparison as well. Focusing on one city allows for an in-depth and accurate portrayal of actors' behaviour across cases, as each case shares a similar context. Moving down a level of analysis from city to within-city cases and limiting the scope of analysis to a seven-year period result in simpler cases. Socio-economic structure and institutions remain the same through each case, allowing for the focused analysis of political behaviour. This method of analysis helps avoid misrepresentation of the cases. In addition, I did not select the cases based on their ability to prove or disprove a theory, thus avoiding selection bias.

This work does not focus on direct comparison between Toronto and other cities (though such comparisons are used throughout for illustrative purposes). Rather, the eight case studies compare the behaviour of certain groups of political actors in Toronto against their typical portrayal in literature using the local political economy approach. I articulated throughout the preceding chapters what this portrayal of behaviour and relationship between actor groups would entail in Toronto due to the influence of the OMB. The eight case studies primarily function as "tests" of this portrayal, and as a means to answer the four questions I introduced in the first chapter.

Compiling Data on OMB Appeals

Neither the City of Toronto nor the Ontario Municipal Board has an authoritative list of OMB decisions and orders or appeals for the City of Toronto. As a result, the data set I used drew on a number of resources. The data set includes only appeals concerning official plan amendments (OPAs), zoning by-law and zoning by-law amendments (ZBLs and ZBLAs), and interim control by-laws (ICBLs). Focusing on only these four types of land use planning disputes excluded the numerous extraneous cases involving minor variances and conflicts between neighbours. While in-depth case studies provide the best means for examining the cause of actors' behaviour, they can be misrepresentative of typical behaviour if not placed in a larger context. The quantitative analysis I conducted offers this larger context, and also aided in choosing the eight individual case studies. In addition, the data offer a means for comparing people's perception of the board against its reality, especially with regard to its decision making.

Only two other studies attempt to document OMB decision making in such a manner.[2] Chipman (2002) provides very general data regarding OMB decisions for the entire province during three periods: 1971–8, 1987–94, and 1995–2000. Each of the periods he addresses provide fairly limited snapshots of which actors the OMB decisions favour. Furthermore, Chipman does not provide a thorough explanation of how he compiled and coded his own data. In particular, he does not explain how he determined which actors the OMB favoured in its decisions.

This fact limits any attempt to replicate and extend his data set. The greater geographic scope of his study and the issue of replicability limit potential comparison between his findings and my findings in this study.[3]

Planning staff at the City of Toronto compiled the other data set. They surveyed OMB decisions from 1999 to 2001 in preparation for a report recommending changes to the OMB's appeals process (Commissioner of Urban Development Services 2002). As with the data set I compiled for this study, city staff focused their effort specifically on OMB appeals regarding OPAs, ZBLAs, and ICBLs.[4] However, the report does not distinguish between appeals made by developers versus appeals made against council's approval of a development. This fact limits the value of the study, as it is impossible to determine whether the City was acting with or against developers at a hearing. The staff report distinguishes between appeals of council decisions and appeals resulting from the failure of city council to render a decision within the ninety-day time frame required (appeals due to neglect).

While the City's report is interesting, it does not indicate how city staff gathered the data they based the report on, nor, as in the case of Chipman, how city staff determined who won an OMB appeal. This lack of explanation proved particularly problematic, as city staff's data for 2000 and 2001 do not correspond perfectly with the data for the same years in the data set I compiled.[5] Significant differences exist between the number of decisions in favour of and against the City, as well as the number of settlements. Table A.1 reflects the data from the staff report for 2000 and 2001, while Table A.2 provides data for the same years drawn from my own data set: In comparison to the City's data, the data set I compiled undercounts the number of decisions on appeals due to neglect (appeals of applications under the ninety days), and over-counts appeals of council's decision. In addition, my data suggest the City fares poorer overall than planning staff's report suggests.

The discrepancies between the two studies could bias quantitative analysis if they represent errors in the data set used for this analysis. However, Tom Keefe, who was responsible for planning staff's report at the time, noted that the tools available to the City when staff compiled the report were limited, and as a result he could not vouch for the report's accuracy. Keefe also emphasized that the report was conducted to provide city staff with a sense of the number of applications and appeals progressing to OMB hearings, as no one at the City had kept track since amalgamation (Keefe interview 2008). The report was

Table A.1. City's data on OMB decisions (from Commissioner 2002)

	2000	2001	Total
Number of OMB decisions on council enacted by-laws	10	15	25
Number of decisions won by the City	8	15	23
Number of decisions lost by the City	2	0	2
Number of OMB decisions on appeals of applications under the 90 days	21	29	50
Number of OMB decisions of 90-day appeals won by the City	5	4	9
Number of OMB decisions of 90-day appeals lost by the City	5	10	15
Number of OMB decisions of 90-day appeals that were settlements	11	15	26

not an in-depth audit of OMB appeals and hearings. Indeed, the staff report, itself, refers to the study as a "general cursory review" of OMB decisions and appeals (Commissioner 2002, 2). In addition, Keefe emphasized the convoluted nature of OMB decisions, as his earlier anecdote highlights, and thus the resulting difficulty in categorizing them. The cursory nature of the City's report and the difficulty city staff faced when coding their data suggest the data I compiled for this study are stronger.

City staff's experience in compiling and coding data on OMB decisions is somewhat reflective of the problems I encountered when compiling the data set for this analysis. Neither the Ontario Municipal Board nor the City keeps a definitive list of OMB decisions. The lists I used to compile this data set included a list of appeals provided by the board and yearly lists of the City's planning lawyers' case assignments.[6] Neither of these sources proved definitive. Searching through OMB decisions on LexisNexis revealed a number of cases missing from the OMB's list. Thus, while I made every attempt to be exhaustive in compiling the data set, some cases (though likely only a few) may be missing.

Table A.2. Data used in this analysis

	2000	2001	Total
Number of OMB decisions on appeals of council decisions*	13	26	29
Number of decisions won by the City	2	10	12
Number of decisions lost by the City	3	8	11
Number of OMB decisions on appeals of applications under the 90 days*	11	10	21
Number of OMB decisions of 90-day appeals won by the City	2	0	2
Number of OMB decisions of 90-day appeals lost by the City	1	6	7
Number of OMB decisions of 90-day appeals that were settlements	8	4	12

*Excludes cases where the outcome is unknown (four in total).

I removed from the data set appeals filed before the 1998 merger of Metro Toronto but decided in 2000 or later,[7] and decisions made after 2006 (the end date of this analysis). I removed an additional twenty-eight cases because, while technically involving an OPA, ZBLA, or ICBL, they did not involve significant development or the development industry. For instance, a number of appeals involved city council's refusal to allow conversion of existing rental apartments into condominiums. The final data set, therefore, comprises 328 cases. Cases were categorized into over eight variables, following a thorough examination of OMB decisions, city staff reports, and decisions on development applications.

Coding the data proved difficult, even with readily available OMB decisions, city staff reports, and City decisions. First, as Keefe's (2008) anecdote suggests, determining whom an OMB decision actually favours is not a simple task. A number of problems emerged early in the process of coding. As a result, and to avoid possibly misclassifying or biasing the results of the data, the data set employs ten possible outcomes of OMB appeals, including withdrawals and settlements. The categories include:

1 Decisions favouring only the developer
2 Decisions favouring only the City
3 Decisions favouring the City and developer
4 Decisions favouring neighbourhood associations
5 Decisions favouring neighbourhood associations and the City
6 Decisions favouring neighbourhood associations and developer
7 Decisions favouring other actors (other businesses and individual citizens)
8 Ambiguous decisions
9 Appeals withdrawn before a hearing
10 Appeals settled before a hearing

Another problem with coding emerged from the classification of developers. Developers usually incorporate new entities for every new development project.[8] While some developers, like Menkes or Minto, include their name within the name of the newly incorporated entity (for example, Menkes Lakeshore Ltd. and Minto YE Inc.), many developers simply create numbered corporations. This fact made categorizing the type of developer difficult. In addition, determining who the developers were in instances where they withdrew their appeal to the OMB proved impossible in many instances, particularly before 2002. While the OMB lists a case when withdrawn, before 2002 the board did not provide any additional information regarding the address of the proposed development or the developer. The board's online database does provide some information after 2002, but, in total, seventy-nine of the cases lacked this information. I categorized these cases as unknown. Though data are missing for seventy-nine cases, the distribution of unknown cases rarely deviates from the overall average of all cases.

Initially, the data set included nine categories of developers. However, due to insufficient data in some instances, the nine categories became six. The categories focus on the geographic distribution[9] of the developer and include:

1 Developers located in and focused exclusively on the City of Toronto (local)
2 Developers based in Ontario, operating in either the entire province or the GTA (city region)
3 Small-time developers
4 Trans-national, continental, national, and foreign developers (extra-regional)[10]

5 Unknown developers
6 Finally, a category for appeals against City by-laws that lack a particular developer

In addition to these two variables (OMB decisions and developer type), the data set includes six other variables. The first variable categorizes the reason for an appeal to the OMB (council's rejection, council's approval, council's neglect, and unknown). The second focuses on who appealed to the OMB (developer, neighbourhood association, other citizens, other corporations, multiple appellants including developers, and multiple appellants excluding developers). The third categorizes neighbourhood association involvement or activity in each case (i.e., whether an association was involved in an appeal or not).[11] The fourth variable categorizes city planners' opinions regarding a specific development proposal (outright support, hesitant support, provisional rejection, outright rejection, and unknown).[12] The fifth focuses on the type of development (residential, office, mixed-use residential, other, and appeals that do not involve a specific development). And the final variable considers whether the OMB cited expert opinion in its decision/order or not.

Coding the data for the above six variables was less difficult than for the first two. However, cases withdrawn before an OMB hearing still proved problematic, particularly before 2002. I could not code thirty pre-2002 cases. No record exists of whether the appellant(s) withdrew the appeals or not. As a result, I did not code them as withdrawn under the OMB decision variable, even though they likely are withdrawn appeals, as the board provides information for all other appeals during this period. The thirty cases are coded as "missing." In an additional twenty or so cases limited information was available. For example, in some instances, it was impossible to determine whether they were withdrawn, the type of developer and type of development involved, and city planners' opinion.

Chart A.1 shows the number of valid and missing cases for each variable. Given the issues with coding and missing data, my data set is in no way a perfect reflection of OMB appeals in Toronto. Nevertheless, there is no other data set as comprehensive, and, regardless of its limitations, it is still a very useful tool of analysis. Beyond providing a broad sense of the OMB and the four actor groups' roles and participation in development and planning, my analysis of the data highlighted the most relevant variables for further exploration in the eight case studies.

Chart A.1. Valid and missing cases by category

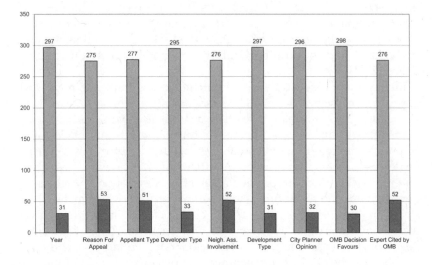

Case Selection, Resources, and Comparison

The primary purpose of the eight case studies is to provide an account of
actors' behaviour for comparison with typical actor behaviour in American local political economy literature. Each chapter from 5 through 8
addresses one of the questions posed in chapter 3. The context of each
case is the same; they take place in Toronto, and exist within an institutional structure where the OMB has the final say on planning disputes.

Chapters 5 through 8 each focus on two case studies useful for examining the behaviour and role of the four actor groups involved in the
politics of urban development in Toronto. These chapters provide in-
depth depictions of actors' behaviour and relationship with each other,
whereas the quantitative analysis in chapter 4 provides a more general
account. Obviously, two cases cannot provide a definitive sense of the
role and behaviour of these actors in the politics of urban development.
However, by examining one major case involving significant media attention and one minor case in each chapter, these studies offer a glimpse
of actors' behaviour both in instances of significant high-stakes conflict and everyday planning disputes. As such, they should capture the
range of behaviour of the four actor groups. In addition, while the focus

of each chapter is on a specific actor group, each actor, except for neighbourhood associations, is actively involved in every case, and thus all eight cases offer some evidence pertaining to all four actors' behaviour. Chapter 9 synthesizes the findings of all eight cases, the data analysis of chapter 4, and any additional information and insights from chapters 5 through 8.

Ideally, these case studies would include cases resulting in an OMB appeal and those that did not. However, finding extensive data recounting actors' behaviour for cases that did not involve appeals proved very difficult. Instead, in order to capture more typical development scenarios, the cases include some appeals arising from city council's neglect and others that resulted in settlement. The case analysis draws on multiple resources to provide a narrative description of each case's development and to capture actors' behaviour. The richest material derives from the OMB archives on each case. Included in the file archives were communications between the various actors (city councillors, neighbourhood associations, and developers), their lawyers, and often members of the OMB. These communications offered some of the best accounts of actors' behaviour and relationship with other actors. Other important materials in the archives include written submissions to the board from neighbourhood associations and individual citizens.

OMB decisions were another important source of information. Some provide detailed accounts of the cases. In addition, they indicate the board's reasoning for a decision, and its attitude towards different actors and experts. Staff reports from City Planning and minutes from community and city council meetings – conveniently available online in most cases – offered insight into the thoughts of planning experts and local politicians. The latter is important because the OMB material rarely includes politicians' reasoning for their decisions in its account or archives. In addition to these sources, the case analyses draw on media accounts, newsletter accounts of discussions between a neighbourhood association and developer, and interviews I conducted between May and August 2008 and in February 2009.

Interviews

In total, I conducted seven interviews for this analysis. The interviewees include two City councillors (now both retired), Michael Walker and Kyle Rae; former vice-president of Urban Development and Planning for MintoUrban, Bob Blazevski; the aforementioned Tom Keefe, director of community planning, Etobicoke York (formerly North York)

District; John Paton, director of planning and administrative tribunal law for the City of Toronto; Peter Smith, private-sector land use planner and partner at Bousfields Inc.; and the board of directors of the Markland Homes Association, a neighbourhood association located in Toronto's west end.

I chose the seven interviewees for being representative of the main actor groups involved in the politics of urban development in Toronto, their significant experience in dealings with the Ontario Municipal Board, and their involvement in at least one of the eight case studies I selected for analysis. Thus, these individuals (and association) offer insight into the broader politics of urban development in the city and the role the OMB plays, as well as into specific cases otherwise unavailable from other sources.

Their representativeness as members of the actor groups central to this analysis was the primary factor driving my choice of individuals to contact for interviews. The quantitative analysis on OMB appeals I conducted shaped these choices as well, by strengthening the argument for a certain actor's inclusion. Paton, Smith, and Keefe represent the different elements of the planning community. Paton captures the insight of a City lawyer with substantive knowledge of planning law and the machinations of the OMB's appeal process. Keefe and Smith represent public- and private-sector planning experts respectively, and offer their take on the board's role in planning and the politics of urban development. Both have substantial backgrounds in planning in the city and dealing with OMB disputes.

Bob Blazevski represents the development industry, having worked at MintoUrban for many years, and was involved in one of the most controversial developments during the period of this analysis, Minto Midtown. The board of directors of Markland Homes Association (MHA) represents neighbourhood associations in Toronto. This particular association is one of the better organized groups in the city, and one of the largest in terms of membership. The MHA has always been involved in issues of planning affecting its neighbourhood, both in working against and working with local politicians, city planners, and developers. Lastly, Kyle Rae and Michael Walker not only represent local politicians in Toronto, they also reflect the two poles in the debate over development. During their ternue as city councillors, Rae was typically pro-growth, envisioning downtown Toronto as a new Manhattan, while Walker was typically anti-growth, focused on representing the interests of his constituents by protecting the integrity of their neighbourhoods. Both have significant experience dealing with controversial developments in their respective wards. Three of the case studies fall within Councillor Rae's ward, while the aforementioned Minto Midtown unfolded in Councillor Walker's ward.

In three instances, individuals arose as potential interviewees because of the regular occurrence of their names in City documents and OMB decisions as I compiled the data set for the quantitative analysis. Both councillors, along with Smith,[13] fall within this category. Keefe emerged as a key interviewee due to his coordination of city staff's report on the OMB, discussed above. His involvement in the Pulse development emerged later in my research. Keefe suggested Paton as a useful interviewee because of his position with the city (he runs the department responsible for OMB hearings) and long history of personal dealings with the board. His involvement in the Minto Midtown case emerged during my interview with him. Councillor Rae suggested Bob Blazevski when asked for potential interviewees to represent the development industry, as his specific role at Minto focused on the planning and development process. His direct involvement in the Minto Midtown case emerged during the interview. Lastly, attempts to contact some of the most prominent neighbourhood associations in Toronto initially failed. However, the limited information available from OMB records on the Bloor & Mill case made speaking with the Markland Homes Association a major priority. Fortunately, the MHA responded, or else neighbourhood associations may have remained the sole group without a direct voice in this analysis.

The interviews consisted of a set of questions regarding interviewees' perceptions of the behaviour and role of each actor group in the politics of urban development, their relationships with one another, and the role of the OMB. I asked additional questions concerning specific cases they participated in, again focusing on the relationship between different actors and their behaviour. The questions were open ended and the responses varied significantly in their focus and insights. The interviews, as a whole, provided a rich source of information for understanding both the broader picture of the politics of urban development in Toronto and the role of the OMB, as well as insight into the eight individual case studies.

Case Selection

Table A.3 provides a general overview of each of the eight case studies. The level of sustained media coverage, City Planning's opinion on the proposal, city council's initial decision or stance towards the proposal, and the neighbourhood association level of involvement were the four main variables I used for selecting the eight cases. Date and location played a secondary role, the first to ensure that the cases encompassed the entire period of my analysis, and the latter to ensure that the cases were representative of the politics of urban development in Toronto as a whole, as opposed to a specific area within the city. Aside from media exposure, the variables were chosen in large part based on the quantitative analysis of OMB appeals. While the type of developer or appellant played a limited role in determining outcomes in most appeals, City Planning's opinion, council's decision, and the involvement of neighbourhood associations emerged as important indicators of the outcome of appeals to the board, and the behaviour of each actor. The importance of the city council's or local politicians' stance on a given project proposal should be self-evident, especially in relation to city planners' opinion and the neighbourhood associations' involvement. City council's choice to support or reject a proposal (and often to support or reject the advice of city planners, or the will of neighbourhood associations) illuminates city councillors' behaviour and strategic thinking. In addition, council's decision often determines the pattern of other actors' behaviour. The appellant in each case necessarily derives from council's decision. Council's decision also reflects the interests or strategic thinking of other actors (where strategy is actually involved). The cases were selected to include both instances where council supported proposals and where it rejected them.

City planners' opinions and other actors' responses to their opinions (including the OMB) emerged as one of the best indicators of actors' relative success at the board. This fact not only reflects the relative importance of city planners, and experts in general, to the politics of urban development in the city, but highlights their central importance to the OMB process. As a result, I selected cases that ensured a variation in City Planning's stance towards the development proposals. Lastly, the involvement of neighbourhood associations in individual cases often relates to the level of conflict surrounding a specific development. Thus, the cases I selected include varying neighbourhood association involvement.

I used media exposure as a variable to determine case selection to ensure the inclusion of some of the city's most high-profile disputes over planning (Four Seasons Hotel, Minto Midtown, 100 Yorkville, and One Sherway) and instances more reflective of the regular workings of planning politics in the city (Aldergreen Estates, Pulse, Bloor & Mill, and Lowe's). Each of four chapters examines one high-profile case and one regular case to capture specific actors' behaviours in both

Table A.3. Case summary

	Chapter 5: Experts		Chapter 6: Developers		Chapter 7: Neigh. Assoc.		Chapter 8: Local Polit.	
Case name	Four Seasons Hotel	Aldergreen Estates	Minto Midtown	Pulse	100 Yorkville	Bloor & Mill	One Sherway	Lowe's
Location (former city)*	Downtown (Toronto)	Downtown (Toronto)	Midtown (Toronto)	North Centre (North York)	Downtown (Toronto)	West (Etobicoke)	South West (Etobicoke)	Midtown (York)*
Date of application	July 2005	Nov. 2004	Dec. 2000	Unknown	Apr. 2002	May 2004	July 2003	Sept. 2005
Developer type	City region & international hotelier	Small-time	Provincial	City region	Local	Small-time	City region	Continental
Development type	Hotel/condo	Office/condo	Condo	Condo	Condo	Town homes	Condo	Retail
Sustained media coverage	Yes	No	Yes	No	Yes	No	Yes	No
Planners' opinion	Support	Reject	Reject	Support	Support	Support	Support	Reject
Council's position	For	Against	For	For	For	For	Against	Against
Neighbourhood association involvement	Heavily involved	Minor involvement	Heavily involved	Minor involvement	Heavily involved	Heavily involved	Heavily involved	Not involved

	Chapter 5: Experts		Chapter 6: Developers		Chapter 7: Neigh. Assoc.		Chapter 8: Local Polit.	
Date of appeal	May 2006	July 2005	Dec. 2001	Oct. 2003	May 2003	Dec. 2004	Feb. 2005	Dec. 2005
Appellant	Neighbourhood associations +	Developer	Developer	Neighbouring resident	Neighbourhood association +	Developer	Developer	Developer
OMB decision	City and developer settled with all but one of the appellants. OMB decided in favour of City and developer. Decision was formality.	Ostensibly, OMB decided in favour of the developer. However, the OMB substantially relied on city planners' opinion.	City and developer settled. However, neighbourhood associations continued to oppose. OMB upheld the settlement.	The OMB threw out the appeal without hearing the case.	OMB decided in favour of City and developer and against neighbourhood association and SAVE Yorkville. Upheld City's original by-law.	OMB decided in favour of City and developer. Only opposition remaining from lone citizen.	OMB decided in favour of developer. Relied heavily on City Planner's opinion.	Settled before board decision. City exempted proposed development from ICBL.
Decision date	Jan. 2007	Oct. 2006	Sept. 2002	Dec. 2003	Apr. 2004	Apr. 2005	Oct. 2005	July 2006

Table A.4. Case selection matrix

	Heavy Neigh. Inv.	Low Neigh. Inv.	City for	City against	Planners support	Planners reject
High media exposure	Four Seasons; Minto Midtown;100 Yorkville; One Sherway	N/A	Four Seasons; Minto Midtown; 100 Yorkville	One Sherway	Four Seasons; 100 Yorkville; One Sherway	Minto Mid-town
Low media exposure	Bloor & Mill	Aldergreen; Pulse; Lowe's	Pulse; Bloor & Mill	Aldergreen; Lowe's	Pulse; Bloor & Mill	Aldergreen; Lowe's
Planners support	Four Seasons; 100 Yorkville; One Sherway; Bloor & Mill	Pulse	Four Seasons; Pulse; 100 Yorkville; Bloor & Mill	One Sherway		
Planners reject	Minto Midtown	Aldergreen; Lowe's	Minto Midtown	Aldergreen; Lowe's		
City for	Four Seasons; Minto Midtown; 100 Yorkville; Bloor & Mill; One Sherway	Pulse				
City against	One Sherway	Aldergreen; Lowe's				

instances. Omitting the high-profile disputes over development from analysis would be misleading, even though they do not represent the norm, as they are an important source in shaping people's perception of the OMB and the politics of urban development in Toronto. Focusing on such cases exclusively would also be misrepresentative, however, as they are precisely not the norm in Toronto.

Four Seasons, Minto Midtown, and One Sherway emerged as candidates for case studies well before the introduction of a specific method of case selection, due largely to their prominence. Excluding any of them from an analysis of the politics of urban development in Toronto from 2000 to 2006 would be to entirely misrepresent the era. Offsetting these cases with others more representative of the normal planning process in Toronto played a large role in the choice of the remaining cases. While it was impossible to provide a case reflecting every possible combination of variables, the choice of the remaining cases ensured some variation. I chose the four less-prominent cases, along with 100 Yorkville, directly from the data set I compiled, to offset the other three cases, and to ensure variation not only within each variable, but in combination with each other. Table A.4 captures this variation. Each box represents the relationship between two variables. Thus, the first box (upper left) includes each case that involves high media exposure and neighbourhood association involvement: Four Seasons, Minto Midtown, 100 Yorkville, and One Sherway. The box to its right includes each case with high media exposure and low neighbourhood involvement. This is the only box that is empty. High media exposure usually results from neighbourhood association opposition to a development, so the lack of a case fitting this box is not an issue. The remaining boxes follow the same pattern. While by no means achieving any form of perfect distribution (whatever that might entail), the cases selected ensure variation among the factors most likely to determine the outcomes of OMB appeals and the politics of urban development.

Overall, the combination of quantitative analysis and case studies, with the assistance of other forms of analysis on occasion, provides both a breadth of scope and a depth of analysis that would be impossible if I only used one method of analysis. The variety of methods I used for gathering evidence and data also ensured a rich pool of resources was available for analysing the politics of urban development in Toronto, and the role of the OMB. Limited data and evidence diminish the strength of analysis, regardless of how many methods of analysis one adopts. Utilising as many source of data and evidence as possible overcomes this problem.

Notes

1. Introduction

1 Only Mexico City, New York, Los Angeles, and Chicago are larger.
2 Metro Toronto was a two-tier system of municipal government which was, prior to its amalgamation into the single-tier City of Toronto in 1998, composed of an upper-tier municipality, the Municipality of Metropolitan Toronto, and six lower-tier municipalities: the City of Toronto, the City of North York, the City of Etobicoke, the City of Scarborough, the City of York, and the Borough of East York.
3 In the United States the most notable authors utilizing the LPE approach include Logan and Molotch (1987), Swanstrom (1988), Stone (1989), Kantor with David (1988), Ferman (1996), and Imbroscio (1997). In Canada they include Lorimer (1972), Sancton (1983), Keil (1998), Cobban (2003), and Leo (2003).
4 For instance, Lorimer (1972) and Ferman (1996) perceive them as a progressive force, while Filion (1999) portrays them in a more negative light.
5 Stone (1989) reflects the first perspective, while Logan and Molotch (1987) reflect the latter.
6 DeLeon (1992b) and Purcell (2000) portray a shift in politicians support in favour of neighbourhood associations in San Francisco and Los Angeles respectively, while Lorimer (1970), writing much earlier, suggests the same occurred in 1960s Toronto.
7 Kantor, in expounding such a view, suggests city councils face an "explosive dilemma" as both groups offer different resources and impose different costs on local politicians depending on which group they choose to support (Kantor with David 1988, 5).

2. Local Political Economy Theory and Toronto

1 Arguably, such literature has always considered the influence of institutions, particularly those governing local governments' ability to raise revenue and central–local relations. However, earlier literature has not always been explicit about their importance.
2 The authors both criticize and draw upon Marxist concepts of the land-owning class in developing their notions of rentiers and place entrepreneurs (Logan and Molotch 1987, 29).
3 In fact, in an article leading up to the publication of his seminal *Regime Politics* (Stone 1989), Stone goes to great length in his attempt to defend and expand upon Floyd Hunter's work on community power structure (Stone 1988).
4 Such criticisms are prolific; see for instance Mossberger and Stoker (2001), Davies (2003), John and Cole (1998), or Denters and Mossberger (2006).
5 See Boudreau (2003), Somerville (2002), Harding (1994), or Keating (1991) for examples of such arguments.
6 Terry Clark and Edward Goetz (1994) actually argue the exact opposite, arguing that regime theory is overly deterministic. While they appear in the minority, their contradictory view suggests an important ontological difference between structurally focused analysts and agency-focused ones.
7 For insightful discussions on this subject see Cobban (2003), Somerville (2002), Leo (1997), Garber and Imbroscio (1996), or Fainstein (2001).
8 The crash, as discussed later in this chapter, led not only to a recession in many parts of the world, but also to the collapse of a number of the world's largest office developers.
9 The anecdote in the previous chapter regarding the politics of urban development in Seattle suggests the opposite is occurring, by contrast, as council becomes increasingly favourable towards development.
10 Interestingly, these events in Toronto parallel, to some extent, the success of young, white middle-class neighbourhoods in Atlanta in defeating the proposed I-485 (Stone 1989, 82–5).

3. The OMB and the Politics of Urban Development

1 Quite often, authors fail to make a clear distinction between structures and institutions because they both function as constraints on human behaviour and play a role in distributing resources among actors. Nevertheless, the distinction is important because the relationships between actors and structures and actors and institutions differ. The main difference between

structures and institutions is intent. Structures, whether economic, social, or cultural, emerge as a result of human behaviour, but not of human intent. They are unintended consequences. In contrast, polities, citizens, or human beings in general create institutions to serve a specific function. They are intentional. Society may create institutions to reinforce existing structures, or in an attempt to change them, but structures remain apart from such institutions (and such institutions may fail). Institutions are always a product of human will, even if their original intent has faded from memory, while structures are simply aggregates of human behaviour.

2 See both Chipman (2002) and Krushelnicki (2007) (esp. chap. 6) for an elaboration on this debate.

3 The McGuinty government made far more significant changes with the Planning and Conservation Land Statute Amendment Act, 2006. However, the period of this study ends before these changes came into effect on 1 January 2007. Whether these more significant changes have altered the board's role in the politics of urban development remains to be seen, though recent decisions of the board suggest otherwise.

4 The most significant changes were the increase in time allowed to municipal governments to render decisions on planning applications, and an increased emphasis on the provincial government's planning policies (which were all but absent during former premier Mike Harris's Conservative government). The additional time provided by the amendment could reduce the number of appeals to the OMB arising from a municipality's failure to render a decision on a development application, but would have limited effect otherwise. The provision requiring the board to address provincial policy in its decisions could have a significant influence for areas where greenfield development is occurring. However, it would have less influence on the City of Toronto, where much of the development in the city involves intensification of existing areas. The OMB typically favoured intensification before McGuinty's changes to the Planning Act; thus, the province's emphasis on intensification would only add impetus to the OMB's usual support for such development in the city.

5 The board, in addition to hearing appeals regarding major zoning variances or amendments and Official Plan amendments, also hears appeals regarding minor variances, which can involve issues as simple as the location of a neighbour's fence. These issues have little to do with the politics of urban development. As a result, I have excluded them from my analysis.

6 The board will not hear from unincorporated neighbourhood associations (ratepayers' organizations), but will hear appeals under the name of a

single member in such instances where the association is not incorporated (OMB n.d.).

7 These rules are available on-line at http://www.omb.gov.on.ca/stellent/groups/public/@abcs/@www/@omb/documents/webasset/ec059424.pdf.

8 For instance, Adler (1971), Frankena and Scheffman (1980), Cullingworth (1987), and Chipman (2002).

9 As of 2007, the board must "have regard to" both the decision of municipal council and any previous documents considered by council in its original decision (Planning Act, 1990, s. 2.1), thus this element of de novo hearings technically no longer applies. However, whether the changes have had significant effect on the board's decisions is unclear at this time.

10 In compiling the data for chapter 4, little evidence emerged suggesting that developers in Toronto completely switch their application once they reach the board. In most instances, changes made to the applications resulted from dialogue between the city's planning department and the developer. However, developers do submit incomplete development applications to the city, which can lead to appeals from neglect, as the city's planning department, not surprisingly, will be unable to assess the application in its original form.

11 City Planning Division is an arm of the City of Toronto responsible for all measures of planning in the city. Its responsibilities include advising council, developing and researching planning policy, promoting quality urban design, planning transportation, and creating and maintaining the City's by-laws. I use the term City Planning when referring to planning experts in the employ of the City. Community Planning, a sub-division of the City Planning Division, is responsible for the reports to City Council. However, those reports rely on the input of multiple arms of the City's bureaucracy.

12 Krushelnicki (2007) argues that despite addressing each case de novo, the OMB regularly scrutinizes both the municipal councils' decisions and any files included with their decisions. He also suggests that the McGuinty government's new requirement that the OMB "have regard to" the municipality's decision only codifies this practice, as the board, while cognizant of the municipality's reasoning, can still decide against it, regardless. (The provincial government, in the same statute, changed the reference to having "regard to" provincial policy because the language allowed the board to make decisions counter to such policy.)

13 The choice of bodies for comparison is based on a survey of relevant state and provincial legislatures and the websites of such bodies where available. In addition, Cullingworth (1993) and Cullingworth and Caves's

(2009) survey of planning practices in the United States also directed my focus on specific jurisdictions, as did other relevant literature.

14 All of Canada's provinces, except British Columbia, have some form of planning appeals body. Alberta's Municipal Government Board is significantly weaker than its counterparts in other provinces and is of less interest for comparison, and so I have omitted it from this discussion. I also omit both the Regulatory and Appeals Commission in Prince Edward Island and the regional boards in Newfoundland and Labrador. They are recent additions to their respective provinces and serve primarily as appellant bodies for planning in smaller municipalities and rural communities (with the exception of St John's, which is neither small nor rural).

15 The SMB is actually a recent merger of a number of appeal bodies and other commissions in Saskatchewan. The Provincial Planning Appeals Board was the precursor of the Planning Appeals Commission (Saskatchewan Municipal Board 2003).

16 The Committee of Adjustment consists of four panels, North York and Toronto–East York each include ten members, though only five preside over a hearing. Scarborough and Etobicoke-York have five members. City Council appoints members from the public. Panels usually include one or two members with prior backgrounds in land use planning (see "Agencies, Boards, Commissions and Corporations," at http://www.toronto.ca/abcc/qj-committee-adjustment.htm).

17 This separation of legislative and administrative roles is common in the United States.

18 Civil law is based on strict law codes and generally does not allow the same type of judicial interpretation typical in the common law tradition.

19 Currently the whole appeal structure in New Brunswick is undergoing change.

20 Additionally, the board conducts hearings in an adversarial and court-like manner, which seems to be typical of most boards in Canada.

21 Along with planning, this super board has a diverse range of functions including the oversight of gaming, electricity, and railways, as well as acting as an appeal body for the likes of fire safety and film classification (Nova Scotia Utility and Review Board n.d.a).

22 These planning boards and commissions are more like Manitoba's planning commissions than Saskatchewan's development appeals boards. However, unlike Manitoba's system, the typical state system, as Cullingworth (1993) notes, does not involve the municipal council acting as a local appeal body for commission decisions.

23 Changes to Florida law in 2011 altered elements of this process. Among other things, the state abolished the Deparment of Community Affairs, replacing it with the Department of Economic Opportunity. The state reduced its role in planning through this process. See FAQs at: http://www.floridajobs.org/community-planning-and-development/programs/comprehensive-planning.

24 For information regarding the companies' respective holdings and distribution, see the following websites: http://brookfieldofficeproperties.com/content/portfolio-2904.html, http://www.cadillacfairview.com/notesdata/hr/cf_lp4w_lnd_webstation.nsf/page/Portfolio+Map.

25 Both companies are currently constructing or recently completed large office buildings in the downtown core and plan for others.

26 For information concerning the property development and holdings in Toronto of the respective developers, see the following websites: http://www.tridel.com/community/list.php, http://www.context.ca/pages/communities/communities.htm, www.canderelstoneridge.com, http://www.menkes.com/templates/condo_living.htm, http://www.danielshomes.ca/our_communities.html, http://www.minto.com/buy-a-condo-in-toronto/projects.html, and for Concord Adex http://www.cityplace.ca/index.asp and http://www.concordadex.com/parkplace/index2.asp.

27 According to Kipfer and Keil (2002), the composition and interest of these associations have marginalized radical and working-class movements in the city (239).

28 For example, the South Eglinton Residents' & Ratepayers' Association, ABC Residents Association, and Active 18, a citizen, residents, and business-owner association, all played major roles in planning disputes (see respectively *Minto YE Inc. v. Toronto (City)* [2002]; *Save Yorkville Heritage Association et al. v. Toronto (City)* [2007]; *2059946 Ontario Limited et al. v. Toronto (City)* [2007]).

4. OMB Appeals in Toronto from 2000 through 2006

1 Data for the number of applications the City received from 2000 through 2002 were not available.

2 As I mentioned in the previous chapter, the OMB categorized OMB appeals by the year of the decision, not by year of the appeal, so the number of appeals for 2003 through 2006 is inexact. However, though my initial attempts to account for the original appeal date in each instance were problematic, the evidence available suggests a typical appeal takes a year or

less from the appeal to settlement or board decision. Thus, data on OMB decisions/settlements from 2003 through 2006 are a reasonable measure of the number of appeals from 2002 through 2005, 188 in total (see chart 4.1). Based on the average number of decisions, one can assume at least forty decision for 2007, resulting in an additional forty or so appeals for 2006. This number may fail to represent the fact that many OMB appeals combine appeals against re-zoning and OPAs. Additionally, some by-laws generate multiple appeals, which may inflate the size of this number.

3 See appendix A, section 4.3 for discussion of the limited withdrawal data.

4 In fact, the most interesting aspect of this table is that trends did not significantly change over the duration of the analysis. Despite the changes the McGuinty government made to the Planning Act (R.S.O. 1990, c. P.13) in 2004, extending the time frame for city council to render a decision on an application, 2006 recorded the second highest percentage of appeals due to neglect over the seven-year span. In fact, both 2001 and 2006 recorded twenty such appeals. Because the cases were categorized by the year the OMB rendered its decision (when applicable), the statistics for 2004 likely reflect a number of appeals made in previous years, given that OMB cases often take over a year to resolve. However, by 2006, most of the appeals due to neglect likely arose after the Province changed the act. While this table by no means offers conclusive evidence that the Province's changes in 2004 are ineffectual, it does raise questions about their effectiveness.

5 These groups are not neighbourhood associations or equivalent to them. Many of Toronto's neighbourhood associations are incorporated entities and are represented as such at the OMB. Even neighbourhood associations that have yet to incorporate are usually recognized by the board, even though, technically, they cannot have party status in a hearing. In these instances, an individual member of the association is party to the hearing, with the understanding that he or she represents the interests of the unincorporated association. The individuals or small groups of individuals that account for so many appeals are rarely as well informed or organized as even the weakest neighbourhood association. Generally, these individuals or small groups have no expert witnesses to support their opposition. In a number of cases included in the data set, the board threw out the appeal without a hearing, and, in rare occasions, also awarded either City or developer (or both) costs (see, for example, *Colonia Treuhand Ltd. vs. Toronto (City)* [2003] O.M.B.D. no. 397 and no. 969).

6 The fourth set of columns includes four OMB decisions favouring a combination of the City and neighbourhood associations. Thus, the City is somewhat more successful against developers than the chart initially suggests.

7 Elkin (1985) does recognize the importance of the bureaucracy to city politics, however.
8 The withdrawn cases are anomalies, as one would expect the board to say
   nothing in such instances, because most withdrawn appeals do not result
   in a hearing or a board decision.
9 In cases resulting in a settlement, the board still renders a decision and
   order. However, the decision and order reflect the agreement between the
   parties involved in the dispute. Thus, the board does not actually impose
   its own decision.
10 The results are based on 270 appeals, the number of cases where reason
   for the appeal was available. City Planning supported the application 140
   times (51% of 270): appeals from approval accounted for 50% of these 140
   appeals; appeals from neglect, 32%; and appeals from refusal, 17%.
11 Part of the reason larger commercial developers are not present relates
   to their absence (as developers) from the development market for many
   years after the crash, primarily in office development, in the late eighties
   and early nineties. They were not excluded intentionally from this analysis, but were absent from the development scene in Toronto for much of
   this period. New office building construction remained much softer than
   the residential market well through the nineties and early part of the millennium. Additionally, city planners and local politicians may view office
   development, now that it is occurring on large scales again, more favour-
   ably than residential development. Finally, as with retail development, office development, particularly on the scale currently in development in the
   city's core, occurs in areas with an absence of neighbourhood opposition
   (or potential for opposition).

5. Experts and the Planning Community in Toronto

1 The coming-into-force of the new official plan should ease some of the bur-
   den of city planners. They are no longer required to consider official plans
   for municipalities that no longer exist in conjunction with a non-binding
   city-wide one.
2 Chipman's (2002) work provides the most comprehensive discussion of
   the OMB's rationale for decision making.
3 The application process technically begins when the developer submits an
   application for approval. However, developers will often approach either
   city councillors or city planners beforehand (Rae interview 2008).
4 The planning consultant was in the hire of the developer. Notably, he or
   she was also a former City employee.
5 See Menkes's corporate website: http://www.menkes.com/.

6 All four proposals were approved by the City and have since been constructed.

7 By-law 330-2006 amended the official plan.

8 The Four Seasons case was not included in the database used in appendix A. Technically, the OMB rendered its decision after 31 December 2006. However, the events leading to the OMB hearing occurred during the time frame of this study, and the board rendered its decision not long after.

9 It is unclear whether the other participants involved in the working committee were involved in the final settlement or not.

10 The list was, in fact, from an appeal of another development (see chapter 7). The SYHA repeatedly referred to Jane Jacobs in its submission to the board (SYHA 2007). In an exchange between Mayor Miller and Councillor Jane Pitfield (one of the councillors who opposed the development) following council's first decision to support the development, Councillor Pitfield asked Mayor Miller whether he was aware of Jane Jacobs's opposition to the development. Mayor Miller responded that he would not dignify the question with a response (Toronto Star 2006), Ms Jacobs having passed away a few days before the exchange.

11 City staff's refusal report lists Colson Investment as the developer behind this proposal, and lists 16 November 2004 as the date of the initial application for development. However, the development approval application on file at the OMB, dated 29 July 2005, lists Aldergreen Estates as the property owner, as does city staff's preliminary report, dated 6 December 2004.

12 Barber's (2006) article suggests that the Litwins were either directly or indirectly involved in all of these developments despite the changes in ownership.

13 In his appeal to the Community Council to oppose the development, Mr Kubbernus noted that "during the numerous meetings with the city, [he] basically discovered that for the most part, area zoning and planning cannot be relied upon and is simply a loose guideline" (Kubbernus 2005, 2 (742)). Mr Kubbernus was correct in his surmise.

14 The ABC Residents' Association was a participant to the hearing, but it does not appear it played a significant role, nor is there any evidence indicating it effectively mobilized against the development.

15 In planning and architecture a setback or setbacks refers to the relation and distance of a structure, wall, floor, or storey, from the property line, floor, or storey below. In this instance, the building plans are referring to 'steps' or 'tiers' in the design. Generally, a building with setbacks of a certain size will cast less of a shadow than a building with the same height and footprint, but no setbacks.

6. The Politics of Toronto's Development Industry

1 Brookfield Properties has head offices in Toronto, New York, and Sydney (contact: http://www.brookfieldofficeproperties.com/content/contact-2908.html; see also Cadillac Fairview, contact: http://www.cadillacfairview.com/Notesdata/HR/CF_LP4W_LND_WebStation.nsf/ContactUs!OpenForm; and Oxford, contact http://www.oxfordproperties.com/corp/utility/contact.htm).

2 Brookfield emerged as one of the worlds largest property holders by acquiring the holdings of many failed development companies during the 1990s (Brookfield Properties history: http://www.brookfieldofficeproperties.com/content/corporate/history-3179.html).

3 Brookfield recently completed the first building of its multi-building Bay Adelaide Centre complex, (http://www.brookfieldofficeproperties.com/content/bay_adelaide_centre/tenant_resources-5266.htmlhome/index.ch2?pageNumber=1). Cadillac Fairview recently completed building the new RBC Centre (http://www.rbccentre.ca/en/Pages/default.aspx).

4 Cadillac Fairview's venture into the condominium market is by no means inconsequential, however. The company is currently constructing two major predominantly residential developments, the Residence at the Ritz-Carlton (a director competitor to the Four Seasons development from chapter 4) and, in partnership with Lanterra and Maple Leaf Sports and Entertainment, Maple Leaf Square. The company is currently planning another major development including another office tower and two large condominium towers. (see Cadillac Fairview, Investment and Development, at http://www.cadillacfairview.com/notesdata/hr/cf_lp4w_lnd_webstation.nsf/page/Development).

5 Monarch: see "Why Monarch?" at http://www.monarchgroup.net/WhyM/WhyM.aspx.

6 All building statistics come from Emporis.com (www.emporis.com).

7 The eight developers include the aforementioned Tridel, Menkes, Daniels, H&R, and Monarch, as well as two other local companies, Canderel Stoneridge (www.canderelstoneridge.com) and Cresford (www.cresford.com), and Concord Adex, a division of Vancouver-based Concord Pacific Developments (www.concordpacific.com). Each of these companies built a minimum of five condominiums in Toronto from 2003–6. Their percentage share of total condominium development is an estimate, because the completion date of a building varies on occasion from the application for condominium approval.

8 As when classifying developers for the data set, clearly distinguishing between developers and other corporations who donated to Ms

Bernardinetti's campaign is difficult, because many of the donations came from numbered corporations. This fact also limited the possibility of more than a cursory exanimation of campaign financing in this study.

9 Following amalgamation in 1998, the City initially established six community councils, which would review certain items before passing them on to the full council. On 1 December 2003, the City reduced the number of councils to four, dividing the Midtown Community Council between the Toronto East York Community Council and the North York Community Council. (Toronto, Community Councils, http://www.toronto.ca/committees/community_councils.htm.)

10 Secondary plans function like an official plan, but are specific to one area. They provide a vision for the future of an area and general guidelines for future development.

11 Section 37 of the Planning Act [R.S.O. 1990, c. P.13] allows municipalities to increase the permissible height or density of a development in return for the provision of services, facilities, or monetary donations in lieu of services or facilities.

12 According to Robert Blazevski, who represented Minto throughout much of the process, this was the first instance that a shadows assessment became a primary issue for a development application. He noted that many of the current planning requirements for new applications in the city arose from the Minto Midtown case (Blazevski 2008).

13 As chapter 3 suggests, FoNTRA's argument might not be wholly inaccurate, despite the fact the board does not technically consider its previous decisions when judging a new appeal.

14 City planning had not submitted its final report based on the focused review at that point.

15 Developers may, in fact, prefer the issue of development not be a salient issue in an election, especially with a number of strong anti-growth–oriented neighbourhood associations in the city.

7. Neighbourhood Mobilization in Toronto

1 These documents were more likely to name neighbourhood associations opposed to development. As the Bloor & Mill case below demonstrates, not all neighbourhood associations participate only when in opposition to development.

2 The City initiated the Zoning By-Law Project in 2003 in a bid to harmonize the 41 zoning by-laws then in place in the city. Stakeholders are groups with vested interests in planning that the City consults with on the project (City Clerk 2004). Ratepayers are the most numerous of such groups,

though of the 315 listed, only 35 actually registered with the City for the project (Tynford 2006).

3 "History of the Annex": http://www.theara.org/Heritage/History.aspx.

4 The BVA encompasses all of census tract 5350305.01, which had a population of 4610 as of the 2006 census, as well as additional territory to south (Statistics Canada 2006: Census tract profile for 0305.01).

5 The city's designated neighbourhoods are not equivalent to the neighbourhoods of the various associations. The city's "neighbourhoods" appear to be only means for monitoring socio-demographics in the city; that each neighbourhood incorporates a number of census tracts and shares its borders with them reflects this.

6 I examined household incomes in this fashion because indicators such as medium or average income, or household tenure, provide a poor indication of the actual presence of either middle- or upper-middle-class residents, a fact emphasized by both Thomas (1986) and Ley and Mercer (1980) in their respective studies of Cincinnati and Vancouver. Many of the city's designated neighbourhoods comprise areas of both great wealth and high poverty; thus, either medium or average income could either mask or overemphasize the presence of upper-middle-class residents. For instance, in Cabbagetown–South St James Town, households making $100,000 account for the plurality of households in the neighbourhood (18%). The next largest group of households, however, are those with incomes between $10,000 and $19,999 (15.4%) (Community and Neighbourhood Services 2004a). While household tenure is probably a good indicator of relative affluence in the suburbs, many of the wealthier downtown neighbourhoods encompass significant rental housing. For instance, in Rosedale–Moore Park, one the city's wealthier areas, 45.4 % of households have incomes of $100,000 or over, but only 53% of households are owner-occupied (Community and Neighbourhood Services 2004b).

7 Map 7.1 includes only seventy-four of the seventy-seven cases, as the locations of three cases were unavailable.

8 The average household income for the entire city in 2000 was $45,345 (Statistics Canada 2002: Census-Community Profiles – Toronto).

9 At some juncture, Invar Building Corporation became a partner to Barclay-Grayson, acquired the land and development proposal, or acquired Barclay-Grayson. The relationship between the two developers is not entirely clear from the material available.

10 In Toronto, a heritage designation explicitly recognizes the historical importance of a building, due to its architecture, history of use, etc. Such a designation limits what the owners of such buildings may do with them.

Generally, such a designation requires the maintenance of at least a portion of the designated original building.

11 Floor plate refers to the shape and dimensions of each floor in a building. A larger floor plate entails more square footage, and a wider tower.

12 Three city councillors asked that the city clerk record their opposition to the development: Peter Milczyn, councillor for a ward in Etobicoke, and proponent of the One Sherway development discussed in the following chapter, and, interestingly, Anne Johnston and Michael Walker (Council Minutes 2003b).

13 SYHA would latter submit a photocopy of the same list of signatures when opposing the Four Seasons Hotel development.

14 This notion of councillors being confused or unsure emerged during the Minto Midtown debate as well.

15 Ownership of the site apparently changed hands two times before the development was finally built, but these changes did not significantly alter the final design of development agreed upon by the developer, City Planning, and the MHA (MHA interview 2009).

16 City staff erroneously referred to the MHA as the Markland Woods Ratepayers' Association in some of their documents.

17 NIMBY stands for Not-In-My-Backyard, and is a derisive term denoting an organization or residents opposed to any type of development in their neighbourhood, seemingly without thought.

18 The development achieved an element of notoriety after construction began. In October 2007, a fire broke out in the development, burning down many of the partially completed houses, and resulting in $3.5 million in damage. City firefighters considered the fire suspicious (Gray 2007). Another fire broke out in two of the unfinished units in March 2008, resulting in an additional $150,000 in damage. Again, some reports suggested someone had deliberately set the blaze (Toronto Sun 2008).

8. Politicians and Urban Development in Toronto

1 Following the 1998 amalgamation, there were six such community councils. On 1 December 2003 the City reduced the number to four: Etobicoke York Community Council, North York Community Council, Toronto and East York Community Council, and Scarborough Community Council (Toronto n.d.a):

2 The importance a ward-based system with a strong council may hold for the politics of urban development is an interesting question, but beyond the scope of this study.

3 To be fair to both councillors, neither is quite as extreme in opposition to or support of development as they are often portrayed. As the Aldergreen Estates case demonstrates, Councillor Rae has opposed developers and City Planning in supporting residents in his ward. As for Councillor Walker, during the interview conducted for this study, it became clear that he is less an ardent anti-growth councillor than an unapologetic populist. His anti-growth sentiment is largely directed by his perception of ward residents' concerns, rather than a specific vendetta against developers.

4 Now Lifetime Urban Development Group, Lifetime Homes began as a developer of housing subdivisions throughout the Greater Toronto Area, but increasingly focused on condo development in the city proper. (see, about LMB, http://www.libertymarket.ca/lifetimeGroup.php; and Lifetime Homes, http://lifetime.homebuyers.com/story.htm).

5 City Planning uses the Floor Space Index (FSI) to express the density of a development. An FSI of 1.5 means that the amount of floor space in a building is 1.5 times greater than the size of the lot. A building can have varying heights on a lot, but the same FSI, depending on the size of the floor plate.

6 Legal statements: http://www.onesherway.com/index.php?n=Condo&o=suites&towerid=4#self.

7 This contradicts the notion of separate fiefdoms in the city, with each councillor determining planning decisions for each ward. However, the site was directly adjacent to Councillor Grimes's ward, and most of the residents opposed to the development came from his ward as well, thus making the issue far more salient for Councillor Grimes than it would otherwise be, much as the Minto Midtown case was salient to multiple councillors due to its location.

8 According to Menkes, despite opposition to the development, neighbourhood residents accounted for the bulk of unit sales in the first two buildings (Raymaker 2006).

9 The same could be said for councils in other cities with wards, a weak mayor, and no parties, like Los Angeles.

10 In the developer's Notice of Appeal to the OMB, the solicitor suggests the developers submitted the application on 23 September 2005. However, all other sources state the 26th (the actual application was not in the OMB's archival material).

11 The company filed the application under Castlefield/Caledonia Developments Inc.

12 See "Our History": http://nadg.com/html/history.php.

13 According to the City of Toronto a "Site Plan Control is an important planning tool that enables the City to approve the design and technical aspects of a proposed development to ensure it contributes to the public realm in a manner that is attractive, functional and compatible with the surrounding area or planned context" (City Planning 2010).

14 This is an interesting argument, as many developers have argued the opposite, suggesting the OMB accept the proposal, because it worked with the new plan, even if it did not conform with the plans still in force (see especially Minto Midtown, chapter 6).

15 Both North American and Lowe's also appealed council's neglect to render a decision on the site plan application within thirty days following its submission (Harbell 2005b; Makuch 2005a).

16 Another owner of a property within the design district appealed these new ICBLs, in large part because they discriminated against other property owners by exempting Lowe's and North American's site (Duguid 2006).

9. The OMB and Local Political Economy

1 This number removes all settlements before a board hearing and any instance where the City supported the developer during the hearing, including the few instances where council initially opposed the development.

2 The number is inexact because of the limits of the data. Note 2 in chapter 4 details the issues of comparing city data for OPAs and ZBLAs and the data from the data set I compiled for this analysis. In addition, of the 284 cases table 4.1 depicts, information regarding neighbourhood association involvement and appeal outcome was only available for 276.

3 I chose Venn's four-ellipse diagram after numerous failed attempts to create a three-dimensional diagram using spheres. The diagram attempts to capture the relationship each factor shares with the other three factors. That is, each factor, to a certain extent, shares an independent relationship with each of the other factors. Actors' behaviour, or action, exists at the confluence of all four.

Appendix A

1 However, Stone (1989) makes a compelling point that as a theory or concept, the urban regime was never intended to remain "frozen at the version" he presents (256). To suggest that theories or concepts cannot or should not evolve is problematic in itself.

2 At least, only two studies are readily available.

3 Chipman (2002) only devotes a paragraph or two to coding in his appendix on methodology. He seems to focus more heavily on categorizing different areas that OMB decisions touch upon. Additionally, Chipman relies
on the Ontario Municipal Board reports, which limits, effectively, his cases
to the more notable decisions, while additionally addressing cases well beyond the bounds of OPAs, ZBLAs, and ICBLs.

4 The data set used in this study also include appeals of new zoning by-
laws, but these account for very few of the total number of appeals (thirteen in total).

5 City Planning's study does not say whether appeals made before 1998 are
included in the data set or not. There inclusion could account for some of
the discrepancy, but not all. See note 7 below.

6 Matthew Bryan, the Citizen Liaison Coordinator for the OMB, and Rita
Marrazzo, legal assistant for the Planning and Administrative Tribunal
Law division of Toronto Legal Services, were kind enough to provide each
list respectively. The OMB's list included every OMB case involving the
above four planning areas for the City of Toronto from 2000 to 2008. The
City's list covered the years 2002, 2004 through 2006, and 2007. Though ru-
dimentary, the City's list afforded a secondary source to cross-check with
the former.

7 These appeals reflect the dynamics of the politics of urban development
and the OMB appeals process of each of the six lower-tier municipalities
that existed at the time, which could vary from the new City of Toronto.

8 Both Paton (interview 2008) and Keefe (interview 2008) suggest they did
so for liability reasons.

9 Determining the size of the corporations based on assets or some other
measure proved very difficult, and given the findings of this analysis,
likely would have been a fruitless endeavour. The geographic distribution
of a developer's portfolio of developments, while not an exact reflection of
size, still functions as a suitable alternative.

10 The data set excludes the large commercial developers such as Brookfield
and Cadillac Fairview. Since 2000, despite the increasing activity of commercial developers in the city, no appeal has resulted from their development plans.

11 Any numbers relating to neighbourhood association involvement are
likely undercounts. I determined neighbourhood association involvement
in a case usually by referring to OMB decisions, which list the parties and
participants involved. Cases withdrawn before the first OMB hearing offer
no such information. In addition, even if a neighbourhood association is

not directly involved in the appeals process, it may have been involved earlier on. Nevertheless, the data do provide an accurate portrayal of the role neighbourhood associations play in the actual appeals process (specifically hearings), and indicates their relative level of success versus other actors.

12 While these categories may seem to be "splitting hairs," there are important differences between each. Outright support indicates that the planners have no issue with the proposal (or very mild ones). Hesitant support indicates that the planners approve the proposal in general, but have reservations regarding certain aspects of it. Usually, in these cases, the planners suggest that council support a development proposal only if the developer makes certain changes. Provisional rejection entails proposals that planners have significant reservations about, but believe can be changed through extensive negotiations with the developer, resulting in something more appropriate. Lastly, outright rejection entails proposals that city planners feel are completely inappropriate for an area (often such rejection revolves around the use of the building, not just the form).

13 Smith happened to be the father of a former student as well, which helped facilitate communications with him.

References

Works Cited

Adler, Gerald M. 1971. *Land Planning by Administration Regulation: The Policies of the Ontario Municipal Board*. Toronto: University of Toronto Press.

Barber, John. 2008. "A silver lining to the zoning mess." *Globe and Mail*, 16 August.

Barber, John. 2006. "Finding clues in the ashes of old St Paul's." *Globe and Mail*, 3 August.

Barber, John. 2005. "High-rise hysteria undermines community council." *Globe and Mail*, 29 January.

Bermingham, Timothy. 2001. "Ontario Municipal Board Jurisdiction." In *Planning for Success before the Ontario Municipal Board*. Toronto: Canadian Bar Association, Ontario Branch.

Bowman, Michael. 2001. "Working with Expert Witnesses." In *Planning for Success before the Ontario Municipal Board*. Toronto: Canadian Bar Association, Ontario Branch.

Boudreau, Julie-Anne. 2003. "Questioning the Use of 'Local Democracy' as a Discursive Strategy for Political Mobilization in Los Angeles, Montreal and Toronto." *International Journal of Urban and Regional Research* 27 (4): 793–810. http://dx.doi.org/10.1111/j.0309-1317.2003.00484.x.

Boyle, Theresa. 2005. "Towers go ahead despite objections." *Toronto Star*, 11 June.

Caulfield, Jon. 1974. *The Tiny Perfect Mayor*. Toronto: James Lorimer & Co.

Charney, Igal. 2005. "Property Developers and the Robust Downtown: The Case of Four Major Canadian Downtowns." *Canadian Geographer* 49 (3): 301–12. http://dx.doi.org/10.1111/j.0008-3658.2005.00097.x.

Chipman, John G. 2002. *A Law unto Itself: How the Ontario Municipal Board Has Developed and Applied Land Use Planning*. Toronto: University of Toronto Press.

Chu, Showwei. 2004. "Vancouver extends hearing on big-box store for Kitsilano." *Vancouver Sun*, 8 July, final edition.

Clark, Gordon L. 1985. *Judges and the Cities: Interpreting Local Autonomy*. Chicago, London: University of Chicago Press.

Clark, Terry Nichols, and Edward G. Goetz. 1994. "The Antigrowth Machine: Can City Governments Control, Limit, or Manage Growth?" In *Urban Innovation: Creative Strategies for Turbulent Times*, ed. Terry Nichols Clark, 105–45. Thousand Oaks, CA: Sage Publications.

Clifford, Patrick J. 2005a. "President's Update." *Marklander* 42 (3): 2.

Clifford, Patrick J. 2005b. "President's Update." *Marklander* 42 (2): 2.

Clifford, Patrick J. 2004a. "President's Update." *Marklander* 41 (9): 2.

Clifford, Patrick J. 2004b. "Letter to the landlords of the property at the corner of Mill and Bloor." *Marklander* 41 (2): 4.

Cobban, Timothy. 2003. "The Political Economy of Urban Redevelopment: Downtown Revitalization in London, Ontario, 1993–2002." *Canadian Journal of Urban Research* 12 (2): 231–48.

Cordileone, Elvira. 2004. "Rae of hope." *Toronto Star*, 28 February [Ontario edition].

Cullingworth, J. Barry. 1993. *The Political Culture of Planning: American Land Use Planning in Comparative Perspective*. New York and London: Routledge.

Cullingworth, J. Barry. 1987. *Urban and Regional Planning in Canada*. New Brunswick, NJ: Transaction Books.

Cullingworth, Barry, and Roger W. Caves. 2009. *Planning in the USA: Policies, Issues, and Processes*. 3rd ed. London, New York: Routledge.

Dahl, Robert A. 1961. *Who Governs? Democracy and Power in an American City*. New Haven, CT: Yale University Press. 2nd ed., with foreword by Douglas W. Rae and new preface by the author. 2005. New Haven, CT: Yale University Press.

Davies, Jonathan S. 2003. "Partnerships versus Regimes: Why Regime Theory Cannot Explain Urban Coalitions in the UK." *Journal of Urban Affairs* 25 (3): 253–69. http://dx.doi.org/10.1111/1467-9906.00164.

Davies, Jonathan S. 2002. "Urban Regime Theory: A Normative-Empirical Critique." *Journal of Urban Affairs* 24 (1): 1–17. http://dx.doi.org/10.1111/1467-9906.00111.

DeLeon, Richard E. 1992a. *Left Coast City: Progressive Politics in San Francisco, 1975–1991*. Lawrence: University Press of Kansas.

DeLeon, Richard E. 1992b. "The Urban Antiregime: Progressive Politics in San Francisco." *Urban Affairs Quarterly* 27 (4): 555–79. http://dx.doi.org/10.1177/004208169202700404.

DeLeon, Richard E., and Sandra S. Powell. 1989. "Growth Control and Electoral Politics: The Triumph of Urban Populism in San Francisco." *Western Political Quarterly* 42 (2): 307–31. http://dx.doi.org/10.2307/448357.

Denters, Bas, and Karen Mossberger. 2006. "Building Blocks for a Methodology for Comparative Urban Political Research." *Urban Affairs Review* 41 (4): 550–71. http://dx.doi.org/10.1177/1078087405282607.

Deverell, John. 2003. "Condo tower foes unite." *Toronto Star*, 11 April [Ontario edition].

DiGaetano, Alan, and Elizabeth Strom. 2003. "Comparative Urban Gvernance: An Integrated Approach." *Urban Affairs Review* 38 (3): 356–95. http://dx.doi.org/10.1177/1078087402238806.

Downs, Anthony. 1981. *Neighborhoods and Urban Development*. Washington, DC: The Brookings Institution.

Elkin, Stephen L. 1987. *City and Regime in the American Republic*. Chicago, London: University of Chicago Press.

Elkin, Stephen L. 1985. "Twentieth Century Urban Regimes." *Journal of Urban Affairs* 7 (2): 11–28. http://dx.doi.org/10.1111/j.1467-9906.1985.tb00080.x.

Environment and Land Tribunals Ontario (ELTO). 2009. *Your Guide to the Ontario Municipal Board*. Toronto: Queen's Printer for Ontario. http://www.omb.gov.on.ca/stellent/groups/public/@abcs/@www/@omb/documents/webasset/ec081184.pdf.

Fainstein, Norman I., and Susan S. Fainstein. 1983. "Regimes Strategies, Communal Resistance, and Economic Forces." In S.S. Fainstein et al., *Restructuring the City: The Political Economy of Urban Redevelopment*, 245–82. New York: Longman.

Fainstein, Susan S. 2001. *The City Builders: Property Development in New York and London, 1980–2000*. 2nd ed., rev. Lawrence: University Press of Kansas.

Ferman, Barbara. 1996. *Challenging the Growth Machine: Neighbourhood Politics in Chicago and Pittsburgh*. Lawrence: University Press of Kansas.

Filion, Pierre. 1999. "Rupture or Continuity: Modern and Postmodern Planning in Toronto." *International Journal of Urban and Regional Research* 23 (3): 421–44. http://dx.doi.org/10.1111/1468-2427.00206.

Frankena, Mark W., and David T. Scheffman. 1980. *Economic Analysis of Land Use Policies in Ontario*. Toronto: University of Toronto Press.

Frisken, Frances. 2001. "The Toronto Story: Sober Reflections on Fifty Years of Experiments with Regional Governance." *Journal of Urban Affairs* 23 (5): 513–41. http://dx.doi.org/10.1111/0735-2166.00104.

Frisken, Frances. 1988. *City Policy-Making in Theory and Practice: The Case of Toronto's Downtown Plan.* London: University of Western Ontario.

Frug, Gerald E., and David J. Barron. 2008. *City Bound: How States Stifle Urban Innovation.* Ithaca, London: Cornell University Press.

Gainsborough, Juliet F. 2008. "A Tale of Two Cities: Civic Culture and Public Policy in Miami." *Journal of Urban Affairs* 30 (4): 419–35. http://dx.doi.org/10.1111/j.1467-9906.2008.00406.x.

Gale, Denis E. 1992. "Eight State-Sponsored Growth Management Programs: A Comparative Analysis." *Journal of the American Planning Association. American Planning Association* 58 (4): 425–39. http://dx.doi.org/10.1080/01944369208975827.

Garber, Judith A., and David L. Imbroscio. 1996. "'The Myth of the North American City' Reconsidered: Local Constitutional Regimes in Canada and the United States." *Urban Affairs Review* 31 (5): 595–624. http://dx.doi.org/10.1177/107808749603100502.

Gillespie, Kerry. 2007. "It's not just the same old OMB." *Toronto Star*, 10 February.

Globe and Mail. 2007. "The curse of the OMB." 22 December.

Goldberg, Michael A., and John Mercer. 1986. *The Myth of the North American City: Continentalism Challenged.* Vancouver: UBC Press.

Goldrick, Michael D. 1982. "The Anatomy of Urban Reform in Toronto." In *The City and Radical Social Change*, ed. Dimitrios I. Roussopoulos, 260–82. Montreal: Black Rose Books.

Government of Manitoba. 2008. *Manitoba Municipal Board: FAQ*, http://www.gov.mb.ca/municipalboard/faqs.html.

Gray, Brian. 2007. "Fierce blaze 'suspicious.'" *Toronto Sun*, 24 October [final edition].

Gray, Jeff. 2006. "School board gets $2-million over shadow hotel could cast." *Globe and Mail*, 4 April.

Greenwood, John. 2004. "Home Depot's Kitsilano project up in air." *Vancouver Sun*, 11 May [final edition].

Harding, Alan. 1994. "Urban Regimes and Growth Machines: Toward a Cross-National Research Agenda." *Urban Affairs Review* 29 (3): 356–82.

Harvey, David. 1989. "From Managerialism to Entrepreneurialism: The Transformation in Urban Governance in Late Capitalism." *Geografiska Annaler. Series B, Human Geography* 71 (1): 3–17. http://dx.doi.org/10.2307/490503.

Harvey, David. 1983. "Class-Monopoly Rent, Finance Capital and the Urban Revolution." In *Readings in Urban Analysis: Perspectives on Urban Form and Structure*, ed. Robert W. Lake, 250–77. New Brunswick,

NJ: Rutgers University, Center for Policy Research. http://dx.doi.
org/10.1080/09595237400185251.

Harvey, Ian. 2008. "Boom town." *Toronto Star*, 24 May.

Hiller, Susanne. 2002. "New towers seen as neighbourhood-killer." *National Post*, 21 September.

Hume, Christopher. 2003. "The Village, upscale and down, still tossed by forces of development." *Toronto Star*, 19 September [Ontario edition].

Hunter, Floyd. 1953. *Community Power Structure: A Study in Decision Makers*. Chapel Hill: University of North Carolina Press.

Imbroscio, David L. 2003. "Overcoming the Neglect of Economics in Urban Regime Theory." *Journal of Urban Affairs* 25 (3): 271–84. http://dx.doi.
org/10.1111/1467-9906.00165.

Imbroscio, David L. 1997. *Reconstructing City Politics: Alternative Economic Development and Urban Regimes*. Thousand Oaks, CA: Sage Puplications.

Jessop, Bob, Jamie Peck, and Adam Tickell. 1999. "Retooling the Machince: Economic Crisis, State Restructuring and Urban Politics." In *The Urban Growth Machine: Critical Perspectives, Two Decades Later*, ed. Andrew E.G. Jonas and David Wilson, 141–59. Albany: State University of New York Press.

John, Peter. 2001. *Local Governance in Western Europe*. London: Sage.

John, Peter, and Alistair Cole. 1998. "Urban Regimes and Local Governance in Britain and France." *Urban Affairs Review* 33 (3): 382–404. http://dx.doi.
org/10.1177/107808749803300307.

Kantor, Paul. 1987. "The Dependent City: The Changing Political Economy of Urban Economic Development in the United States." *Urban Affairs Quarterly* 22 (4): 493–520. http://dx.doi.org/10.1177/004208168702200402.

Kantor, Paul, with Stephen David. 1988. *The Dependent City: The Changing Political Economy of Urban America*. Glenview, IL: Scott, Foresman and Co.

Kaplan, Harold. 1967. *Urban Political Systems: A Functional Analysis of Metro Toronto*. New York: Columbia University Press.

Kaplan, Harold. 1965. "Politics and Policy-Making in Metropolitan Toronto." *Canadian Journal of Economics and Political Science* 31 (4): 538–51. http://
dx.doi.org/10.2307/139829.

Keating, Michael. 1991. *Comparative Urban Politics: Power and the City in the United States, Canada, Britain and France*. Aldershot, UK: Edward Elgar.

Keil. Roger. 1998. Toronto in the 1990s: Dissociated Governance? *Studies in Political Economy* 56 (Summer): 151–68.

Kipfer, Stephan, and Roger Keil. 2002. "Toronto Inc? Planning the Competitive City in the New Toronto." *Antipode* 34 (2): 227–339. http://dx.doi.
org/10.1111/1467-8330.00237.

Krushelnicki. Bruce. 2007. *A Practical Guide to the Ontario Municipal Board*. 2nd ed. Toronto: LexisNexis.

Leo, Christopher. 2003. "Are There Urban Regimes in Canada? Comment on Timothy Cobban's 'The Political Economy of Urban Redevelopment: Downtown Revitalization in London, Ontario, 1993–2002.'" *Canadian Journal of Urban Research* 12 (2): 344–8.

Leo, Christopher. 1998. "Regional Growth Management Regime: The Case of Portland, Oregon." *Journal of Urban Affairs* 20 (4): 363–94. http://dx.doi.org/10.1111/j.1467-9906.1998.tb00428.x.

Leo, Christopher. 1997. "City Politics in an Era of Globalization." In *Reconstructing Urban Region Theory: Regulating Urban Politics in a Global Economy*, ed. Mickey Lauria, 77–98. Thousand Oaks, CA: Sage Publications.

Levy, Sue-Ann. 2003. "Develop this: Yorkville residents battle to save area charm and tourist dollars." *Toronto Star*, 20 April [final edition].

Levy, Sue-Ann. 2001. "High stakes: Young and Eglinton faces major development." *Toronto Star*, 4 May [final edition].

Ley, David, and John Mercer. 1980. "Locational Conflict and the Politics of Consumption." *Economic Geography* 56 (2): 89–109. http://dx.doi.org/10.2307/142929.

Liberty, Robert. 1998. "Planned Growth: The Oregon Model." *Natural Resources and Environment* 13: 315–8, 367–9.

Logan, John R., and Harvey L. Molotch. 1987. *Urban Fortunes: The Political Economy of Place*. 20th anniversary ed. with new preface by authors, 2007. Berkeley: University of California Press.

Logan, John R., and Gordana Rabrenovic. 1990. "Neighborhood Associations: Their Issues, Their Allies, and the Opponents." *Urban Affairs Quarterly* 26 (1): 68–94. http://dx.doi.org/10.1177/004208169002600104.

Logan, John R., Rachel Bridges Whaley, and Kyle Crowder. 1997. "The Character and Consequences of Growth Regimes: An Assessment of 20 Years of Research." *Urban Affairs Review* 32 (5): 603–30. http://dx.doi.org/10.1177/107808749703200501.

Lorimer, James. 1972. *A Citizen's Guide to City Politics*. Toronto: James Lewis & Samuel.

Lorimer, James. 1970. *The Real World of City Politics*. Toronto: James Lewis & Samuel.

Lorinc, John. 2007. "Moving the building blocks." *Globe and Mail*, 26 May.

Macdonald, Greg. 2007. "Yorkville towers approved." *National Post*, 20 January.

Magnusson, Warren. 1990. "Progressive Politics and Canadian Cities." In *Challenges to Local Government*, ed. Desmond S. King and Jon Pierre, 173–94. London: Sage Publications.

Magnusson, Warren. 1983. "Toronto." In *City Politics in Canada*, ed. Warren Magnusson and Andrew Sancton, 94–139. Toronto: University of Toronto Press.

Mesch, Gustavo S., and Kent P. Schwirian. 1996. "The Effectiveness of Neighborhood Collective Action." *Social Problems* 43 (4): 467–83. http://dx.doi.org/10.1525/sp.1996.43.4.03x0151u.

Mollenkopf, John H. 1983. *The Contested City*. Princeton, NJ: Princeton University Press.

Molotch, Harvey. 1993. "The Political-Economy of Growth Machines." *Journal of Urban Affairs* 15 (1): 29–53. http://dx.doi.org/10.1111/j.1467-9906.1993.tb00301.x.

Molotch, Harvey. 1976. "The City as a Growth Machine: Toward a Political Economy of Place." *American Journal of Sociology* 82 (2): 309–32. http://dx.doi.org/10.1086/226311.

Mossberger, Karen, and Gerry Stoker. 2001. "The Evolution of Urban Regime Theory: The Challenge of Conceptualization." *Urban Affairs Review* 36 (6): 810–35. http://dx.doi.org/10.1177/10780870122185109.

Nova Scotia Utility and Review Board. n.d.a. *Nova Scotia Utility and Review Board: About Us*, http://www.nsuarb.ca/about/index.html.

Nova Scotia Utility and Review Board. n.d.b. *Nova Scotia Utility and Review Board: Planning*, http://www.nsuarb.ca/functions/adjudicative/planning/index.html.

Ontario. Ministry of Municipal Affairs. 1985a. *A Citizen Guide*, no. 6. *Ontario Municipal Board*. Queen's Printer for Ontario.

Ontario. Ministry of Municipal Affairs. 1985b. *A Citizen's Guide*, no. 2, 1985. *Official Plan*. Queen's Printer Ontario.

Ontario Municipal Board (OMB). 2006. *Rules of Practice and Procedure*. http://www.omb.gov.on.ca/stellent/groups/public/@abcs/@www/@omb/documents/webasset/ec059424.pdf.

Ontario Municipal Board (OMB). n.d. *Your Guide to Ontario Municipal Board Hearings*.

Orr, Marion E., and Gerry Stoker. 1994. "Urban Regimes and Leadership in Detroit." *Urban Affairs Quarterly* 30 (1): 48–73. http://dx.doi.org/10.1177/004208169403000103.

Painter, Joe. 1995. "Regulation Teory, Post-Fordism, and Urban Politics." In *Theories of Urban Politics*, ed. David Judge, Gerry Stoker, and Harold Wolman, 276–95. London: Sage.

Peter, John. 2001. *Local Governance in Western Europe*. London: Sage.

Peterson, Paul E. 1981. *City Limits*. Chicago, London: University of Chicago Press.

Pierre, Jon. 1999. "Models of Urban Governance: The Institutional Dimension of Urban Politics." *Urban Affairs Review* 34 (3): 372–96. http://dx.doi.org/10.1177/10780879922183988.

Porter, Catherine, and Paul Moloney. 2005. "OMB okays massive project." *Toronto Star*, 3 June.

Purcell, Mark. 2000. "The Decline of the Political Consensus for Urban Growth: Evidence from Los Angeles." *Journal of Urban Affairs* 22 (1): 85–100. http://dx.doi.org/10.1111/0735-2166.00041.

Purcell, Mark. 1997. "Ruling Los Angeles: Neighborhood Movements, Urban Regimes, and the Production of Space in Southern California." *Urban Geography* 18 (8): 684–704. http://dx.doi.org/10.2747/0272-3638.18.8.684.

Quine, Kelley. 2004. "Appellate Ruling a Blow to Developer." *Chicago Daily Law Bulletin*, 1 September.

Raymaker, Derek. 2006. "Condominium influx aids neighbourhoods in transition." *Globe and Mail*, 13 October.

Reese, Laura A., and Raymond A. Rosenfeld. 2004. "Local Economic Development in the United States and Canada: Institutionalizing Policy Approaches." *American Review of Public Administration* 34 (3): 277–92. http://dx.doi.org/10.1177/0275074004264293.

Reguly, Eric. 2006. "T.O.'s new height of hypocrisy." *Global and Mail*, 27 April.

Rochon, Lisa. 2005. "Welcome to Sin City." *Globe and Mail*, 10 December.

Rooney, John Finley. 2004. "Jutices Won't Cast Shadow over Zoning." *Chicago Daily Law Bulletin*, 24 November.

Rose, Albert. 1972. *Governing Metropolitan Toronto: A Social and Political Analysis, 1953–1971*. Berkeley: University of California Press.

Rusk, James. 2005. "New authority means council must grow up." *Globe and Mail*, 17 December.

Sachdev, Ammet. 2006. "Justices boost stalled tower plan: Gold Coast highrise stuck in legal battle." *Chicago Tribune*, 22 December.

Sancton, Andrew. 2000. *Mergia Mania: The Assault on Local Government*. Montreal, Kingston: McGill-Queen's University Press.

Sancton, Andrew. 1983. "Conclusion: Canadian City Politics in Comparative Perspective." In *City Politics in Canada*, ed. Warren Magnusson and Andrew Sancton, 282–317. Toronto: University of Toronto Press.

Sanders, Heywood T., and Clarence N. Stone. 1987. "Development Politics Reconsidered." *Urban Affairs Quarterly* 22 (4): 521–39. http://dx.doi.org/10.1177/004208168702200403.

Saskatchewan Municipal Board. 2003. *Saskatchewan Municipal Board: Planning Appeals Committee*, http://www.smb.gov.sk.ca/planning_appeals.htm.

Saunders, John. 2001. "Size matters to residents angry over midtown skyscraper plan." *Globe and Mail*, 6 June.

Savitch, H.V., and Paul Kantor. 2002. *Cities in the International Marketplace: The Political Economy of Urban Development in North America and Europe*. Princeton, NJ: Princeton University Press.

Scrivener, Leslie. 2007. "Sculpting by numbers." *Toronto Star*, 10 June.

Sellers, Jefferey M. 2002. *Governing from Below: Urban Regions and the Global Economy*. Cambridge, UK: Cambridge University Press. http://dx.doi.org/10.1017/CBO9780511613395.

Sewell, John. 1972. *Up Against City Hall*. Toronto: Lewis & Samuel.

Shields, Jeff. 2008a. "City's tallest building gets Council committee approval." *Philadelphia Inquirer*, 4 December [CITY-D edition].

Somerville, C. Tsuriel. 2002. "Institutional features of Canadian real estate." CUER Discussion Paper 02-05 (November). Centre for Urban Economics and Real Estate.

Sommerfeld, Julia. 2003. "Coalition to stand up for neighborhood plans: New groups contends Seattle Mayor shirking 'contact' with citizens." *Seattle Times*, 2 June [4th ed.].

Sommerfeld, Julia. 2008. "Tallest building in U.S. proposed for Phila." *Philadelphia Inquirer*, 20 June.

State of Florida. 2012. *Florida Department of Economic Opportunity – Division of Community Planning & Development: Comprehensive Planning: Amendment Submittal and Processing Guidelines*. http://www.floridajobs.org/community-planning-and-development/programs/comprehensive-planning.

State of Oregon. 2008. *Land Use Board of Appeals: Frequently Asked Questions*, http://www.oregon.gov/LUBA/FAQ.shtml.

Statistics Canada. 2002. Table: Toronto, Ontario. 2001 Community Profiles. 2001 Census. Statistics Canada Catalogue no. 93F0053XIE. Released 27 June 2002. Last modified 30 November 2005. http://www12.statcan.ca/english/Profil01/CP01/Details/Page.cfm?Lang=E&Geo1=CSD&Code1=3520005&Geo2=PR&Code2=35&Data=Count&SearchText=toronto&SearchType=Begins&SearchPR=01&B1=All&Custom=.

Stoker, Gerry. 1998. "Governance as Theory: Five Propositions." *International Social Science Journal* 155 (50): 17–28. http://dx.doi.org/10.1111/1468-2451.00106.

Stone, Clarence N. 2001. "The Atlanta Experience Re-examined: The Link between Agenda and Regime Change." *International Journal of Urban and Regional Research* 25 (1): 20–34. http://dx.doi.org/10.1111/1468-2427.00295.

Stone, Clarence N. 1993. "Urban Regimes and the Capacity to Govern: A Political Economy Approach." *Journal of Urban Affairs* 15 (1): 1–28. http://dx.doi.org/10.1111/j.1467-9906.1993.tb00300.x.

Stone, Clarence N. 1989. *Regime Politics: Governing Atlanta, 1946–1988*. Lawrence: University Press of Kansas.

Stone, Clarence N. 1988. "Preemptive Power: Floyd Hunter's 'Community Power Structure' Reconsidered." *American Journal of Political Science* 32 (1): 82–104. http://dx.doi.org/10.2307/2111311.

Strom, Elizabeth. 2008. "Rethinking the Politics of Downtown Development." *Journal of Urban Affairs* 30 (1): 37–61. http://dx.doi.org/10.1111/j.1467-9906.2007.00373.x.

Strom, Elizabeth. 1996. "In search of the growth coalition: American urban theories and redevelopment in Berlin." *Urban Affairs Review* 31 (4): 455–81.

Swanstrom, Todd. 1988. "Semisovereign Cities: The Politics of Urban Development." *Polity* 21 (1): 83–110. http://dx.doi.org/10.2307/3234925.

Thomas, John Clayton. 1986. *Between Citizen and City: Neighbourhood Organizations and Urban Politics in Cincinnati*. Lawrence: University Press of Kansas.

Toronto Star. 2006. "Dark dreams." 30 April.

Toronto Sun. 2008. Sunflashes column. 10 March [final edition].

Vancouver Sun. 2004. "Mindless store size limits will drive business away." 14 July [final edition].

Vincent, Donovan. 2008. "One councillor accused, as another is vindicated." *Toronto Star*, 22 October.

Vogel, Ronald K., and Bert E. Swanson. 1989. "The Growth Machine against the Antigrowth Coalition: The Battle for Our Communities." *Urban Affairs Quarterly* 25 (1): 63–85. http://dx.doi.org/10.1177/004208168902500106.

Won, Shirley. 2005. "Four Seasons digs in as competition grows." *Globe and Mail*, 25 July.

Young, Bob. 2003a. "Community leaders lose influence at City Hall: Nickels push on jobs rankles neighborhoods." *Seattle Times*, 10 August [4th edition].

Young, Bob. 2003b. "Much ado over city's obscure L52: South Lake Union proposal runs into growth policy." *Seattle Times*, 7 June [4th edition].

City of Toronto Documents

City Clerk. 2006a. Consolidated clause in Toronto and East York Community Council report 3, which was considered by City Council on 25, 26, and 27 April: 2.

City Clerk. 2006b. Consolidated clause in North York Community Council report 2, which was considered by City Council on 14 February: 17.

City Clerk. 2005a. Consolidated clause in Toronto and East York Community Council report 9, which was considered by City Council on 5, 6, and 7 December: 12.

City Clerk. 2005b. Consolidated clause in Etobicoke York Community Council report 2, which was considered by City Council on 16 February: 25.

City Clerk. 2005c. Consolidated clause in Etobicoke York Community Council report 1, which was considered by City Council on 1, 2, and 3 February: 29.

City Clerk. 2004. Consolidated clause in Planning and Transportation Committee report 5, which was considered by City Council on 20, 21, and 22 July: 5.

City Clerk. 2003a. Clause embodied in report no. 5 of the North York Community Council, as adopted by the Council of the City of Toronto at its meeting held on 24, 25, and 26 June: 16.

City Clerk. 2003b. Clause embodied in report no. 4 of the Humber York Community Council, as adopted by the Council of the City of Toronto at its meeting held on 21, 22, and 23 May: 7.

City Clerk. 2003c. Clause embodied in report no. 2 of the Toronto East York Community Council, as adopted by the Council of the City of Toronto at its special meeting held on 24, 25, 26, 27, and 28 February: 3.

City Clerk. 2002a. Clause embodied in report no. 5 of the Midtown Community Council, which was before the Council of the City of Toronto at its meeting held on 18, 19, and 20 June: 1.

City Clerk. 2002b. Notice of motion I(2), which was before the Council of the City of Toronto at its meeting held on 18, 19, and 20 June.

City Clerk. 2002c. Clause embodied in report no. 3 of the Midtown Community Council, as adopted by the Council of the City of Toronto at its meeting held on 16, 17, and 18 April: 15. OMB Archive, Case no. PL011652, Exhibit 2.

City Clerk. 2002d. Clause embodied in report no. 1 of the Midtown Community Council, as adopted by the Council of the City of Toronto at its meeting held on 12, 14, and 15 February: 29.

City Clerk. 2001. Clause embodied in report no. 18 of the Administrative Committee, as adopted by the Council of the City of Toronto at its meeting held on 4, 5, and 6 December: 18.

City Clerk's Department. 2002. Minutes of the Midtown Community Council, Meeting no. 2, clause no. 14, report no. 14 (25 February).

City Clerk's Division. 2003. Minutes of the North York Community Council, Meeting no. 5, report no. 5, clause no. 15 (11 June).

City Clerk's Division. 2001a. Minutes of the Midtown Community Council, Meeting no. 6, clause no. 12, report no. 5 (12 June).

City Clerk's Division. 2001b. Minutes of the Midtown Community Council, Meeting no. 4, report no. 4, clause no. 35 (3 April).

City Clerk's Office. 2006. Minutes of the North York Community Council, Meeting no. 2, report 2, clause no. 17 (7 February).

City Clerk's Office. 2005a. Minutes of the Toronto and East York Community Council, Meeting no. 9, report no. 9, clause no. 12 (15 and 16 November).

City Clerk's Office. 2005b. Minutes of the Etobicoke York Community Council, Meeting no. 2, report no. 2, clause no. 25 (8 February).

City Clerk's Office. 2004a. Minutes of the Etobicoke York Community Council, Meeting no. 10, report no. 9, clause no. 40(i) (16 November).

City Clerk's Office. 2004b. Minutes of the Etobicoke York Community Council, Meeting no. 8, report 7, clause no. 56(q) (14 September).

City Clerk's Office. 2003. Minutes of the Toronto and East York Community Council, Meeting no. 2, report no. 2, clause no. 3 (20 February).

City Planning. 2010. Notice: Site Plan Control Applications. New 1:50 Scale Elevation Drawing Requirement.

City Planning. 2005. *Overview in Development Portfolio of Major Projects, 2005.* Toronto: Toronto City Planning.

City Planning. 2004. *Project by Planning District in Development Portfolio of Major Projects, 2004.* Toronto: Toronto City Planning.

Clerk's Department. 2002. Minutes of the Toronto and East York Community Council, Meeting no. 6, report no. 8, clause no. 44(b) (4 June).

Commissioner of Urban Development Services. 2002. Report on a review of Ontario Municipal Board decisions (7 March).

Community and Neighbourhood Services. 2004a. *Cabbagetown–St. James Town (71), Social Profile #3 – Neighbourhoods, Households and Income.* Toronto: City of Toronto. http://www.toronto.ca/demographics/pdf3/cpa71.pdf.

Community and Neighbourhood Services. 2004b. *Rosedale–Moore Park (98), Social Profile #3 – Neighbourhoods, Households and Income.* Toronto: City of Toronto. http://www.toronto.ca/demographics/pdf3/cpa98.pdf.

Community and Neighbourhood Services. 2004c. *South Parkdale (85), Social Profile #3 – Neighbourhoods, Households and Income.* Toronto: City of Toronto. http://www.toronto.ca/demographics/pdf3/cpa85.pdf.

Community Planning. 2004a. Preliminary Report: Official Plan Amendment & Rezoning Application 04 192570 STE 27 OZ.

Community Planning. 2004b. Final Report: OPA and Rezoning Applications 03 035379 WET 05 OZ, 700 Evans Avenue, Sherway Gate Development Corp. (27 October).

Community Planning. 2004c. Preliminary Report: OPA and Rezoning Application 04 135814 WET 03 OZ, 4325 Bloor Street West, PMG Planning Consultants. (23 August).

Community Planning. 2003a. Final Report: Application to Amend the Zoning By-law, 5566 Yonge Street. (26 May).

Community Planning. 2003b. Final Report: Application to Amend the Official Plan and Zoning By-law 438-86, 76, 88R, 92 & 100 Yorkville Avenue, Yorkville (2001) Ltd. (5 February).

Community Planning. 2002a. Preliminary Report: Application to Amend the Zoning By-law, Sun Life Assurance Company c/o Pat Berne, 5566 Yonge Street. (19 June).

Community Planning. 2002b. Preliminary Report: Application to Amend the Official Plan and Zoning By-law and Application for Site Plan Approval, Yorkville (2001) Ltd., 76, 92, and 100 Yorkville Avenue. (16 May).

Community Planning. 2001. *Status Report: Focused Review of Yonge-Eglinton Part II Plan and Application by Minto YE Inc. (3 October)*. Toronto: City Planning, Urban Development Services.

Condominium Application. n.d. UDYC-348 (55CDM-99-508). Symphony Square Limited – 23 Lorraine. (Clause adopted by City Council without amendment on 4, 5, and 6 July 2000).

Council Minutes. 2006. Item 8.95. Notice of motion J(31) in Minutes of the Council of the City of Toronto, 27, 28, and 29 June: 163–5.

Council Minutes. 2005a. Item 4.118. Notice of motion J(20) in Minutes of the Council of the City of Toronto, 12, 13, and 14 April: 138–9.

Council Minutes. 2005b. Item 1.50, Etobicoke York Community Council report no. 1, clause no. 29, in Minutes of the Council of the City of Toronto, 1, 2, and 3 February: 101–4.

Council Minutes. 2003a. Item 4.135. Planning and future development of the Village of Yorkville in Minutes of the Council of the City of Toronto, 14, 15, and 16 April: 195.

Council Minutes. 2003b. Consideration of reports: Clause with motions, votes, etc., S2.6 in Minutes of the Council of the City of Toronto, 24, 25, 26, 27, and 28 February and 3 March.

Council Minutes. 2002. Attachment no. 5 [Enquiry (3)(a)] in Minutes of the Council of the City of Toronto, 21, 22, and 23 May: 167.

Dill, Paula M., and Paul Bedford. 2000. *Toronto Plan Directions Report: Toronto at the Crossroads: Shaping Our Future*. Toronto: City of Toronto, Urban Development Serivces.

Four Seasons Working Committee (FSWC). 2005a. Minutes of the Four Seasons development application working committee, meeting on 13 December.

Four Seasons Working Committee (FSWC). 2005b. Minutes of the Four Seasons development application working committee, meeting on 16 November.

Four Seasons Working Committee (FSWC). 2005c. Minutes of the Four Seasons development application working committee, meeting on 3 November.

GTA Task Force. 2003. Report of the GTA Task Force on OMB Reform: Recommendations for reforming the Ontario Municipal Board and Ontario's planning appeal process. (7 March).

Policy and Research. 2007. *Profile Toronto: How Does the City Grow?* Toronto: Toronto City Planning.

Policy and Research. 2006. *Development Portfolio of Major Projects: Highlights of Development Activity in the City of Toronto, January 1, 2006 to December 31, 2006.* Toronto: City Planning, Policy & Research.

Silva, Mario, District School Board. 2005. To Steve Daniels, Planner, Urban Development Land Use Planning Officer, Toronto Services. (19 August).

Toronto. 2006. Elections. *Councillor, 2006 poll by poll results.* Toronto: City of Toronto. http://www.toronto.ca/vote2006/results/councillors.pdf.

Toronto. 2003. Elections. *Councillor, 2003 poll by poll results.* Toronto: City of Toronto. http://www.toronto.ca/vote2003/results/councillors.pdf.

Toronto. n.d.a. *Community Councils.* Community council profiles. http://www.toronto.ca/committees/community_councils.htm.

Toronto. n.d.b. *Toronto city councillors.* Ward 23 Willowdale, John Filion. http://www.toronto.ca/councillors/filion1.htm.

Tynford, Ted, Chief Planner. 2006. Staff Report: Status Report on the Zoning by-law Project (15 February).

Tyndorf, Ted, Chief Planner. 2005. Proposed Planning Study and Interim Control Bylaw, Castlefield Caledonia Design and Décor District. (26 October).

Urban Development Services. 2003. *Ward 35. Ward profiles, City of Toronto.* Toronto: City of Toronto. http://www.toronto.ca/wards2000/pdf/wardprofiles_35.pdf.

Urban Development Services. 2000. Final report: 92–100 Yorkville Avenue, renewal of temporary use by-law (Midtown). (16 May).

City of Toronto By-laws

City of Toronto. By-law no. 1126-2007 (OMB). To amend Chapters 320 and 324 of the Etobicoke Zoning Code with respect to lands municipally known as 4325 Bloor Street West.

City of Toronto. By-law no. 643-2007 (OMB). To amend Chapters 320 and 324 of the Etobicoke Zoning Code with respect to lands municipally known as 4325 Bloor Street West.

City of Toronto. By-law no. 331-2006. To amend General Zoning By-law no. 438-86 of the former City of Toronto with respect to lands municipally known as 36, 38–48 Yorkville Avenue, 1263 Bay Street and 55 Scollard Street.

City of Toronto. By-law no. 330-2006. To adopt Amendment no. 361 to the Official Plan for the former City of Toronto with respect to lands municipally known as 36, 38–48 Yorkville Avenue, 1263 Bay Street and 55 Scollard Street.

City of Toronto. By-law no. 863-2005. To effect interim control for the lands shown on Schedule "1" to this By-law being the portion of Castlefield Caledonia Design and Décor District located in the former City of York.

City of Toronto. By-law no. 862-2005. To effect interim control for the lands shown on Schedule "1" to this By-law being the portion of Castlefield Caledonia Design and Décor District located in the former City of North York.

City of Toronto. By-law no. 248-2004 (OMB). To amend the General Zoning by-law no. 438-86 for the former City of Toronto respecting lands known municipally as 2195 Yonge Street.

City of Toronto. By-law no. 247-2004 (OMB). To adopt Amendment no. 249 to the Official Plan for the former City of Toronto respecting lands known municipally as 2195 Yonge Street.

City of Toronto. By-law no. 192-2003. To amend By-law no. 438-86 of the former City of Toronto, as amended with respect to lands known municipally as nos. 76, 88R, 92 and 100 Yorkville Avenue and nos. 95, 115, 119 and 121R Scollard Street.

City of Toronto By-law no. 191-2003. To adopt an amendment to the Official Plan for the former City of Toronto respecting lands known as 76, 88R, 92 and 100 Yorkville Avenue and 95, 115, 119 and 121R Scollard Street.

Ontario Municipal Board Archives

ABC Residents' Association (ABC). 2006. To the Ontario Municipal Board and City Clerk. Notice of appeal. (24 May). OMB Archive. Case no. PL060496. Lead file.

ABC Residents' Association (ABC) Executive. 2003. To Mayor Mel Lastman and Members of Council. (4 April). OMB Archive. Case no. PL0304085. Additional file folder. Loose leaf.

Affleck, Marnie. 2005. To Marie Hubbard, Chair, Ontario Municipal Board. ([Day obscured] October). OMB Archive. Case no. PL050120. Lead file.

Aldergreen Estates. 2005. Development approval application. (29 July). OMB Archive. Case no. PL050775. Lead file.

Ball, Stacey Reginald. 2003a. To Natalie Horn. Withdrawal of appeal. (29 October). OMB Archive. Case no. PL0304085. Lead file.

Ball, Stacey Reginald. 2003b. To City Clerk. Notice of appeal. (14 May). OMB Archive. Case no. PL0304085. Lead file.

Brown, Adam. 2006. E-mail to Sheila Latham. (10 November). OMB Archive. Case no. PL060496. Lead file.

Caliendo, John. 2003a. To City Clerk. On behalf of the ABC Residents' Association. Notice of appeal. (20 May). OMB Archive. Case no. PL0304085. Lead file.

Caliendo, John. 2003b. To Councillor Kyle Rae. On behalf of the ABC Residents' Association. (19 February). OMB Archive. Case no. PL0304085. Additional file folder. Loose leaf.

Chu, Linda. 2003a. To City Clerk. On behalf of the SAVE Yorkville Committee. Notice of appeal. (16 May). OMB Archive. Case no. PL0304085. Lead file.

Chu, Linda. 2003b. To Mayor Lastman and Members of City Council. On behalf of the SAVE Yorkville Committee. (6 April). OMB Archive. Case no. PL0304085. Additional file folder. Loose leaf.

Chung, Gee. 2003. To Councillor Rae and Council Members of the Toronto East York Community Council. On behalf of the Greater Yorkville Residents Association. (18 February). OMB Archive. Case no. PL0304085. Additional file folder. Loose leaf.

DeBacker, William. 1996. On behalf of the Edithvale-Yonge Community Association. To Paula Dill, Commissioner of Planning, City of North York. (27 July). OMB Archive. Case no. PL031123. Binder in brown box.

Devine, Patrick J. 2005. To Clerk's Department. On behalf of Aldergreen Estates Inc. Notice of appeal. (28 July). OMB Archive. Case no. PL050775. Lead file.

Diamond, Stephen H. 2005a. To David Miller and Members of Council. Applications for Official Plan and zoning by-law amendments. (27 July). OMB Archive. Case no. PL060496. Lead file.

Diamond, Stephen H. 2005b. Mary Clark, Ontario Municipal Board. On behalf of Sherway Gate. (15 March). OMB Archive. Case no. PL050120. Lead file.

Diamond, Stephen H. 2005c. Ulli Watkiss, City Clerk. On behalf of Sherway Gate Development Corp. Notice of Appeal. (4 February). OMB Archive. Case no. PL050120. Lead file.

Diamond, Stephen H. 2003. To Mayor Mel Lastman and Members of Council. On behalf of Lifetime Homes. Application for Official Plan and zoning by-law amendment, 700 Evans Avenue. (11 June). OMB Archive. Case no. PL050120. Lead file.

Diamond, Stephen H. 2002. To Mayor Mel Lastman and Members of Council. On behalf of Yorkville (2001) Ltd. (8 April). OMB Archive. Case no. PL0304085. Lead file.

Diamond, Stephen H. 2001a. To Ulli Watkiss, City Clerk. On behalf of Minto YE Inc. Notice of Appeal. (7 December). OMB Archive. Case no. PL011652. Lead file.

Diamond, Stephen H. 2001b. To Members of Midtown Community Council. On behalf of Minto YE Inc. Review of terms of reference. (15 May). OMB Archive. Case no. PL011652. Additional file.

Dickie, Randal. PMG Planning Consultants. 2004a. To secretary, Ontario Municipal Board. On behalf of Bloor & Mill Co. Consolidation of appeals. (10 December). OMB Archive. Case no. PL041189. Lead file.

Dickie, Randal, PMG Planning Consultants. 2004b. To Urban Development Services. On behalf of Bloor & Mill Co. Revised plans. (6 July). OMB Archive. Case no. PL041189. Lead file.

Director of Education, Office of the Metropolitan Separate School Board. 1995. To Paula M. Dill, Commissioner of Planning, City of North York. (16 October). OMB Archive. Case no. PL031123. Plastic bound file in brown box.

Donald, John, and Linda Chu. 2006. To City Clerk. Notice of appeal. (28 May). OMB Archive. Case no. PL060496. Lead file.

Duguid, Brent K. 2006. To City Clerk, North York Community Council. On behalf of Rexton Developments Ltd. Notice of appeal. (27 November). OMB Archive. Case no. PL051301. Additional folder.

"Exhibit A." 2000. Information and material to be provided in an application under Subsection 22(4) of the *Planning Act*. (22 December). OMB Archive. Case no. PL011652. Additional file.

Federation of North Toronto Residents Associations (FoNTRA). 2001a. FoNTRA remarks to Midtown Community Council. (23 October). OMB Archive. Case no. PL011652. Additional file.

Francoz, Jeff, and Michael Freel. 2001. To Mel Lastman, Mayor. On behalf of the Federation of North Toronto Residents Associations (5 March). OMB Archive. Case no. PL011652. Additional file.

Grimes, March. 2005. To Mary Clarke, Ontario Municipal Board. OMB Archive. Case no. PL050120. Lead file.

Haley, Brian. 2006. To S. Schiller, Member, Ontario Municipal Board. On behalf of the City of Toronto. (30 June). Settlement of appeal. OMB Archive. Case no. PL051301. Lead file.

Harbell, James W. 2005a. To City of Toronto, City Clerk's Office. On behalf of Lowe's Companies Canada, ULC. Notice of appeal. (22 December). OMB Archive. Case no. PL051301. Lead file.

Harbell, James W. 2005b. To Ontario Municipal Board. On behalf of Petroff Partnership Architects and Lowe's Companies Canada, ULC. Site plan referral. (22 December). OMB Archive. Case no. PL051301. Folder (2 of 2).

Heisey, A. Milliken. 2006. To Jan de P. Seaborn and Michael Barncz. Procedural order – 1263 Bay Street, 36, 38–48 Yorkville Ave., and 55 Scollard Street. (17 October). OMB Archive. Case no. PL060496. Lead file.

Heisey, A. Milliken. 2005. To Janet Davis and members of Toronto East York Community Council. 121 Avenue Road, Toronto, Ontario. (9 November). OMB Archive. Case no. PL060496. Black O-ring binder from box.

Horosko, Barry A. 2003a. File to Regina Ip. On behalf of 2015174 Ontario Inc. (3 December). OMB Archive. Case no. PL031123. Lead file.

Horosko, Barry A. 2003b. To Patrick Hennessy, Board Secretary, Ontario Municipal Board. On behalf of 2015174 Ontario Inc. (10 November). OMB Archive. Case no. PL031123. Lead file.

Howe, Robert D. 2003. To City Clerk. On behalf of 1191777 Ontario Ltd. Notice of appeal. (16 May). OMB Archive. Case no. PL0304085. Lead file.

Ip, Regina. 2003. To City Clerk. Notice of appeal. (4 November). OMB Archive. Case no. PL031123. Lead file.

Ip, Regina. 2002. To Thomas Keefe, Acting director, Community Planning, and Dennis Glasgow, Senior planner, Community Planning, North District, Urban Development Services. (11 December). OMB Archive. Case no. PL031123. Additional file.

Jacobs, Jane. 2003. To Frances Pritchard, Administrator, Toronto East York Community Council. (18 February). OMB Archive. Case no. PL0304085. Additional file folder. Loose leaf.

Jaenisch, Manfred. 2004. Toronto Urban Development Services, Development approval application. (14 May). OMB Archive. Case no. PL041189. Lead file.

Kubbernus, Robert. 2005. To Janet Davis and members of Toronto East York Community Council. (10 November). OMB Archive. Case no. PL060496. Black O-ring binder from box.

Kusser, Barnet H. 2005. To Mary Clark, Planner, Ontario Municipal Board. On behalf of Alderwood Community Involvement Inc. (11 March). OMB Archive. Case no. PL050120. Lead file.

Latham. Sheila. 2007. Letter sent by e-mail to Michael Barnycz, OMB case worker. (10 Jan.). OMB Archive. Case no. PL060496. Lead file.

Latham. Sheila. 2006. E-mail to Adam Brown. (10 November). OMB Archive. Case no. PL060496. Lead file.

Latham. Sheila. 2003. To Natalie Horn. On behalf of the SAVE Yorkville Heritage Association. Notice of Incorporation. (30 June). OMB Archive. Case no. PL0304085. Lead file.

Macaulay, Robert. 2006. Affidavit of Robert Macaulay. Sworn before Aaron Isaac Platt at the City of Toronto, 30 June. OMB Archive. Case no. PL051301. Lead file.

Makuch, Stanley. 2006. To City Clerk. On behalf of Jesse Ketchum Public School Parent Council. Notice of appeal. (29 May). Lead file.

Makuch, Stanley. 2005a. To Ulli Watkiss, Clerk, City of Toronto. On behalf of Castlefield/Caledonia Development Inc. Notice of appeal. (21 December). OMB Archive. Case no. PL051301. Lead file.

Milbrandt, George. 2003a. To Mayor Lastman and Members of City Council. On behalf of the Federation of North Toronto Residents' Association. (4 April). OMB Archive. Case no. PL0304085. Additional file folder. Loose leaf.

Milbrandt, George. 2003b. "Prominent Leaders of Toronto Voice Concerns" (Prominent Leaders). To Mayor Lastman and Members of City Council. (28 March). OMB Archive. Case no. PL0304085. Additional file folder. Loose leaf.

Rovazzi, P., and David E. Shelton. 2006. To the City of Toronto. On behalf of Lowe's and North American. Proposed terms of settlement. (21 June). OMB Archive. Case no. PL051301. Lead file.

Saunderson, R.S. 2001. To Graham Baker, President, Barclay Grayson. On behalf of the Bloor-Yorkville Business Improvement Area Board of Management. (30 November). OMB Archive. Case no. PL0304085. Additional file folder. Loose leaf.

Save Yorkville Heritage Association (SYHA). 2007. Presentation to the Ontario Municipal Board. (8 January). OMB Archive. Case no. PL060496. Lead file.

Save Yorkville Heritage Association (SYHA). 2006. To City Clerk. Notice of appeal. (24 May). OMB Archive. Case no. PL060496. Lead file.

Stoffman, Nicole. 2003. To Mayor Lastman, Toronto East York Councillors, and City Staff. (17 February). OMB Archive. Case no. PL0304085. Additional file folder. Loose leaf.

Tyacke, John. 2001. On behalf of the Federation of North Toronto Residents Associations. Presented during the Midtown Community Council meeting of 12 June. OMB Archive. Case no. PL011652. Lead file.

Tyndorf, Ted, Chief Planner. 2006. Extension of interim control by-law for the Castlefield Caledonia Design and Décor District. (21 August). OMB Archive. Case no. PL051301. Additional folder.

Walker, Michael. 2002. To Midtown Community Council. (28 January). OMB Archive. Case no. PL011152. Lead file.

Walker, Michael. 2001a. To Robert Blazevski, Vice-president, Planning, Minto YE Inc. (22 October). OMB Archive. Case no. PL011152. Additional file.

Walker, Michael. 2001b. To Councillors Flint, Pitfield, Mihevic, Johnston, and Minnan-Wong. (2 April). OMB Archive. Case no. PL011152. Additional file.

Whicher, Gordon J. 2005. To Mary Clark, Ontario Municipal Board. On behalf of the City of Toronto. OMB Archive. Case no. PL050120. Lead file.

Ontario Municipal Board Decisions

1191777. Ontario Ltd. v. Toronto (City) [2003] O.M.B.D. no. 1198.

Aldergreen Estates Inc. v. Toronto (City) [2006] O.M.B.D. no. 1011.

Colonia Treuhand Ltd. vs. Toronto (City) [2003] O.M.B.D. no. 397 and no. 969.

Davenport Three Develco Inc. v. Toronto (City) [2006] O.M.B.D. no. 637.

Minto YE Inc. v. Toronto (City) [2002] O.M.B.D. no. 291.

Minto YE Inc. v. Toronto (City) [2002] O.M.B.D. no. 703.

Save Yorkville Heritage Association v. Toronto (City) [2006] O.M.B.D. no. 1110.

Save Yorkville Heritage Association v. Toronto (City) [2006] O.M.B.D. no. 1242.

Symphony Square Ltd. v. Toronto (City) Committee of Adjustment [1999] O.M.B.D. no. 1453.

Toronto (City) Interim Control By-law 862-2005 (Re) [2006] O.M.B.D. no. 941.

Toronto (City) Official Plan Amendment No. 252 (Re) [2004] O.M.B.D. no. 430.

Toronto (City) Official Plan Amendment No. 361 (Re) [2007] O.M.B.D. no. 33.

Toronto (City) Official Plan Redesignate Land Amendment (Re) [2005] O.M.B.D. no. 406.

Toronto (City) Official Plan Redesignate Land Amendment (Re) [2005] O.M.B.D. no. 595.

Toronto (City) Official Plan Redesignate Land Amendment (Re) [2005] O.M.B.D. no. 1059.

Toronto (City) Official Plan Site-Specific Exemption Amendment (Re) [2006] O.M.B.D. no. 1342.

Toronto (City) Zoning By-law No. 944-2003 (Re) [2003] O.M.B.D. no. 1269.

Provincial and State Legislation

Florida. Growth Management Act, F.S. 1985, c. 163, p. II.

Manitoba. Planning Act, C.C.S.M. 2005, c. P80.

New Brunswick. Assessment and Planning Appeal Board Act, S.N.B. 2001, c. A14.3.

New Brunswick. Community Planning Act, R.S.N.B. 1973, c. C-12.

Nova Scotia. Municipal Government Act, S.N.S. 1998, c. 18.

Ontario. Greenbelt Protection Act, 2005, S.O. 2004, c. 9.

Ontario. Municipal Election Act, 1996, S.O. 1996, c. 32, Sched. 35.

Ontario. Ontario Municipal Board Act, R.S.O. 1990, c. O.28.

Ontario. Place to Grow Act, 2005, S.O. 2005, c. 13.

Ontario. Planning Act, R.S.O. 1990, c. P.13.

Ontario. Planning and Conservation Land Statute Law Amendment Act, 2006, S.O. 2006, c. 23.

Ontario. Statutory Powers Procedures Act, R.S.O. 1990, c. S.22.

Ontario. Strong Communities (Planning Amendment) Act, S.O. 2004, c. 18.

Oregon. Oregon Land Use Act, O.R.S. 1973, c. 197.

Quebec. Loi sur la commission municipale, L.R.Q., c. C-35.

Quebec. Loi sur l'aménagement et l'urbanisme, L.R.Q., c. A-19.1.

Saskatchewan. Planning and Development Act, R.S.S. 2007, c. P13.2.